EMOTIONS OF MENACE AND ENCHANTMENT

Emotions of Menace and Enchantment examines four pivotal human emotions. It explores what defines these emotions, how they interact, and how they impact the experience of self-boundary. All four feelings speak to the boundary around the self, to whether we stiffen that boundary, relax it or worry about its fraying.

Psychoanalysis has looked closely at conflicts that human beings experience, but has paid relatively less attention to the specific emotions through which conflict is known and managed. The disgust emotion is unique in operating like a gatekeeper that manages what approaches us closely. Disgust appears prominently in our relationship with the physical world, but surprisingly, is just as common in the world of politics. It moves people to action, including deeds of great violence. Horror occurs when we feel invaded and altered by something that leads to profound insecurity. Human beings behaving inhumanly is one common source of horror. While disgust is a moral emotion, horror makes no judgments but speaks to the misery of being unsafe. Awe opens the self to the outside world, and creates moments that sustain us through times of stress. Fascination also involves openness but its characteristic attitude and attention shows its differences from awe. It forms the foundation for deep learning. All four emotions find their way into psychopathology; for example, fascination plays a role in addiction and awe in masochism and cult formation.

Emotions of Menace and Enchantment will help mental health professionals in psychoanalysis, psychotherapy, psychiatry and social work to better parse clinical encounters with the four emotions and to think as well about defensive patterns aimed at blunting contact with them. It will engage anyone interested in examining the roles these emotions play in politics, societal violence, addictions, and everyday joys and suffering.

Susan Beth Miller is a clinical psychologist in private practice in Ann Arbor, Michigan. She enjoys writing fiction as well as non-fiction and has published the novel, *Indigo Rose*, in addition to *The Shame Experience, Shame in Context, Disgust: The Gatekeeper Emotion* and a book for teenagers with troubled parents entitled *When Parents Have Problems*.

EMOTIONS OF MENACE AND ENCHANTMENT

Disgust, Horror, Awe, and Fascination

Susan Beth Miller

LONDON AND NEW YORK

First published 2018
by Routledge
2 Park Square, Milton Park, Abingdon, Oxon OX14 4RN

and by Routledge
711 Third Avenue, New York, NY 10017

Routledge is an imprint of the Taylor & Francis Group, an informa business

© 2018 Susan Beth Miller

The right of Susan Beth Miller to be identified as author of this work
has been asserted by her in accordance with sections 77 and 78 of the
Copyright, Designs and Patents Act 1988.

All rights reserved. No part of this book may be reprinted or
reproduced or utilised in any form or by any electronic, mechanical,
or other means, now known or hereafter invented, including photocopying
and recording, or in any information storage or retrieval system,
without permission in writing from the publishers.

Trademark notice: Product or corporate names may be trademarks
or registered trademarks, and are used only for identification
and explanation without intent to infringe.

British Library Cataloguing in Publication Data
A catalogue record for this book is available from the British Library

Library of Congress Cataloging in Publication Data
A catalog record for this title has been requested

ISBN: 978-1-138-57880-7 (hbk)
ISBN: 978-1-138-57881-4 (pbk)
ISBN: 978-1-351-26376-4 (ebk)

Typeset in Bembo and Stone Sans
by Florence Production Ltd, Stoodleigh, Devon, UK

For my father, my dear friend

CONTENTS

Acknowledgments		*ix*
1	Entering the world of emotion	1
2	The gatekeeper emotion: disgust	27
3	The breakdown emotion: horror	73
4	The imbibing emotion: awe	109
5	The fixed eye of fascination	135
6	Concluding comments	151
Notes		*155*
References		*157*
Index		*163*

ACKNOWLEDGMENTS

I received help from a number of friends, family members, and colleagues in writing this book, many of whom read and critiqued portions of it or offered input in other ways. My thanks to Irv Leon, Nancy Leon, Deb and Michael Jackson, Lisa Sablosky, Laura Eligator, Howard Erman, Kathy Tuta, Jay Radin, Moses Everett, Rose DiLiscia-Everett, Randy Milden, Rick Ochberg, Julia Davies, Juan Ramos, Carole Symer, Judy Gray, Brian Ashin, Judith Saltzman, Ann Pearlman, Jane Hassinger, Pat Bommarito, and Glenn Groustra. I especially want to thank Tracy Munn, whose editorial input was of great value, and George Rosenwald, who put me in touch with Tracy and, as always, along with Gay, lent enthusiasm for my project.

My thanks to Charles Bath and Kate Hawes, of Routledge, and Lorna Wilkinson of Florence Production Ltd, for patiently addressing a multitude of questions and working past obstacles during the preparation of my manuscript.

Special thanks to the many patients who over the years have fascinated and taught me and especially to those generous individuals who gave me permission to discuss our work in these pages.

I am grateful to the research participants whose narratives enriched my under-standing of emotions and added texture to the book's treatment of those emotions.

Excerpts from Daphne Du Maurier's *Rebecca* in Chapter 3 are reproduced by permission of Curtis Brown Group Ltd, London on behalf of the Chichester Partnership. Copyright © The Chichester Partnership, 1938.

"Beside the Waterfall," "The Sea Mouse," and "Porcupine" in Chapters 3 and 4 are taken from *White Pine: Poems and Prose Poems* by Mary Oliver. Copyright © 1994 by Mary Oliver. Reprinted by permission of Houghton Mifflin Harcourt Publishing Company. All Rights Reserved.

Excerpt from "October Maples, Portland" from *New And Collected Poems* by Richard Wilbur featured in Chapter 4. Copyright © 1998 by Richard Wilbur. Reprinted by permission of Houghton Mifflin Harcourt Publishing Company. All Rights Reserved.

1

ENTERING THE WORLD OF EMOTION

Disgust, horror, awe, and fascination stir us boldly when a subject seizes our interest. They move us bodily, as when disgust motivates us to step back and fascination to lean in. They rouse us socially, as they stimulate or stem our engagement with others. The four emotions at the center of this study assign potent characteristics to what is in the world; they ascribe value or worthlessness, security or menace. In contrast with an emotion such as shame that attends primarily to my self, or a feeling such as embarrassment that splits its attention between self and other, the four considered here most often focus on something outside that is engaging, affecting, or altering me. The stimulating subject may be a part of me but, if so, it is split off from the observing self and perceived as something at which I can look: I am fascinated by my own dreams or disgusted by a suppurating wound on my foot.

Emotions speak of how the world outside appears to us. They also reconfigure the experiencing self. Under the influence of a feeling, I may become a door that is opening or a wall of muscle. I am a flowing stream, an ice cube, a tattered dress, or a sky filled with sparkles. The self is a highly flexible state of body awareness, images, implicit metaphor, and idea. The four emotions at issue affect particularly the boundary component of self, which imagines us to be open or closed, expanding or narrowing, invaded or launching weapons from a defined base.

Disgust, horror, awe, and fascination often join forces. The negatively-toned emotions – disgust and horror – speak to our attention to a threat and our felt urgency in protecting ourselves from it, so they may work in concert. The "positive" emotions – fascination and awe – both intensify contact, attention, and eager absorption of what I have encountered, so they, too, co-mingle. States that seem to be in opposition team up as well. Confrontation with power evokes mixed emotions. What has the intensity to disgust us will fascinate as well. What horrifies with its destructiveness often awes by dint of that same force. The man horrified

2 Entering the world of emotion

by a movie has chosen to stay up late to witness what disturbs him, so we can infer some fascination keeping company with his horror. All four feelings concentrate on what we regard as powerful and thus commanding of interest and, not infrequently, that shared focus brings all four emotions into play.

Extreme fascination and awe commonly draw into play opposing and limiting forces. When interest is fanatical and self-indulgent, it courts dangers that drop us onto the terrain of horror or disgust. Cautionary tales in horror stories speak to such overreach (Day, 1985) and show us how fascination and awe cooperate with disgust and horror.

An emotion's momentary, highly idiosyncratic alterations in the sense of self may tell us a great deal about who a person is, has been, and aims to be. We can look at a 27-year-old Detroit man's particular way of experiencing horror. The narrative is a sample of the data on which this study depends. In this and all other uses of research data, I use the participant's narrative with no correction of spelling, typing, or sentence structure:

> If there is something that am always afraid of is a nightmare. This is the reason why I have not had a nightmare for a really long time but the joy was short lived. A few days ago, I slept late watching "Nightmare on Elm Street." Now this is the first time I was watching the movie and worse still, very late into the night. Once I went to bed, I took some time before I could actually get some sleep but when I did, I was living my own nightmare on Elm Street.
>
> The movie resonates with my situation because the plot is about people sleeping and dying in their sleep. Before I even entered my room, there was an eerie feeling and I was very terrified. There was this chilling feeling of horror as if someone was watching me. I cannot even tell how I fell asleep but I wish I didn't. When I woke up the next day, I could not believe that I was still alive and for some reason vowed to stick to the kind of movies am used to.

The horror stimulus is the complex narrative and imagery of a film, one about people dying in their sleep, in an exposed, unguarded state. We might wonder about any personal history that sensitizes the young man and note the line "[t]he movie resonates with my situation." This man lives in a city known for violence. Is his vulnerability as he lies down to sleep influenced by any broader experience of defenselessness?

The beginning of his story is confused. He says he slept late but seems to mean he stayed up late. He states that he hasn't had a nightmare in a long time because he is afraid of them, which is another perplexing statement. Perhaps his cognition is shaken by fear. A threatening outside world has invaded inner space. What was happening out there will occur internally so that a movie seen becomes a movie directed, in a nightmare.

He fantasizes he is being watched by a malign presence, which is a common horror trope. To be surveilled by something that has not openly declared its presence, its nature, or its intentions is a theme found in a number of narratives. Great power inheres in the gaze, which is the expression of your deep interest in me and my activities, and perhaps your power to harm me. If you do not identify yourself and your purpose, I know you to be peculiar, not normal. I assume evil intent.

He is *chilled* by horror, another common avowal, one that tells us that horror is a deep disturbance of self that perturbs the experience of a normally warm, safely energized body. He experiences himself as small and feeble, depleted of strength and heat. His condition is a body and mind affair.

We can see in this story and others to follow both idiosyncratic and universal elements in the reaction to a horror stimulus, or in a person's belief that a stimulus is horrific. A responsive consciousness shapes the world, while also self-reflecting and detailing inner changes, especially with respect to boundaries.

The concept of taboo is an integrator of the four emotions. Taboo has been the subject of intensive study by anthropologists (Douglas, 1966; Leach, 1964) and was considered as well by Freud (1913). To regard a subject as taboo means to see it as holding and emanating great and dangerous power. Taboo is a status, not an emotion, but Freud endorsed a definition of the word – "holy dred" – that points us toward emotional aspects of our engagement with what is taboo, and signals the relevance of the feelings, awe and horror. Disgust may join the mix when people approach the taboo. Fascination may as well; consider, for example, the complex feelings stirred by stories about incest.

Emotion has been defined in a variety of ways. Along with the word, *feeling*, people use *emotion* to designate the conscious component of processes that psychoanalysis, in somewhat shifting ways, calls *affect*, from the German, Affekt. Studying the definitional complexities of the term, affect, André Green (1999) concludes, "Affect, therefore, should be understood essentially as a metapsychological term rather than a descriptive one" (p. 8). He suggests that, when looking for descriptive language, "the term affect may be replaced by another, more adequate one, one closer to the reality that it designates" (p. 8). Despite Green's recommendation, psychoanalysts do, at times, continue to use affect rather than (or in addition to) emotion or feeling to designate felt experience (Spezzano, 1993).

Some nonpsychoanalytic scholars avoid the word affect, and treat emotion as synonymous with feeling (LeDoux, 2015). They restrict emotion and feeling to conscious experience (a useful if redundant phrase) that characterizes how an individual *is* in the moment, to his or her state of mind, which has bodily aspects and attitudal elements. I join those who avoid the use of the term, affect, as historically confusing, and speak instead of emotion and feeling, which denote consciousness. Talking about nonconscious processes relevant to emotion, I will label them as such. A useful definition of emotion was put forth by Levinson (1997):

4 Entering the world of emotion

> At present there appears to be some consensus that in perhaps the majority of cases an emotion is best thought of as a bodily response with a distinctive physiological, phenomenological, and expressive profile, one that serves to focus attention in a given direction, and that involves cognition to varying degrees and at various levels.
>
> (p. 21)

The words, emotion and feeling, can be used almost synonymously although emotion can connote slightly more weighty and abiding experience than feeling does. Emotion entails a sense of reification and a tilt toward a full, multi-faceted experience that feeling, for me, often lacks. They differ in their verb forms, too, with "I feel" designating an inner state and "I emote" emphasizing expression that others can read, nevertheless, in their noun forms, their meanings are too close for me to try to differentiate them.

As I work to define emotion and feeling, and look at others' definitions (Levinson, 1997), I recognize that the experience of feeling contains something irreducible. A feeling is what is felt. It is uniquely itself as much as vision and hearing are, as the color blue, or the taste of an olive. Experientially, these cannot be defined in other terms though we can refer to the physiological events that associate with them and undergird the experience, or to external triggers or cognitive elements. Speaking of emotion, we can address aspects of the experience such as tension in the muscles, or ideas filling the mind, but assembling those elements does not amount to a feeling: the whole is not the sum of the parts. I can say that disgust is a pushing-away and pulling-back feeling, but the core of what it means to *feel* remains irreducible.

Speaking of and attempting to delineate particular emotions is easier than defining what it is to feel. Each emotion to be considered in this book has a structure, that is, elements without which we ought not to say the feeling exists in the moment. Each has as well certain variations that occur with frequency and deserve to be noted but are not essential to defining the state. These structures and their variants designate orientations toward an object – an other, a part of the self, or the self as a whole – and speak to changes in the self that aim to increase or reduce contact, to draw back, shake off, or drink in and absorb.

Also of note are precursor states. These are early developmental states that may be part of the lineage of one of the four feelings, but are not the full emotion. The person feeling them may lack self-awareness that recognizes "I am in this state," and may be absent the ability to assign a name to what he or she feels. Such cognitive acts are a necessary part of adult and later childhood experience of discrete moments of emotion. *Naming* is itself an important element in the achievement of emotional maturity. It shapes our experience, as described by Philip Fisher (2002), who tells us that "naming always remembers only certain details about an object, thrusting them to the front whenever we want to think about it at all, with certain lines of thought already favored, the table tilted even before thought begins to roll" (pp. 112–113).

Entering the world of emotion **5**

Many moments of life experience defy labeling with a nameable emotion with its clear structure. Feeling or emotion can be rapidly shifting, akin to a flickering flame, so that we move between one state and another and cannot simply say, *it is this*. Or perhaps we cannot get hold of the thing we want to denote: it slips in and out of cognitive definition as if it were a tree viewed in light so shifting that it throws complex shadows. We do not know what the moment is. Is it disgust? Horror? Both at once? Some emotion is subtle and entails little ideation or bodily bent. It calls forth none of the common labels we use for "the" emotions. It is a darkness or a brightness, a fog, or a bogged-down condition. Though it is feeling, it does not rise to the level of "a" feeling. I might have great difficulty describing it and no confidence that I could elicit an image of it in another person through descriptive words. It is as challenging to convey as a dreamscape.

Emotions are not all or nothing, present or absent; they come in partial forms and gradations. The fear I feel while reading a book about climbing Mt Everest and the fear I know scaling a mountain of rock and scree differ in important respects. Reading of a risky ascent, I maintain an awareness of my own physical safety that is absent when my foot slips on shingle and stone. I am in a state that has been called "mental simulation" (Walton, 1997, p. 38) Both, however, have elements that lead me to call them fear, though philosophers of art debate whether the emotion aroused by fiction is "actual" fear (Walton, 1997, p. 38).

In the chapters to follow, I will focus on four emotions that have names and identifiable structures; they have relatively clear form rather than vague contours that resist delineation. I will look at the moment of emotion and also at the life occurrences that stimulate it. In both tasks, three related concepts will be of help: each involves attention to important boundaries within human experience.

The first concept is that of *category-breaching*. Category-breaching is a term that characterizes certain events that stimulate emotion. Within this broad concept are four narrower ideas: the *intercategorical*, the *marginal*, the *category-bursting*, and the *alien*. The *intercategorical* breaches the boundary by lying between two defined concepts. Anthropologists (Leach, 1964; Douglas, 1966) have considered this terrain as has the psychoanalyst, Theodore Lidz (1973). An example of the intercategorical is the gender concept of hermaphroditism, which designates what sits between male and female. Categories are human constructions and so are malleable, and are influenced by culture and history. Contemporary feminist thinking (Butler, 1993, 2002; Dimen, 2002, 2003; Goldner, 2002; Layton, 2002) might move hermaphroditism out of the intercategorical realm and simply consider it a category unto itself.

Assigning something an intercategorical status affects what emotions it arouses. Consider the human fetus, which can be seen as lying between the categories of baby and tissue mass in a middle space that for many arouses a very uncomfortable confusion of emotions if abortion is under consideration. In an ethnography of rural north India, Jeffery and Jeffery (1996) speak of women, in the first months of pregnancy, who refer to miscarriage bleeding as a late period. "Women will say, 'there was no pregnancy' merely a 'blob of flesh' . . ." (p. 24). Women avoid

6 Entering the world of emotion

the troubling intercategorical realm of early pregnancy. In Jamaican culture, denying the reality of early pregnancy enables abortions that would otherwise be conflictual. In the case of a wanted child, it mitigates grief (Sobo, 1996, p. 52).

The second variety of category breach is *marginality*, an idea much-explored in modern psychoanalytic and feminist theory (Benjamin, 1995; Corbett, 2009, 2016; Creed, 1993). Like the intercategorical, the marginal takes shape in relation to existing category. It positions an experience just outside a familiar grouping so that the parent-classification stays within our field of view. In some societies, a gay man would be thought of as categorically marginal in deviating from a familiar definition of male. In many cultures, a childless woman is marginal (Cecil, 1996). An adult woman should be a mother. One who is not has no comfortable, alternative category such as "child-free by choice." We see how crucial cultural forces are: some people, in some times and places, would not see the gay man or child-free woman as marginal. The weight of culture is not a problem for our conceptualization, but is a primary reality of it.

Douglas (1966) explores the power that marginality has to evoke emotions. She considers, for example, the margins of the human body:

> [A]ll margins are dangerous. If they are pulled this way or that the shape of fundamental experience is altered. Any structure of ideas is vulnerable at its margins. We should expect the orifices of the body to symbolise its specially vulnerable points. Matter issuing from them is marginal stuff of the most vulnerable kind.
>
> (p. 122)

Matters at the margin can elicit fear, due to their dangerousness. We will see as well the role of marginality in the elicitation of disgust and sometimes horror.

The third type of category breach is *category-bursting*. This term refers to an active or explosive rupture of a classification. Category-bursting occurs when something new is formed by destroying an existing structure. An apposite image would be a seed pod that erupts, sending seeds into the air and tearing the pod itself. A short story too big for its genre would belong as well. A man whose mother elicits disgust by infantilizing him in a way that disturbs the category, "my adult self," would also be an example.

The fourth category breach is *alien status*. To categorize something as alien is to say it does not fit in any familiar class of things, thus it merits its own grouping. The status of alien says that the most salient thing about the person, thing, or experience is difference from the familiar. The word familiar contains "family" and the alien is not of the family or self. It is foreign. The power of the word, alien, and concept has been marshaled in efforts to exclude or deport those without legal status within a country. In the US, arguments over the use of the word reflect understanding, on both sides, of its power to dehumanize.

Looking at these categorizations and attempting to use them, we quickly learn that I can construe an occurrence as intercategorical or as category-bursting, even

Entering the world of emotion **7**

alien, depending on how I conceive of it. Nevertheless, the classifications are useful if not taken to be mutually exclusive.

The second core concept I will use is *self*, an experience of delineation of what is and is not me in any given moment. The feeling that a border exists, containing the self, is shifting and can be elusive but is an important element in human consciousness that has relevance to all four emotions. The self implies a nonself, so there exists intercategorical space that can be occupied between the two states. Things and experiences can also be defined in a way that emphasizes their marginality with respect to self. Substances that have just come out of the body, such as tears, are marginal, as are certain growing things within the body. These include the baby in utero, as well as a cyst or tumor. Puberty is a transformation of self that is category-bursting, since the old self no longer exists once the process has been completed. The alien is not just nonself; it is remote from self and difficult to comprehend.

The self-border has an active quality as it opens to experience or extrudes it. Both awe and fascination involve softening the self-border so that new experience is absorbed; horror means that what is inside the border – fully or partially – is now awful due to an invasion or overtaking. Like someone whose meal is hard to digest, I am laboring to absorb what is now within me. Disgust, in contrast, refuses integration and insists that what is bad remains outside the self-border. In the passage below, illustrative of awe, we see someone who opened himself to new aspects of life. What transpired changed him. The experience is category-bursting and the category is self. Self-boundary is softened as he "soaked it all in":

> I remember my first trip out to the mountains. I was on a road trip with a couple of buddies and we were driving through Virginia. We traveled all the way from New Mexico. I never really get out much so everything was new to me. I'd never seen so many trees, so many stars, so many birds. I was in awe as we drove across each state. Everyone had something different to offer. The best part was seeing the mountains. I had only seen mountains in books and movies but I'd never actually seen one up close. We were driving on the road around the mountain and at first I didn't even realize it. That made it even more amazing. I jumped up like a child when I realized that we were in the mountains. We stopped at a rest stop and kind of took a walk though the mountains. I just stood there in awe and gazed at everything around it and soaked it all in and for the first time I felt free.

The last line of the story is striking: *for the first time I felt free*. The moment of awe has situated itself in relation to a life narrative. We wonder what his life has been like, what kind of constriction he felt that led him to characterize this glorious instance as his first experience of freedom.

To find a counterpoint to the awe stories, we can look at what happens to the self-border in this brief portrayal of disgust. The comments are not from the research collection, but were emailed to me and are thus verbatim. The writer is an older woman:

8 Entering the world of emotion

> Kelly and I went to the Chinese restaurant on Friday. Food was wonderful BUT the waiter (who was a good waiter) had the most disgusting white liquid on his lips. I'm wondering if he was on Lithium.
>
> I can't think of him without feeling DISGUSTED. I think we already talked about this. So Joe and I may have to find another restaurant. Maybe go back to Espacio which is quiet.
>
> I keep seeing his mouth with the white foam in the corners.
>
> How do I get rid of that image??????

She knows the waiter was good at his job but she cannot help her acute disgust. She wants to purge the image and stay away from the place that elicited it once and might do so again. She needs to shut herself off from the intrusive pictures. She ends with the expressed desire to go to a place that is quiet. What does quietness have to do with the story? I wonder if it is a quiet mind she seeks, because hers is so aroused by her disgust. She thinks the waiter is on lithium, which portrays the man himself as someone with an unquiet mind, perhaps someone strange, which is another motivator to respond with repulsion. She goes on to say:

> Yes, I have quite a few "disgust" data.
> I hate seeing anyone floss his/her teeth.
> Even seeing it coming out of its holder is oh, oh.
> Yuck.
> I'll let you know as I remember.
> Oh yes. That ad about ??? where the woman has her intestines etc. Showing.
>
> Lipstick smears on cups or glasses.
> People sticking their fingers into their mouths after eating to clean their teeth.
>
> A lot of my disgust has to do with the mouth which I feel is a very intimate part of our body.
> More so than the p word.

She is starting to reflect on her experience, to note the prominence of the mouth, to compare oral disgust to genital disgust, which is less profound. As more and more images emerge, the cadence of her writing changes. Phrases are clipped. Elaboration drops away. She seems to be trying to communicate with the reader without stirring too much emotion in herself. While the awed person is trying to extend a pleasurable emotion by drinking in experience, this woman is trying to protect herself from noxious, evocative images that confuse inside and outside, as in the picture of intestines showing or those of something that emerges from the mouth or enters it. She wants to curtail her exposure and cordon off the self (though she also wants to confront and understand her experience, as conveyed by her writing about it). She is attempting to build a wall. She feels entitled to her wall. It is her prerogative to assign devalued status and to close off self-access. The assertion that she is thus warranted helps define her personality.

The third core concept I will use is that of *humanity* or *humanness*. Just as self is a key category, humanity is a special class in relation to which experiences are positioned. Some monsters sit at the edge of humanity whereas others occupy the intercategorical realm between the human being and another defined entity, such as a machine or an angel. To classify something as alien often means it is less than fully human thus not deserving of normal consideration. Trauma plays a category-bursting role in relation to the idea of humanity by doing damage to the classification; trauma will have relevance to the study of horror. Awe shows us the best of what is human and may lead to the redefinition of the category itself so that we feel, *ah*, to be human is more wonderful than I had thought.

Each of the three concepts will help us to approach the feeling states of interest here. They are especially important to an understanding of the attentional and physical *energy* instilled in the emotions. Concept-borders are high-energy places (Douglas, 1966), whether the concept is self, humanity, or another idea such as youth. Imagine the 40-year-old who is anxiously looking in the mirror, searching for (but hoping not to find) signs she is transiting out of the category, youth, and into a new category, middle-aged. Strong feeling attends this attempt to remain within the known, valued category of youth.

Emotion research

I came to the study of disgust as a graduate student in clinical psychology in search of a research area that would advance my progress toward a doctoral degree. Like most of my classmates, I was grasping for a suitable topic. I knew I wanted something that would feel substantive and would give me some contact with people in a reasonably natural setting. One day, casting my net broadly, I had a memory of my mother interacting with her father, my grandfather, in which a moment of disgust was central. I was curious about the memory and began to wonder, could I find in others' disgust stories something in which I could invest some investigative energy? Just maybe. I might explore what meanings attach to moments of disgust and try to get a close look at the fabric of those moments.

In that initial study, I asked people to write about disgust. First, I had them locate and describe a memory of feeling disgust. Next, I asked them to describe the disgust emotion itself. Finally, I requested that they describe the "key feelings and sensations" in their memory. That was the research design, beginning to end. The fanciest instrument of measurement at my disposal would be my own judgment – informed by reading – about what the data held.

The stories, written by college students at the University of Michigan, were rich and thought-provoking and took me deep into the study of an emotion that had not, at that time, received much attention in the field of psychology, though much has changed since then. In the chapters to follow, I will present a bit of early data and a tranche of newer data, similarly collected, using volunteers

10 Entering the world of emotion

from Craigslist Detroit and Ann Arbor, but covering horror, awe, and fascination as well as disgust. In the more recent collection, I asked for an example of each of the four emotions and asked what about the moment elicited the particular feeling.

A sample of the data from the 1974 collection will give us an initial look at the kind of material that first emerged when I asked people to talk about their experiences of disgust. The responses below (Miller, 1986) were written by a young woman in a university class:

> [Describe the memory.] When I was in the third grade my teacher showed a movie about people with elephantitus [sic]. I don't know what country this was filmed in – but as I recall it was some poor, underdeveloped country. The people in the movie had this disease – some of the people had feet or legs or arms that were huge and out of proportion with the rest of their bodies – they looked swollen, but also very hard, crusty almost, and very dry. These people were very sad looking, and the ones that were not wore very blank expressionless faces. The narrator just kept talking about elephantitis [sic] – I can't recall what he said, but as he talked the film would focus in on the afflicted limbs of the individuals. At first this sight repulsed me so much I didn't want to look. but I didn't look away or close my eyes – it was sickening, but somehow it fascinated me, never having seen such things before. Then I started looking more at the faces of these people – and coupled with the repulsion I felt very sad – and quite angry, too; for the man just kept repeating and repeating the disease and showing all the ugliness of it. I recall feeling that the man was extremely mean for doing this – making this movie – I guess I thought he was making fun of them . . . I kept wishing that the movie would end – and that people would be nice to these sick men and women.

> [Describe the disgust feeling.] Anger and sadness – anger at anyone in the world having to be so sick and unhappy; and at the crazy teacher for showing it to a bunch of small kids – I *never* could figure out the purpose behind it – it strikes me as being pretty stupid on her part. I can see the faces – sad – makes me sad that there is absolutely nothing in my power that could possibly help these people in the least bit. A kind of lost feeling – I don't even know the people's country, worse than that – they're probably all dead now anyway. It's pathetic no matter how I look at it.

> [Describe the key feelings and sensations.] Helpless, insignificant, repulsive, sad, anger.

At the center of this woman's disgust are the distorted, damaged, abnormal limbs of elephantiasis victims. These images "repulse" her; her words convey disgust. But as she explores her experience, she reveals its complexity and the interplay of a number of different feelings. The body damage and distortion disgust her, but

Entering the world of emotion **11**

fascinate as well so that she does not look away. The victims also arouse great compassion; they come from a "poor" and "underdeveloped" country, and are victimized both by disease and by the pitiless attention of camera and narrator. The narrator angers her; he seems unkind and relentless as he "kept repeating and repeating the disease." She feels sad and also impatient; she wants the movie to end, the torment to patient and observer to cease.

Of note are the flux and variety of emotions identified – all experienced within a short time period and recalled (and thus re-experienced) in a briefer span still – a matter of minutes. Asking for disgust, I got an aggregation of emotions, some easily named, some not. The emotions are subtle and chiaroscuric and the search for meaning drives her use of one emotion-label, then her abandonment of that identifier for another descriptor or cluster of them. The meanings she finds are personal and nuanced.

We should note as well that when asked to focus closely on the disgust feeling and describe it, she abandons her concentration on the bodies and attends instead to the interpersonal; she speaks of the emotional condition of the victims, the narrator, and herself. She does not say so directly, but she implies that she feels disgust toward the narrator and the teacher. The disgust is now a moral judgment against cruelty. So the feeling, or its conception, has mutated. It has taken another one of the shapes disgust frequently takes, which we will discuss in the next chapter. The disgust also is entangled with or indistinct from other emotions. She is asked to describe "the disgust feeling" and she names two other emotions, "anger and sadness."

When articulating feeling, we may start with something internal that is inchoate and look for a label. When we get one that's "right," we grab it, as if it were a good-enough suit on the rack. But what does it mean for the label to be "right?" Probably it is close enough, so we put it on and wear it around. That suit we're wearing now starts to shape our experience a bit. If we lived in a different country, spoke a different language, we'd have chosen a slightly different garb, a different label with its own connotations and shaping power.

Gender studies theorists have, in recent decades, trained sharp attention on how the containers or categories we call "male" and "female" give shape to our preconceptual experience; they have produced a rich literature on the subject (Butler, 1993; Corbett, 2009, 2016). Once I realize I am a girl, I may then think that the way I already smile, run, talk are by definition girl ways of doing things; they are aspects of being a girl. Or I may look around at other girls and at the media and define my category through those observations in such a way that I conclude I am failing in girlness; I am not a correct girl. I may even conclude I am not *really* a girl. Analogous conversation about the interplay of emotion labeling and feeling life helps us think about how the designating of an emotion dictates aspects of what we see, feel, and communicate and controls as well what we fail to notice, experience, and convey.

The elephantiasis story can be glossed from the perspective of self-boundary. The boundary has collapsed between the respondent and the subjects of the

12 Entering the world of emotion

film. Both she and they are helpless. She and they are sad. She and they are lost. Her empathy has erased the interpersonal boundary. We will see later that such breakdown of distinction between a troubled exterior and interior does not in fact point to the emotion, disgust, but is characteristic of horror. Thus while she is disgusted by the bodies and morally repelled by the narrator, disgust only speaks to an aspect of her experience.

Humanity is also important to the narrative. The demarcation between callous narrator and teacher has blurred and together they sit at the edge of the category, human. The teacher is "crazy" and "stupid" and her motives are beyond understanding. The narrator is "mean." Both are disreputable adults in relation to vulnerable others: sick, poor people and "little kids." Her harsh judgments are characteristic of disgust. Her sense that the world she inhabits is inhuman signals horror. Perhaps she is also saying something about her experience as a research subject. The investigator, like the narrator and childhood teacher, has asked her to look at something she may not want to view.

Since we are just setting out, I want primarily to draw attention to the complexity and shifting nature of the emotion accompanying a remembered event, which includes easily-named, cognitively-elaborated states and objectless, cognitively-unelaborated feeling. The sadness seems to belong to the latter category; it holds steady while foreground feelings such as disgust coalesce and disband. We don't know whether the sadness preceded the showing of the film and influenced its viewing, or whether it is solely a response to the film. Also noteworthy is the young woman's struggle in trying to parse the meaning the memory has for her. In order to answer the research questions, she has to squint inward, draw out a shrouded experience, disentangle its fibers and assign, then reassign, labels. The research question bends her attention toward disgust, even though her memory includes other emotions.

A psychotherapist's eye turned toward the elephantiasis story might yield a different set of questions; these would center on wishes, fears, and defenses that grow out of an idiosyncratic history. Why did this particular half-hour of experience make such a profound impression on this child and remain a highly-charged memory for the adult? How did those moments of youthful exposure relate to the totality of the child's experience? Did those ugly, scrutinized, sick people evoke someone or something in the child's current life? Did they gain salience from related self-images, images of a parent, or fantasies the child had, or did they belong within a cluster of fears the child held about damage that can befall the human body? Did the focus on particular, peculiar body parts and the belief that the disease is "elephantitus" mean something in relation to the child's experience of her body or others' bodies, perhaps their sexuality? Does guilt over fascinated voyeurism play a role in her compassionate, even depressed merger with the victims?

Let us now place our undertaking in the context of some emotion concepts that will be important to the chapters ahead. Some of these concepts have been major foci of academic psychology.

Emotion concepts

Emotional opposites?

It is tempting to see disgust and fascination, horror and awe as two pairs of opposites. Literature professor Philip Fisher (2002) speaks to the long history of identifying emotion opposites, saying, "Ever since the work of Aristotle, the passions have been arranged and discussed systematically. . . . First, pairs of passions are regarded as opposites. . . . The discovery of opposites is one preoccupation of earlier philosophical work on the passions" (p. 28). Fisher mistrusts the notion of opposites (p. 29) and I share his skepticism. The idea of one opposite to each emotion appears flawed. Disgust and fascination might be seen as opposites, but so too might disgust and love. Opposition depends on which of disgust's dimensions we highlight. Is it the idea of badness, in which case goodness would be the opposite condition and admiration or love might be seen as the opposing emotion? Or is it the idea of wanting distance, in which case fascination, which reduces distance, would be an opposite? The dimension, *movement*, is another worth examining. We can move toward and we can move away. We can also move in tandem. If these differing movements are represented in emotion, we have, when moving toward, what Tomkins (1962, 1963) calls "interest-excitement" – which undergirds fascination and awe – and we have, when moving away, disgust or aversion. We have as well feelings such as *esprit de corps* that suggest synchronized movement. The "elephantitus" story-teller placed disgust and fascination in opposition as she talked about wanting to attend or to close her eyes. Rather than posit that each emotion has one opposite, and only one, it seems more accurate to say that we are considering emotion pairs, such as disgust and fascination, which have opposing vectors we can specify.

Emotional modes

Named emotions often involve other persons, or at least other agents, including God and fortune, though many exceptions exist: joy, for example, or interest, need not involve other beings. Our feelings toward others adopt different modes. I may feel fascination and may hope that you will *share* it, so I extend an invitation that says, come look at what I am looking at and see if you feel what I feel. A second mode asserts *control* over the other person. I feel disgust and expect you to share it; I insist that you must feel what I feel and am angry or hurt if you do not. A television ad spoofs this attitude by portraying a raccoon who has eaten something disgusting (Geiko, 2016). "Oh, this is awful, try it," he says to a second raccoon. "Oh no, that looks gross, what is that?" queries the second raccoon. "You gotta try it, it's terrible," the first says. "I don't want to try it if it's terrible," demurs the second. The first raccoon finally screams, JUST TRY IT. He demands that his friend share in his experience. In the third mode, you are the *direct object* of my emotion. My attention trains on you as one who, I believe, stimulated my emotion. You disgust me, or horrify me, or inspire my awe.

14 Entering the world of emotion

Each of these modes is used in everyday interactions; they are important to note and, at times, comment upon, in psychotherapy as well. A mode may offer hiding places for impulses. Think about the woman who targeted the waiter who had white liquid on his lips. She couldn't stand this image and attacked it through disgust. Are hungry, "oral" desires hiding behind such a need to target one who allows white fluid or foam (derivative of milk?) to sit on his lips? Coercing another to feel something also communicates strong impulses and relationship dynamics. If I insist my child feel fascination with the bonsai plants that delight me, what am I saying about our separateness or about my inclination to use aggression to force compliance?

Developed and evolutionarily-conserved structures

Psychoanalysts sometimes succumb to a developmental fallacy that suggests that everything that exists in the adult developed out of infantile experience, so, for example, every adult moment of disgust must have specific and extensive roots in childhood exposures. Evolutionists speak of evolutionarily-conserved or bio-logically-prepared responses (Seligman, 1971). Their concept moves us away from individual life history and toward predictable pairings of key exposures with emotional response. From this perspective, an adult moment of horror watching a film about disease-damaged limbs might draw on an evolutionarily-conserved emotional response that would appear in almost all people by a predictable age. A middle ground position is that evolution conserves some responses in a way that promotes their appearance when the right life experience stimulates them. From that perspective, we might conjecture that exposure must develop our investment in body integrity – which will happen in any life that is remotely normal – before horror can emerge at a diseased body. That position seems most defensible. To it I would add that every moment of adult emotion – even for a near-universal stimulus – will carry some influence from idiosyncratic endowment and history that makes each person a unique center of experience. The elephantiasis story can be examined from the point of view of universal reactions with idiosyncratic elements. So can the awe story of the young man whose first view of the mountains led him to feel free.

Psychoanalyst Charles Spezzano (1993) wrote a masterful book on psychoanalytic affect theories and noted evolution's influence on emotion in this way:

> The specific array of affective states with which human beings have come to be equipped is precisely the array we need to make sense of the inherently complex and conflictual world of the other human beings awaiting us at birth – a relational world of opportunities and constraints that welcomes attempts to adapt to its order and resists attempts to subvert its order. . . .

(p. 4)

Entering the world of emotion **15**

I would suggest a modification of Spezzano's statement to allow for evolution preparing us to live in a physical as well as an interpersonal world. Awe is regularly a response to nature. Why would evolution not prepare us for *many* dimensions of experience, including the human dyad, communal life, and our place in a complex physical world? Ultimately, we have to establish relationships at multiple levels and we are equipped for all these tasks.

The interplay of feeling, thought, and action

Feeling without thought?

Feeling and thought intertwine deeply in our experience; it is difficult to conceive of one without the other. It is especially hard to imagine feeling that has no attendant ideas, that is pure emotion. Though some would disagree, I do believe the two spheres are separable; at least theoretically it is possible to experience thought-free feeling (as nonhuman species might) and emotion-free thought. But since both activities are ongoing, they mingle as readily as two bodies of water directed down the same channel and they tend to lose their separate identities.

Given that near-constant entwining, is the separation so theoretical it is not worth stating? One reason I maintain a distinction is that the thought-feeling differentiation points to a meaningful *typology* within the sphere of emotion. Some emotions are easily named and represent one group. Even if little language attends the initial moment of experience, these feelings are readily assigned names and associated concepts. For example, a person who experiences what he instantly or subsequently labels as shame will soon find language to designate and characterize his feeling. He will say he feels small in comparison to others or is less worthy than his friends or she wishes she could run away and hide from everyone's gaze. The named emotions often are verbalized with an attendant prepositional phrase that speaks to a relationship, for example, I am angry *at* Fred, I am disgusted *by* mold, horrified *by* war, ashamed *of* myself. Again, there exist exceptions. Happiness and sadness need not have an object.

Not all feeling is easy to name, map relationally, and discuss. Some emotion defies language or attracts single word descriptors such as dark, bright, carefree, or foggy. It lacks more complex explanations of what it is. I generally refer to these states as *cognitively-unelaborated feelings* rather than moods, because moods connote a somewhat lasting state, whereas cognitively-unelaborated feelings can be prolonged or persist only for seconds. If pressed to give a more complete accounting of such feelings, people may do so. They will say, I feel down because the weather is gray or I feel cheerful because it is my daughter's birthday. But we have little cause for confidence in the verbal links people make between their cognitively-unelaborated feelings and their situations. The human mind is a meaning-making machine and we want to account for what we feel, so in the absence of solid knowledge, we freely fabricate, often in blithe ignorance of what we are doing. One patient frequently and emphatically explained her moods with reference to

16 Entering the world of emotion

weather, diet, vitamins, and local news. I found the explanations very unconvincing. The data seemed weak, the inferences strained and inconsistent. But she was certain she knew. Her mind had delivered its verdicts.[1]

Experiential reports support the occurrence of emotion with minimal attendant cognition in adult moments that are feelingful but are not organized into named emotions. One patient talked of being in such a sharp state of emotional distress that he "inhaled pain and exhaled pain." I asked if he could say what the pain was "about." He could not. I asked if he could characterize the pain further. He found that impossible. One could cite some cognitive elements in the act of naming an experience "pain" or in the notion of pain as something that could be breathed, but the kind of detailed cognition typical of our named emotions was absent. Later he speculated about a remote cause for the suffering – an acute personal disappointment – but the connection was conjectural, not felt. His supposition turned on a personal theory of mind that allowed for fragmentation of experience such that his pain and some meaningful trigger for suffering were dissociated from one another. He himself had no confidence that the attribution of cause was not a fabrication.

Even a gifted novelist, William Styron (1990), could not describe clinical depression, an acute and individually-variable cluster of feelings. He saw the problems such descriptive hurdles create:

> That the word "indescribable" should present itself is not fortuitous, since it has to be emphasized that if the pain were readily describable most of the countless sufferers from this ancient affliction would have been able to confidently depict for their friends and loved ones (even their physicians) some of the actual dimensions of their torment. . . .
>
> (pp. 16–17)

Perhaps the commonly-named emotions are really no easier to describe than Styron's depression but, because they are commonplace, we point to them and identify their bare bones with regularity and with confidence that our listener knows the thing we designate and will "catch our drift" enough to generate a useful internal picture. Thus the communication process is more one of recognition than of full apprehension of the details of description.

Knowing why we feel what we feel

Fabrication about cause is possible with the commonly-named emotions, but seems less likely than with feelings that first present as cognitively unelaborated. We are apt to know why we feel shame, anger, or guilt; the *why* of the emotion is generally embedded in its very fiber, since the emotion specifies its object saying, for example, "I feel ashamed of my performance." Also, many times a day we have the opportunity to correlate event and emotion, to say, I thought about that politician and felt disgusted; I read the article on genetics and was fascinated. Only occasionally will the commonly-named emotions lack all sense of causation, so that

Entering the world of emotion **17**

a person says, "I just feel ashamed – I don't know why" or "I've been angry all day and haven't a clue."

Can we make inferential errors with respect to the named emotions? Indeed. We might listen to a story about a dishonest politician, not notice the offensive smell of cooking cabbage filling the room, and conflate two stimuli for disgust. Casey (2016) discusses the literature on self-reported elevations in moral judgment that occur after an incidental exposure to a physical disgust stimulus such as an odor. Such confusion of stimuli clearly does occur; nevertheless, opportunities to learn the structure of our own emotional lives are abundant and, I suggest, would lead over time to fairly accurate appraisal for people who do not have special impairments affecting brain function. Let me hasten to add that we often do not understand precisely *why* a particular person's voice evokes disgust in us or *why* robots fascinate us, but we should be pretty good at linking immediate stimulus and response. We also may fail – regularly and at times spectacularly – to understand why anger instead of grief, contempt instead of compassion fills our hearts, and we fail to comprehend the layers of meaning that may attend a moment of emotion, including psychological needs and defenses at work and the personal and cultural history in play. We grasp a great deal about the surface structure of our emotional lives, much less about the depth, which might encompass remote psychological causes, defenses, and biological influences such as sunlight, hormonal changes, medication effects, and brain dysfunction.

As a clinical example of misunderstanding a remote cause of an emotion, I think of a college student who was worried that her teacher would find a paper she had written racist and offensive and would excoriate her and withhold credit for her work. She knew she was feeling ashamed of the paper, worried about the teacher's response, and preoccupied with fantasies of disturbing outcomes. She had no awareness however that the catastrophic forebodings followed after and banished her excited fantasies that the paper was exceptional and would draw extravagant praise. And she had no sense of why such delightful fantasies could not simply be enjoyed but had to be effaced by feelings of impending disaster. She easily understood an immediate cause for her feelings, but not the more remote levels of explanation, which related to guilt over surpassing the capabilities of a disabled sibling.

Feelings without awareness?

Action can occur without awareness, but what about feeling without consciousness? Given the frequent psychoanalytic references to unconscious feelings, one could be excused for believing that this concept is widely accepted and theoretically pivotal. However, Spezzano (1993) traces Freud's position on the question and reminds us that Freud consistently rejected the idea that affect or feeling can be unconscious:

> Yet Freud, introducing the id–ego–superego structural model in 1923, was quite specific about continuing to reject the notion of unconscious feelings.

18 Entering the world of emotion

> He said then, as he had in 1915, that analysts, including himself, had "come to speak, in a condensed and not entirely correct manner, of 'unconscious feelings,' keeping up an analogy with unconscious ideas which is not altogether justifiable".
>
> (p. 22)

Freud acknowledges the clinical encounters that tempt us to refer to unconscious feelings but considers it best to avoid this usage.

Eschewing the idea of unconscious feeling is not easy, in part because emotional experience tends to occur in fragmented form. Imagine, for example, that I am seeing a client who asks me about my feeling state. I believe I am relaxed and attentive, but the patient has noticed that I am shaking my foot vigorously and believes I am anxious. When my patient comments on this suspicion, I recall certain threat-themed images that had flitted through my mind during the course of the session. I also notice the tension in my foot. What is the status of my anxiety? It is difficult to say, given the disjointed experience. Behaviorally, I was anxious. Using the definition of feeling as awareness, I would have to say that, emotionally, I was not anxious but that my motor and cognitive behavior suggest unconscious processes associated with the potential for me to become anxious.

W.E.B. Du Bois (1986) gave an excellent example of what psychoanalysts often call unconscious emotion or affect. Du Bois wrote of the initial emotional toll of coming to understand that he belonged to a shunned race. He explored his habitual experience of contempt:

> In a wee wooden schoolhouse, something put it into the boys' and girls' heads to buy gorgeous visiting-cards – ten cents a package – and exchange. The exchange was merry, till one girl, a tall newcomer, refused my card, – refused it peremptorily, with a glance. Then it dawned upon me with a certain suddenness that I was different from the others; or like, mayhap, in heart and life and longing, but shut out from their world by a vast veil. I had thereafter no desire to tear down that veil, to creep through; I held all beyond it in common contempt, and lived above it in a region of blue sky and great wandering shadows. . . . Alas, with the years all this fine contempt began to fade; for the worlds I longed for, and all their dazzling opportunities, were theirs, not mine.
>
> (pp. 363–364)

Du Bois came to understand that his "common contempt" was self-protective; it was what psychologists often call defensive emotion. Some would say that such emotion points to unconscious feeling but the usage, as Freud saw, is problematic. We encounter the difficulty of having no idea what to call this theoretically extant unconscious emotion. Is it shame? grief? anger? humiliation? hurt? All would be appropriate to the situation, but none are actually felt.

Neuroscientists may well prove some day that a feeling can be deprived of consciousness but continue to exist in the form of a specific neurological program running outside of awareness (Shevrin, 2000). Until we have some compelling evidence of a specifiable unconscious neurological process that partners reliably with a particular emotion, it seems best to eliminate references to unconscious or nonconscious emotion, feeling, or affect. Clinical understanding does not require them but does demand a notion such as the *potential* to feel. Thus, rather than saying of Du Bois that he is unconsciously ashamed or angry, we might say that his contempt may operate as a barrier to the development of potential feelings.

Despite the challenge of barring reference to unconscious feeling, doing so helps us, clinically, to avoid an omnipotent stance in which we present ourselves as knowing a great deal more about the patient's feelings than she herself knows, which assertion invites a patient to defer to the therapist's authority about what she, the patient, feels. Sensitive interpretations respect a patient's felt experience and do not flood, coerce, or dominate a person with a therapist's special knowledge. Shunning references to unconscious feeling also helps to promote appropriately cautious inferences from narrative research data.[2]

Language and the experience of emotion

Anthropologists have long called attention to the cultural differences in how people label their life experiences. Geurts (2002) examines how the Anlo-Ewe people of Ghana label their sense experience and in light of her inquiry the idea of five human senses suddenly does not seem so definitive or inevitable. Whether talking of senses, landscapes, or emotions, labels categorize. Importantly, those classifications do not just reflect back what exists in our inner and outer worlds; they shape our worlds by telling us where one thing begins and another ends (Leach, 1964). Those lines, like magicians, lure our attention toward what lies within specified boundaries and distract our focus from what lies outside, between two delineated things. I asked the writer of the elephantiasis story to share "a disgust memory." Did she then simply *find* a disgust memory in her storage chest of recollections? Or did she shape her elephantiasis memory to fit the labeled emotion I had specified?

Leach (1964) questions the intuitive assumption that language simply takes note of natural categories and distinctions and names them:

> I postulate that the physical and social environment of a young child is perceived as a continuum. It does not contain any intrinsically separate "things." The child, in due course, is taught to impose upon this environment a kind of discriminating grid which serves to distinguish the world as being composed of a large number of separate things, each labeled with a name. This world is a representation of our language categories, not vice versa.

(p. 34)

20 Entering the world of emotion

Leach likely overreaches in seeing the world as categoryless before language. I doubt that all cataloguing of early experience awaits parents' instructions about what is distinct from what. That education is part of the process of conceptualizing, but natural sorting of things that have relatively fixed contours likely also occurs. A chair, for instance, doesn't flow into a floor but remains distinct according to features such as texture, color, transportability, and form. A feeling of rage separates itself from a feeling of sadness. The early, intrinsically separable feelings or feeling-rich actions likely also help to establish one of the most fundamental of categories – self – since "I feel," "I kick," or "I cry" begins to describe how and who I am.

Leach (1964) tells us that cultures place a taboo on what lies between our linguistic categories. We don't just fail to notice what falls between the lines of, for example, the living and the dead or the guilty and the innocent. We shun and punish contact with these spaces. I would add that such taboo is more powerful when the categories at issue are fundamental ones. No one will get too excited if you talk about something that is neither desk nor cabinet, but try talking about someone neither male nor female. These taboos serve to keep our categories more distinct than raw experience might warrant and they help us pretend that whatever we experience in life is either fish or fowl, seldom flying fish.

Our need to defend these stark divisions points us toward the anxious emotions we use in responding to mixed gender states, atypical body shape, and other category-defying experiences. We protect the divisions in part because they protect us. To call a 12-week-old gestation a baby elicits different emotion than calling it a fetus. Depending on where one stands on abortion rights, one or the other label is preferred. If the labeling precedes a decision about pregnancy termination, the characterization may affect the choice made.

Words that organize experience and place taboos have importance to emotion study in two ways. Experience gets divided by labels such as guilt, shame, and disgust in somewhat crude or approximate fashion, but we hold tight to our identifiers nonetheless and avoid ambiguous terrain. Second, a few of our named emotions – especially, disgust and horror, as we shall see – are called into play to characterize the taboo area between major categories. So disgust might itself be an imperfect category, nonetheless, it is used to label things that fall between other categories, especially essential ones such as self and nonself.

In analyzing the social structure of the Nazi concentration camps or Lagers, Primo Levi (1989) spoke of our natural resistance to grasping what lies between the reassuring ideas of the entirely good or bad man, the friend or foe:

> The greater part of historical and natural phenomena are not simple, or not simple in the way that we would like. Now, the network of human relationships inside the Lagers was not simple: it could not be reduced to the two blocs of victims and persecutors. Anyone who today reads (or writes) the history of the Lager reveals this tendency, indeed the need, to separate evil from good, to be able to take sides, to emulate Christ's gesture on

Judgment Day: here the righteous, over there the reprobates. The young above all demand clarity, a sharp cut; their experience of the world being meager, they do not like ambiguity.

(p. 37)

The psychoanalytic concept of "splitting" refers to reality distortions aimed at maintaining a clear divide between good (all-good) and bad (all-bad) people. Splitting is seen as a primitive defense often associated with pathology (Mahler, Pine, and Bergman, 1975, p. 82), but Leach's (1964) work with regard to language structure and taboo shows us that a tendency toward good–bad cataloguing is engrained in our cultures and languages, likely in the genetics that structure our minds.

Whether a taboo controls the space between emotion categories – for example, blends of affection and envy – is an open and intriguing question. The English language provides us with a great many, nuanced words for emotion and does not – as research science and some languages might – restrict us to a handful of tight emotion boxes. The type of taboo Leach (1964) discusses may be most active when we have a limited number of well-defined categories such as male and female, living and dead, self and nonself – binary classes that leave a lot in the margins – and less so when we have a rainbow of possibilities.[3]

Reading about taboo objects in earlier or simpler societies suggests to me the possibility that an evolution may have occurred in some societies such that certain objects once taboo and handled emotionally primarily through fear, possibly awe, may have developed a more nuanced array of attendant feelings and an associated reduction in taboo status. In other words, the more one can talk about something and feel about it, the less it is strictly off limits, so taboo status gives way, at least partially, to an emotionally-enriched state (e.g., an object becomes disgusting and horrible). An example would be the wearing of another person's clothes, taboo in Polynesian culture (Freud, 1913). In our own society, some restrictions still apply to donning another's garments, but the act is no longer seen as powerfully dangerous. A more nuanced set of reactions includes the idea that such an act might be improper, unclean, or unappealing, though might also be seen as enhancing, for example, when an adolescent wants to wear her older sister's clothing.

Basic emotions theory

A debate has swirled within psychology about whether a set number of "basic emotions" circuits are hard-wired into the human brain such that appropriate triggers lead to the experience of these core feelings. Darwin (1872), Ekman (1992, 1999, 2003), Izard (1971, 1992), Tomkins, (1962, 1963, 1992), Plutchik (1980), and others going back to Plato (LeDoux, 2015) have argued for this position. A second tradition – more recently labeled "constructionist" or "constructivist" and represented early on by William James (1890/1950) and currently by Barrett (2015), Russell (2015,

22 Entering the world of emotion

2003), and others – has refuted evidence that such basic emotions exist. The constructionists see the categorization of emotion as a cultural and interpersonal achievement built upon a substrate of biological systems that do not separate emotions into a universally fixed group (Jianzhong, 2003). Basic emotions proponents have disagreed about what emotions are fundamental, though a small group of states, including one on our list, disgust, regularly appear. The other three emotions I am exploring might be considered by some to be subtypes of basic emotions, for example, horror is a variety of fear and both awe and fascination might be viewed as types of interest-excitement, another emotion some see as basic (Tomkins, 1962, 1963).

One area of focus in the argument for basic emotions has been facial expressions that some believe are universally recognized and indicative of common experience. Recently, the case for universal facial expressions has been punctured, so that many no longer accept it or they see it as needing modification. Russell (2015) tells us:

> [O]ne prediction from basic emotion theory was so much a part of common sense that it was rarely tested. An emotion results in the corresponding facial expression: happy people smile, and so on. So, it has been a surprise that this prediction has repeatedly failed to be supported. . . .
>
> (p. 190)

A number of facial expressions exist across cultures that do seem to be useful signals of emotion states, but the feeling can occur without the facial expression and the expression without the feeling, so correspondence between the two is unreliable. The smile, the disgust face, and the scowl all are facial expressions that have communicative value, yet even these have variable import. People commonly smile when they are socially anxious or when they are talking about serious, perhaps uniquely painful matters. These smiles seem aimed to misdirect the witness or disarm the observer, to say, "See, I am happy and friendly – I'm not angry, scared, or upset." They do not communicate simply or straightforwardly that the basic emotion of joy has been aroused.

Panksepp (1998, p. 46) notes that some emotions are commonly represented on psychologists' lists of basic emotions due to their apparent correlation with facial expressions (e.g., surprise and disgust), however, research subjects frequently fail to designate these same feelings as basic types. Other feelings, for example, guilt, have no predictable facial expression, seldom show up on psychologists' lists of basic emotions, yet are widely experienced (Spezzano, 1993, p. 122). We must conclude that the ligaments between facial expression and emotion are not so sturdy as we once suspected, nor is there much agreement on which emotions are "basic" and may rely on inherited, hard-wired circuitry.

Neuroscientist LeDoux (2015) differentiates the brain's "survival circuits" – which give rise to nonconscious responses such as freezing – from circuits associated with specific conscious feelings. He notes that we have found evidence for survival circuits, but no evidence for emotion-circuits in the brain. In his opinion, there exists no spot or cluster of locations a neurosurgeon can stimulate to produce anger, joy, shame, surprise, or disgust and no chain of neurons, in every brain, known to reliably associate with these feelings.

LeDoux (2015) wants us to understand that humans and other animals can and do – without consciousness – detect threats and engage in certain protective behaviors, such as freezing or startling. But feeling, which is a conscious state by his definition, does not automatically flow from those nonconscious survival circuits. When activated, do some of the survival circuits lead, in humans, to awareness of what our bodies and faces are doing, to amalgamation of information from the body with information about our interpersonal world and environment, all of which data coalesce into a basic emotion? In LeDoux's opinion, that remains to be seen.

Panksepp's (1998) theory of emotion refers to "emotional operating systems" that consist of subcortical, precognitive responses that quickly incite cortical, cognitive events. The core circuitry he has thus far identified does not relate in any one-to-one fashion to the typically-identified "basic emotions" but does intersect them, for example, the separation distress he sees as subcortically initiated shares some ground with fear, often considered a basic emotion.

Neither LeDoux (2015) nor Panksepp (1998) adheres to the idea of a set list of emotions hard-wired in infancy, but Panksepp goes further than LeDoux in pointing to known neurological systems that underlie specifiable, conscious emotions. He sees some "emotional tendencies" as available in early infancy whereas others come on line maturationally, as late as adolescence. If neuroscientists can demonstrate neurological processes associated with triggered emotions – whether basic or constructed – they may indeed learn that neurologic elements of those emotion processes can continue to be activated when deprived of consciousness (Shevrin, 2000).

The emerging data from neuroscience seem to support a system of emotion states that is more complex, more environmentally-interactive, and more layered with both nonconscious and conscious elements than the original basic emotions theories would predict. That picture corresponds well to what we see in the elephantiasis story and others we shall examine, which are not easily understood as sequences of well-defined and distinguished emotions. Neuroscience data also allow for later childhood, even adult emergence of new emotion experience and support significant cultural influence on the organization and expression of emotions, while acknowledging as well the influence of inherited circuitry such as seeking (Panksepp, 1998) or survival (LeDoux, 2015) systems that may begin as nonconscious responses but lead, under some circumstances and in some species, to conscious feeling.

As a comprehensive theory of feeling, basic emotions theories fail to describe much of our emotional experience. At best, they partially delineate our episodes of nameable emotion but they do not account well for the cognitively-unelaborated emotion that constitutes much of the flow of everyday life, for example, the tonal

24 Entering the world of emotion

sadness in the elephantiasis story or the depression William Styron tries, with difficulty, to describe. If basic emotions do exist, a second system might account for the cognitively-unelaborated emotion.

If we disregard the cognitively-unelaborated and turn our attention exclusively to episodes of cognitively-enriched, foregrounded feeling, emotion words seem reliable as rough guides. Each word maps a range of experiences. Constructionists call this range "the variability problem" (Scarantino, 2015). Word use depends on the individual's make-up and even on the moment in the person's life, but core elements can be identified across individuals. Such identification is one of the tasks of this book.

Disgust is the only one of the four emotions that regularly appears on lists of basic emotions. The data suggest that it shows about the same variability of use as the three emotions that do not appear on lists of basics. None of the words was met with difficulty by the research subjects. Some blurring of fascination and awe occurred, as did some conflation of disgust and horror. We need also to remember that not all languages have precisely equivalent emotion words and categories. Each culture has some idiosyncratic aspects to its language of emotion (Schieffelin, 1985).

Despite reservations and provisos about emotion words, these words, as crude guides, offer a good entree into the realm of emotion and I will use them to stake out territories for exploration. Yes, they are employed somewhat variably person to person and moment to moment, and different societies slice up the pie of emotional life a bit differently, but rough though they are, and uncertainly linked to states that are neurologically hard-wired, the words have stood the test of time in designating felt experience, with some evolution of meaning along the way.

Levels of analysis and the way forward

When I say I am in awe of the night sky, what am I saying about my relationship to my subject matter? What does this moment have in common with other instances of awe? Are some things more likely to awe a person than others? What happens to the self-experience when I feel awe? These questions speak to the basic structure of an emotion and I will examine that composition for each of the four feelings. Recognizing ground shared between two feelings will also be of interest. Might I feel horror at the same time I feel awe? What does that convergence tell us about each state?

Earlier, I defined three concepts: category-breaching and two special categories, self and humanity. These notions help us to understand what triggers an emotion experience and assist us in thinking about qualitative aspects of the experience itself; for example, disgust is often initiated by an encounter with the intercategorical and involves stiffening the self-boundary. Horror at an aged, deteriorated individual might say that we no longer see humanity in the person. I will use the three concepts as lenses through which to view disgust, horror, awe, and fascination in order to enrich our understanding of each state.

The impact on the individual of maturation over the lifespan is another meaningful point of view with which to approach the four emotions. Separation-individuation focuses children on boundaries, and that preoccupation sometimes engages disgust. Adolescence brings profound personal change and associated experiences of awe. Senescence may usher in self-revulsion and elicit horror or disgust from others. Psychoanalysis and general psychology inform us about such maturational change and I will make use of psychoanalytic and related concepts to examine the impact of maturation on the life of each emotion.

Social and cultural life form broad contexts for an emotion. Awe appears when we contemplate religion. Disgust keeps company with politics. Fascination is a response to celebrity. Horror responds to revolutionary socio-political change. Understanding an emotion's core contexts gives us a stronger grasp of the feeling's purpose and value.

The individual life story also deserves our attention as a context for the four emotions. Life trajectories follow not just from normative maturation, but from moments of idiosyncratic experience occurring to a person who has a unique genetic and epigenetic make-up. The child who has a disturbingly intrusive mother will make different use of disgust than the one whose mother respects his autonomy. The bereft person may be a stranger to awe and fascination. In the area of individual dynamics, the concepts and clinical data provided by psychological theorists and practitioners are indispensable. We will consider how each emotion might weave itself into the personal life story, and what role it plays in psychopathology.

In the pages to follow, I will at times illustrate emotion concepts using excerpts from fiction. Some might take issue with this practice and feel that fictional characters and plots do not represent "real" psychologies. My response is that fictional characters are in many respects as veridical as case examples: both have merit and limitations as exemplars of human psychology. Case examples are curated by the individual therapist present in the consulting room and they are further shaped for presentation to a reader when we want to advance a clinical argument. Fiction examples come word for word from the text, so are less curated, though they are isolated from their original context. In using fictional examples, we are ignorant about certain organizing principles of the text. We do not know whether the assignment to a character of a cluster of traits is deliberate and conscious on the part of the author, unconsciously selected, or – most likely – some combination of the two. Though it derives from a mix of conscious and unconscious choices, a character created by a fiction writer – whose exact words we have – seems to me as likely to convey a meaningful psychological gestalt as the character "created" by a psychotherapist.

2

THE GATEKEEPER EMOTION

Disgust

Disgust is a cluster of emotional experiences that have in common the sense of being faced with something in the world that is bad or awful, in some cases also worthless as, for example, trash can be seen as both bad and worthless. When disgusted, I feel threatened and want no contact with that badness, which I experience as dangerous, because it will contaminate me with its foulness and may put me at risk physically or spiritually. But I feel forced into contact by a number of possible realities, including my own wishes, curiosities, and anxieties and the invasive or otherwise compelling nature of the stimulus. I am trying to end the contact by pushing away the thing, person, or idea. I want to label as bad, and thus condemn, what I experience and to create concrete or imagined boundaries. These are the bones of disgust, the basic and predictably present elements.

The psychoanalytic literature trains close attention on interpersonal dynamics, but hasn't attended as sharply to the *map of emotions* that delineate – and construct – our relational options. As a core category for analyzing the four emotions in focus here, I introduced, in Chapter 1, attention to the concept of self. Disgust is an emotion that stiffens the experience of boundary around the self and it associates expulsive energy with that boundary. Psychoanalysis has explored the idea of self-boundary from a number of perspectives. Hartmann (1958) and Mahler, Pine, and Bergman (1975) saw the boundaried self as emerging from a period of undifferentiation between mother and infant. Stern's later (1985) assessment of infant research suggested to him that the separate self exists in some form from birth, or even prenatally. Since disgust is the boundary emotion par excellence, it is noteworthy that we see so much psychoanalytic discussion about boundary-setting processes and anxieties but hear scant reference to disgust in these contexts. Some boundary-forming activities bring no disgust and others are awash in the emotion and it is worthwhile differentiating these and exploring the basis for such difference. The more we can delineate the emotional terrain, the better we capture the individuality of the person in his or her world.

28 The gatekeeper emotion: disgust

Psychoanalytic theory's tendency to underrepresent the emotional surface of life may flow in part from attending more to the internal structure of human experience than to the nature of the external world that elicits our responses. Freud (1905, p. 177) talked of disgust as a reaction-formation and, in doing so, was focused on internal wishes and prohibitions with which one person approaches another. Those wishes and fears color greatly a person's perception of an encounter, because distorting inner processes including transference, projection, and externalization are brought to bear. This level of analysis is critical to understanding moments of experience, especially interpersonal engagement, but undervalues key elements in the stimulus itself, which also impact our responses to it. In looking here at disgust, I will consider the internal psychological processes that affect how we approach a stimulus, but also the key characteristics of the thing itself, as commonly perceived, which call at times for the particular response, disgust.

Self-protection in the physical and social spheres

Disgust is an emotion of self-protection. The feeling represents both the wish to get rid of something and the *effort* to be rid of that thing. The feeling is muscular; it is energetic; it is a command to "go away now." Disgust operates like a living cell wall. It may create a concrete separation, as when I physically walk away from something and keep its odor from entering my nostrils. It may alter the self to limit contact; for example, a reaction-formation against desire – which results in disgust – orients me to attack what was once an object of longing. Or disgust may simply involve an idea and feeling of boundary when it says to the offending thing or being, I don't want you near me.

The notion of disgust as an emotion of self-protection needs some elaboration. By *self*, I mean to represent the human's awareness of his or her own existence and the opinion that some of what *is* is me and some is not-me; I designate as well the awareness of myself as an actor in my environment who exists in space and time. Once we have self, we have boundaries that divide self from nonself. These boundaries will be shifting and uncertain – today's self is not tomorrow's – and the self can be subdivided into parts that allow for the experience, "I am disgusted with myself," which structurally replicates a self–nonself relationship. In a given moment, the self might be conceived of as largely bodily and bounded by skin (Anzieu, 1989), primarily spiritual or emotional, or some fusion of domains. Boundary-linked imagery that appears in disgust descriptions might include walls and barriers or stretched or pressured barricades; contrasting imagery includes merging, sucking in, or enveloping. Anzieu described a 1958 Rorschach study by psychologists, Fisher and Cleveland, that defined and gave examples of the disgust-relevant variables, "barrier" and "penetration of boundary" (p. 31).

Because disgust traffics in assessing what is good and what is bad, it readily turns against the self and expresses self-blame and associated disturbance in self-esteem. It also works to protect self-regard by attributing badness to what is distinct and

The gatekeeper emotion: disgust **29**

distant from the self, saying, in effect, the badness is hers and not mine, over there and not here.

Of the four emotions, disgust is the one most wedded to the flesh – our own and others'. Ask a child about disgust and he or she is likely to think first of "yucky stuff." The matter itself has a powerful physicality. It has mass, texture, consistency, smell, appearance, perhaps taste (only seldom sound, which speaks less to materiality than the other senses do). Often it is organic and may come from an animal or human body – often one that has ruptured, has broken its bounds. Frequently, the contact *moves us* physically – it calls the nose to wrinkle back, the tongue to push forward, the skin to beg for a hand to wipe it clean. Disgust is an emotion of proximity. The stuff that offends us is coming close, often to the body and its surfaces or orifices.

Disgust centers on physical substance, but its story doesn't end there. It is also among the most social, interpersonal, and political of our emotions and may be stone silent about physical "stuff" or the body, which concern it neither as stimulus nor as response. Disgust is our reaction to what we judge to be unethical behavior in the public sphere; it is our rebuke to another's disregard for life or sanctity. Among the research subjects, one woman who was asked to describe the experience of disgust gave a response that highlighted her moral sense. Research data were collected in the fall of 2016:

> Sad to say, I feel disgust for my fellow Americans who are supporting Donald Trump for president of the United States. It is beyond my comprehension that there would be untold millions of people who support someone so unqualified – by background, knowledge, and temperament – and dangerous – to take on the most important job in the world. I am disgusted that his supporters devalue thinking, reasoning, and learning to such a degree that they enthusiastically rally behind a narcissist who would lead us all over the abyss.
>
> What is disgusting about their support of Trump? Their racism, sexism, xenophobia, seat-of-the-pants decision-making, and lack of a concept of citizenship in the true ("we are all in this together") sense.

Where is the body in this woman's words? Where is the yucky stuff? These are nowhere to be found. We are squarely in the realm of values, public action, and adult responsibility. We are also in the sphere of adult emotion that is inconceivable without concepts and relationships inscribed by language. This level of disgust does not exist preconceptually. Ideas are its nerves and arteries.

Why does disgust engage both bodily experience and socio-political experience that is asomatic? Despite the apparent dissimilarity of bodily and moral disgusts, the latter contains allusion to food or to skin sensation. Even when we feel political disgust, as in the above example, we experience the embedded analogy to bodily life. Some have conjectured that stimulus generalization is the developmental route

30 The gatekeeper emotion: disgust

from the body to the body politic (Rozin, Haidt, and McCauley, 1999). Another pathway would involve similar forms serving dissimilar purposes and would not require early oral and tactile experience to set the stage for later political and interpersonal disgust. The presence of embedded oral and tactile imagery in political and moral disgusts lends some support to the idea of stimulus generalization from early oral and tactile experience.

Researchers Rozin, Haidt, and McCauley (2000) argue that disgust is not a fully formed response very early in life when emotionally evocative interactions with oral and tactile stimuli are frequent; thus we might suppose that those infantile contacts are milestones along a developmental path that leads to all varieties of disgust, including those that center on the experience that my body feels disturbed and those that focus on interpersonal disruption or breached values. An alternative hypothesis would be that human beings are hard-wired to utilize the imagery of bodily extrusion and do so largely independent of early exposures.

Disgust's frequent association with the moral sphere might suggest that it is a guardian of good behavior and high values, but we should not jump too quickly to that conclusion. Disgust can be a decidedly bad actor with respect to human relationships. It aims to protect us but may do so with devious and destructive methods. What we do not wish to bear internally – our ignorance, our weakness, our wickedness – we quickly give over to others. We pull back our hands and will have none of it. We induce another to feel the self-loathing we prefer not to entertain. Psychoanalysis calls this defense *projective identification* and disgust is the specialist in that technique of self-protection, which teams up well with sadism. Disgust also enforces questionable values. It is not a sign of discriminating taste, in porridge or in politics; it is just a sign of taste. I will elaborate later on disgust as a destructive force and on the mechanism of projective identification in individuals and groups.

Let us look at a 23-year-old research participant's response when asked to describe a disgust experience and notice what the young woman, whom I shall call Penelope, does with the moral and physical elements of experience:

> I remember the time someone ran over my daughters dog Snowflake. They hit her right in the driveway and left her for dead. My daughter was actually the one who found her. When she came to me crying, I walked outside to see what was going on and there lay Snowflake. Her ran over body was still trembling. I immediately started gagging as I felt so much disgust and also so much anger inside. The fact that her body was in our driveway lets me know that someone was being careless and hit her. She wasn't running in the street. No one even said anything or tried to help her and that is what disgusts me the most.

Penelope associates her disgust both with the physical and the moral. She smoothly transitions from one subtype to the other with no apparent awareness of the shift in her attention. The first disgust trigger is the trembling body of the

The gatekeeper emotion: disgust **31**

dying dog. This disgust is a response to a physical stimulus and likely contains an element of near-universal sensitivity to carnage as well as an idiosyncratic response to this particular, highly meaningful death. But she concludes her story condemning the carelessness and inhumanity of whoever hurt the dog and left her unattended. Now she is operating in the moral sphere, but she has not noted that her disgust has mutated. This mingling of disgust's multiple domains or subtypes is commonplace. Because two aspects of the situation – one physical, one moral – elicit a similar emotional response, the person is unaware that the emotion has multiple meanings and that rejection is occurring on more than one level. All planes of reaction form an experiential gestalt.

At times, one subtype of disgust appears to be a product of the other. For example, a woman talked of feeling revulsion at the idea of dancing with Donald Trump and cited his bodily grossness in great detail. But when I questioned her, it became clear that her disgust with his politics was primary and undergirded her view of his body. The situation is perhaps complicated and made less unidirectional by observing that it is not just the content of his political philosophy that offends her, but also the manner of its conveyance, which includes physical elements such as bodily encroaching on a debate opponent's space. At times the physical and the socio-political are an essentially inseparable whole.

In Chapter 1, I highlighted some problems of the basic emotions theories. Here I would like to consider the *biological primacy theories*. These build from the premise that emotion development – even if not hard-wired into discrete, universally identifiable units – proceeds from the human organism's physical survival needs (LeDoux, 2015). These needs are assumed to be more foundational than social and emotional exigencies. In the literature on disgust, Rozin, Haidt, and McCauley (1999) view disgust as evolving from our need for protection against ingested or touched pathogens; theirs is a biological primacy theory. Schaller and Murray (2010) expand the idea of physical self-protection to include a "behavioral immune system" that helps groups protect against infectious disease by instituting physically protective behaviors. Their emphasis is on risks to the body, thus would be a biological primacy theory. We might propose instead, as do many anthropologists (Douglas, 1966; Leach, 1964), that management of interpersonal life may be as fundamental for human beings as the handling of pathogens. From that position, we would simply observe the correspondence in form between disgust at the dog Snowflake's trembling body and disgust over the human agency that led to such damage and would note that the two structurally similar experiences easily mingle to form a composite disgust feeling. Even if social disgust contains an embedded analogy to body contact, the physical need not be seen as foundational.

The research narrative that follows has similar lines of construction to the Snowflake story and shows again the fusion of physical and moral responses:

> There was a time, as a child, when I felt disgust towards my second grade teacher. The way he sloppily showed up to school with his greasy dripping

32 The gatekeeper emotion: disgust

> hair and unshaven face was just unprofessional and disgusting to me. I would cringe any time he walked past me, fearing being touched by him, and holding my breath to avoid injesting his foul stench. The way he treated students was cruel; grabbing and yelling at them if they spoke out of turn or acted out. His anger and appearance made students frightened of him. I had never felt so disgusted by the attitude and appearance of a person until having been in his classroom.

The teacher is disgusting because he has greasy hair, is unshaven, and smells bad. But he also repels because he is cruel. The writer doesn't show awareness that her disgust inhabits two spheres; she simply catalogues the disgusting elements. One wonders how independent the observations are from each other. Is he disgusting because his hair is greasy or is his hair oilier and more disgusting than another person's might be because he is hated for his meanness? Often we remain unaware of how one element in an experience colors another.

Disgust also moves freely between the particular and the general. One woman talked of visiting a shabby restaurant that felt questionable to her. She saw an unappealing looking dish served and suddenly felt disgusted and unwilling to eat there. She believed that the particular dish of food had nauseated her, but it seemed clear that her inclination to reject the restaurant's offerings had already been stimulated by her sense that it was disagreeably run down.

Contagion

Rozin and Fallon (1987) observed that disgustingness is contagious. If a disgusting thing touches another object, the object contacted becomes repellant. An imagined disgusting essence – a badness and worthlessness – can even be passed from person to person, as conveyed in the old childhood game of "cooties" in which a child gets cooties by being touched by the one who has them. Cooties is a word for lice, though I doubt most children know that; however, they do understand that something yucky on you (some invisible substance or creature) can jump over to me through touch. Such contagion operates within the disgust imagery itself. Disgust moves from the greasy hair to the reprobate character and back again, or from the grungy restaurant to the food served. To see contagion at work, we can look at another research protocol, which centers on animal life:

> The place I was forced to live in growing up was a filthy hellhole. Disgust was always the overriding emotion but it's the only thing I've felt for the trash that call themselves my parents for over 15 years now.
>
> With 30+ cats no surface was safe or sanitary ever. The stench that no amount of showers or laundry would wash off of us. Their utter refusal to get them fixed or get rid of them, or clean up after them. Plus the constant screaming about nothing and the abuse and the responsibility for all of it

The gatekeeper emotion: disgust **33**

that they heaped on me and let my brother abuse me for years and punished me when I defended myself. And all the lies that they told and the money they stole from me. And all the times they used my sister who was like my child to manipulate me.

In this alarming story of early-life privation and violation, we see the physical contagion of disgust. If I live in an abhorrent environment, I pick up the stink of that place and it will not wash out; I am disgusting. But as important as physical contagion is a communication of essence that says, I am like the world I occupy or create. The badness spreads from the dirty environment to the child who inhabits it. Regarding the parents, I would argue that disgustingness transmits as much from the parents to the cats and surfaces as vice versa. The parents are essentially "trash," not just because they live in a dirty setting, but because they chose to foster that environment, with regard to the cats and, more importantly, with regard to the abuse of a child, the narrator. So the house is trashed and disgusting and the parents are garbage (worthless stuff) as well.

Douglas (1966) questions the biological nature of our concerns about contamination. She thinks that impurity anxieties that preceded knowledge of pathogens related to *symbolic* systems, not instinctive responses to danger. Her thinking contrasts with that of those who assume an inherent, likely nonconscious knowledge of pathogenicity (Schaller and Murray, 2010). Douglas states:

> The bacterial transmission of disease was a great nineteenth-century discovery. It produced the most radical revolution in the history of medicine. So much has it transformed our lives that it is difficult to think of dirt except in the context of pathogenicity. Yet obviously our ideas of dirt are not so recent. We must be able to make the effort to think back beyond the last 100 years and to analyse the bases of dirt-avoidance, before it was transformed by bacteriology. . . .
>
> (p. 36)

The following narrative, too, animates the contagion principle and, once again, shows the fusion of physicality and morality:

> I remember when I felt disgust because it was just the other day. I was stepping outside from a full day's work, managing the office of the non profit I work at. And then there was that man, always there, but sometimes looked different saying objectifying words to me as I went about my business. I remember wanting to run, faster than ever, from his words, his eyes that were leering at me. I remember wanting to take a hot shower on a hot day to wash away the disgust. The reason it makes me disgusted is because no one should treat another human as property.

34 The gatekeeper emotion: disgust

The writer says she is disgusted by the man's objectification of her. She points to her values and his violation of them. But clearly she also feels that he is disgusting in a physical way that communicates to her through his leering eyes as well as his words. His words have the weight and substance of the bodily. They make her run. They make her want to wash herself. She says she wants to wash away the disgust but I think it is the disgustingness – his awful essence – that she feels she has caught through the power of his eyes and words and so she must wash it off as if it were a substance on her skin. A profound analogy between physical badness and moral badness reigns and allows the two spheres to merge in the mind of the narrator.

In this woman's experience, what may also be at issue, though unspoken, are the man's intention and desires, as she conceives of them, and these wishes themselves conflate the physical and moral. Embedded in her reactions is her understanding that the man wants to violate her personal boundaries, either through literal rape or through visual or mental encroachment. Disgust speaks to her need to protect the good, clean self by establishing and guarding a powerful self-boundary. Generally, we have little awareness of self-boundary until a feeling of invasion occurs, at which point we will feel and protect the experience of separate self.

Contagion dynamics also occurred in a teenaged psychotherapy patient, violently raped, who repeatedly talked of feeling "repulsive" when describing the assault. She could not protect her body integrity and felt herself to be ruined by the forced contact. Her views were bolstered by her family's belief she should not speak of what happened, as if it were her fault and her repulsiveness. In these examples of responding to aggression with disgust, classical psychoanalysis would have us examine unconscious, forbidden wishes. We should do that, since wishes are possible in any moment and circumstance, but analysis based on the boundary-transgressing danger posed by the aggressor, who brings a behavioral reality to the exchange, is also crucial to understanding disgust.

A passage from Jean-Paul Sartre's (1948) study of twentieth-century French anti-Semitism underscores the primitive thinking that associates with ideas of contagion, which rest on the irrational idea of a personal essence that can be physically conveyed and will pass through one physical medium into another:

> The same action carried out by a Jew and a Christian has a different meaning in each case, and the Jew communicates to everything he handles something execrable and vile. The swimming baths were the first places the Germans closed to the Jews, since they thought that the body of a Jew taking a swim would render the bath wholly unclean. Literally, the Jew infects everything, even the air that he breathes.
>
> (p. 28)

Those familiar with the Jim Crow laws in the US know that the same notion of contagion through bathing water, water fountains, surfaces, even air prevailed. A very light-skinned African-American woman interviewed about her Jim Crow

The gatekeeper emotion: disgust **35**

experiences (Thompson-Miller, Feagin, and Picca, 2015) shows us the devastating emotional impact of a white man's conviction that some essential dirtiness might transfer from a dark-skinned woman to his merchandise. The African-American respondent was observing the interactions between a white merchant and a dark-skinned customer, under cover of her own light skin:

> And I had tried on a dress and something else. And this black lady was in the store . . . looking at some stuff and she was picking it up and the man that owned the store came in and said, "Don't be touching the items you gonna get 'em dirty." Ah, that just hurt me so much, and here I am . . . I can't remember . . . if he knew that I was colored or not. But here I am trying on the dress, and the girdle, and all that stuff . . . you know, intimate stuff. And here's this lady that's just touching it. And he told her she's gonna dirty it. Look like that lump got in my throat, and it just look like I couldn't go back in. It just would hurt so bad. It just got to me.
>
> (pp. 143–144)

In this pain-suffused narrative, we hear the brutality of the commonplace Jim Crow fusion of black skin with contagiously dirty and inferior essence and we easily imagine humiliation and rage in the chastised woman, as well as the anguish of the bystander. We see as well the primitive, profoundly irrational logic of contagion that can attend interpersonal disgust reactions, which masquerade as reasonable concern (over soiled merchandise) when generated by systemic racism.

Stimulus characteristics

What in the nature of the disgust stimulus – whether perceived or defensively-constructed – gives it the power to stir disgust, a boundary-reinforcing emotion? In addressing this question, the core concepts of boundaried self and category-breaching, introduced in Chapter 1, will be of help as will a concept to which I will turn later, that of "too much life," introduced by William Ian Miller (1997).

Since disgust is about fending off invasion, it follows that anything with the power to overrun what I experience as my self might disgust. Just about anything powerful can be perceived as encroaching, so disgust stimuli are abundant and even include split-off, internal parts of the self. That said, we can narrow the field somewhat. In this pursuit, I have found two sets of ideas particularly useful. One is the focus on category-violations explored by anthropologists, especially Edmund Leach (1964) and Mary Douglas (1966). Leach looks at disgust reactions while Douglas looks primarily at the idea of "pollution," but both sets of ideas help us consider what things we find powerfully threatening, thus motivating us to close the gates to the self. We should keep in mind here that invasiveness runs the gamut from something that might concretely enter the body, such as muck on the skin, to an idea we find disturbing, which "invades" us simply by virtue of its impact on our sense of security.

36 The gatekeeper emotion: disgust

The intercategorical and the alien

Of the category breaches introduced in Chapter 1, those most important for disgust experience are the intercategorical and the alien. The marginal and the category-bursting also make some appearances among disgust stimuli. Occupying any of these statuses gives things the power to invade and disgust.

Leach (1964) talked of things that fall between established categories as especially threatening to the human mind. This idea has been abundantly represented in modern psychoanalytic theory, especially in the exploration of distress people feel when asked to consider gender-atypical states (Corbett, 2009, 2016). Something that challenges cornerstone categories such as male and female, living and dead, or guilty and innocent will have great salience for us. These in-between experiences disturb our sense of order and often bring powerful rejection and labeling, through disgust, as highly devalued substances or experiences. Kristeva (1982) highlights this terrain of admixture when she talks of abjection as "The in-between, the ambiguous, the composite. The traitor, the liar, the criminal with a good conscience, the shameless rapist, the killer who claims he is a savior . . . (p. 4)." Kristeva's treatment of category-disturbance resonates with the topic at hand, as does Sartre's (1966) masterful treatment of the liminal status of slime, a substance of in-between status, and Lidz's (1973) exploration of the role of intercategorical thinking in schizophrenia.

Leach (1964) related what lies between categories to what is taboo, a topic to which Freud (1913) gave consideration, but Freud attended to what stirs ambivalent feelings rather than to structural qualities of a stimulus. Leach wanted us to understand that the human passion to organize experience in identifiable units leads us to regard as unacceptable, often taboo, what violates those categories by falling between them. The in-between material is a powerful disrupter and may elicit various distress emotions, among them disgust.

Leach (1964) offers a theory of why we might be disgusted at the idea of eating a dog, but not a deer. The animals are assigned to different categories. The dog is a companion to man and too close to the inedible-man category for us to consider it food:

> In actual fact, of course, dogs are perfectly edible, and in some parts of the world they are bred for eating. For that matter human beings are edible, though to an Englishman the very thought is disgusting. I think most Englishmen would find the idea of eating dog equally disgusting and in a similar way. I believe that this latter disgust is largely a matter of verbal categories. There are contexts in colloquial English in which man and dog may be thought of as beings of the same kind. Man and dog are "companions"; the dog is "the friend of man." On the other hand man and food are antithetical categories. Man is not food, so dog cannot be food either.
>
> (p. 34)

The gatekeeper emotion: disgust **37**

Leach rightly emphasizes the importance of disturbed categories but perhaps should consider more fully the daily emotional realities that form the experiential basis for the category. A dog is classified differently from a deer for complex reasons that implicate our deep relationship with the dog as a part of the human household, both source and recipient of affection. We are not dealing here with categorization for its own sake but with grouping that reflects emotionally powerful meanings. We need though to be careful with this reasoning, lest it become circular, in that deep significance is part of what defines and preserves categories. Suffice it to say that order per se is important, but the personally meaningful content of a category also motivates its preservation. Also worth noting is that once we get inside the meaning of a category we want to protect – let us stay with "dog" – we can begin to integrate the type of significance Freud (1913) explored with his work on taboo. He was evaluating the role of ambivalent feelings about a taboo object, for example, a king or a corpse. Such mixed feelings arise once our thoughts of particular canines accompany the idea of eating a dog.

The research narrative below illustrates disgust as a response to matter that has lost its typical form and now inhabits an in-between or intercategorical state:

> I remember about two months ago, I visited my favorite seafood restaurant, "Mama's". I normally only order shrimp and fries but that particular day I was tired of the usual. I decided to go out on a limb and try something new. I ordered the general tso and yes it was my first time trying it. When I got home I sat at the table and began eating. The food was delicious. Absolutely delicious! But for some reason, it did not agree with my stomach afterwards. I started to get that watery feeling in my mouth that I normally get when I know I am about to puke and I puked everywhere. It was so disgusting. I couldn't even stop. What made it even more disgusting is that on top of me already feeling bad, you could actually see the food that I was throwing up. It didn't digest properly. And to make matters worse, I was home alone and had to clean up myself. The smell itself was disgusting enough.

The act of vomiting is immediately disgusting to the young woman. What belongs inside the body and is nourishing internally does not belong outside. Inside stuff coming out is vile. The critical self–nonself border is at risk and will demand reinforcing, for example, by quickly cleaning away any food on the lips. Equally problematic, the vomit is a melange of digested and undigested food pieces. It is a mess of intercategorical (food–nonfood) junk. The food pieces are matter in decomposed state, but having, still, some of their original form clinging. Also unsettling is the fact that the food source was Mama's, her favorite restaurant, and the food tasted delicious, so the experience was an unsettling mix of goodness and badness. Because the disturbing episode involved what likely is one of the earliest disgust stimuli – bad food – revulsion is all the more likely.

38 The gatekeeper emotion: disgust

This next research narrative also concerns what Mary Douglas (1966) calls "matter out of place" or dirt – roughly, the intercategorical or marginal – and shows a role for disgust when encountering it. It speaks as well to the social fears that may spur the assignment of disgustingness:

> It was April of this year and a beautiful day. I was outside walking my dogs and had set off running toward one who was pooping about 75 yards away. It's not that I like seeing my dogs poop, but I knew with the shade and all the leaves I'd never find it to clear up if I wasn't close by. As I was sprinting, almost flat out I planted my right foot in a hole I knew full well the dog I was chasing after had dug a few days earlier. It was covered in leaves and I was lying face up before I even realized it was there. When I got up, I noticed my back was covered in poop. I was so disgusted! It was green and it stunk really bad and I was so embarrassed. This had never happened before and I was in a park full of people. Everyone was laughing at me and I had to walk home covered in dog poop. It was the worst.

With the exception of tears, all former body substances tend to be experienced as mildly or powerfully disgusting: feces, urine, nail clippings, nasal secretions, and so forth (Leach, 1964, p. 38). Feces epitomize the intercategorical or, in Douglas's (1966) terms, leftover matter. They are stuff transiting from inside to outside, self to nonself. They are also organic, a topic to be discussed later. Even though feces are disgusting, we get used to managing them if we have dogs. We cover the hand in protective plastic bags and do what we must. Disgust is subdued. But this woman's experience defeated all the usual protections against intercategorical stuff. The feces were on her person which meant that she herself – by contagion – was disgusting and might be seen by others as disgusting (thus her mortification). She had become that awful stuff we try to keep at arm's length.

One interesting detail of the woman's story is her quip, "It's not that I like seeing my dogs poop." It seems she noticed herself describing taking off at a run in pursuit of her defecating dog and got a bit anxious; why would someone run to see her dog poop unless that person was a disgusting poop-seeker? She had better disavow that wish. The allusion to the possible role of a wish to encounter the forbidden evokes Freud's (1913) concept of ambivalent feelings as the source of taboo. One must consider, however, that ambivalence may turn as much on the intercategorical status of an experience as on tensions between love and hate. Perhaps the best way to conceive of the young woman's relationship to feces is to think of a layering of motives that sees the human need to avoid the intercategorical as a base layer, but one that is attended as well by high interest. These fears and wishes structure a social universe in which we feel we must shun feces or we will encounter punishing emotions, among them shame and disgust. So the Freudian reaction-formation rests here on a primary discomfort with the intercategorical.

What we perceive to be *alien* is also likely to disgust. Alienness is a complex appraisal rather than a simple judgment and as such may overlap other category

The gatekeeper emotion: disgust **39**

breaches. We might see something dramatically different from the self as alien, but also might call the intercategorical or marginal alien. Our assessments are highly dependent on our emotional needs and wishes, so we might take someone or something whom we hate (perhaps out of envy, or uneasy identification) and "perceive" that person to be alien, or marginal, or both in order to rationalize disgust. I think as an example of a woman who had an identical twin. The woman regarded this twin as completely different from her in personality and saw her as despicable and repulsive. She had an overpowering need to assert this alienness and the associated disgust, perhaps because both twins had suffered from severe mental illness and dysfunction and she feared accepting her twin as a mirror of the self.

Alienness frequently operates in relation to the category, humanity, introduced in Chapter 1. We often think of the alien as not quite human. We may attribute alienness to another in order to justify dehumanization. At times, violence is rationalized as well.

These classification statuses hold in common agency in giving a stimulus great power to cause emotional disruption. That power may incline me to pronounce the stimulus invasive and bad, that is, disgusting. Neither intercategorical status nor any of the other category disturbances I discuss *prescribe* disgust but they increase the likelihood that tension will be handled by introducing an emotion, disgust, that labels a stimulus as bad and pushes it away as if it were spoiled food or gross substance. They represent one way to assess what gives power to experiences.

Male and female: keeping categories straight

With noteworthy exceptions (Cohen, 2017), male and female have historically been foundational category divisions. At this moment in cultural history, in the US and beyond, that categorization has been questioned. We are asked to doubt whether male and female are fundamental at all. Can we rightly ask the obstetrician, Is it a boy or a girl? We are encouraged to consider intercategorical space, as male transitions into female, or an individual eschews the male–female division altogether. This interrogation of category is rich ground for disgust. Reactions we now see to transgender people are much like those that have long been directed at homosexuals, who also defy our society's preferred groupings by refusing their "normal" sexual object and, at times, presenting themselves to their fellow humans in ways that dismiss valued notions of how a man "is" or how a female "ought to be."

In his dissertation study, Logan Casey (2016) looked at emotional responses to LGBT imagery and found a high incidence of disgust reactions in all categories of atypical sexuality, but the highest disgust score was in the transgender stimulus category. Casey surveyed about 1,000 people using Amazon Mechanical Turk, an online sample pool. He had participants read a fictional news story about an LGBT-related policy. Then, after thinking back on how the article made them feel, respondents were asked the extent to which they experienced 15 different emotions; they rated their feeling intensity from none to extremely strong. Finally, respondents

40 The gatekeeper emotion: disgust

answered a short series of relevant policy questions, such as, "Do you favor or oppose employment discrimination protections for transgender people?" Casey concluded: "[J]ust a basic story about LGBT politics makes some people feel disgusted, and when they feel disgusted, they are much less likely to support those policies."

Ken Corbett's (2016) book, *Murder Over a Girl*, considers the true story of a teenage boy who shot and killed a boy who wanted to be a girl. The killer, Brandon, spoke of his disgust for Larry, a girlish boy who called himself Leticia and seemed to be experimenting with gender crossing. Leticia sat near Brandon, looked at him, uttered a phrase to him that was reported to contain the word, "baby." Leticia barely acted in relation to Brandon. Mostly she just lived in Brandon's sight. Her very existence seemed to enrage Brandon, to overwhelm him with the idea that a boy's masculinity might wobble and quake, might be unworthy of pride. Brandon reacted with disgust:

> Dr. Donald Hoagland, a psychologist hired by the defense to interview Brandon, told us that Brandon had felt "squeezed and disgusted" when Larry sat down at the same lunch table on Monday, February 11 (p. 70) . . . Dr. Donald Hoagland told us that following the lunch incident, Brandon's brewing malice and disgust spiked. Dr. Hoagland held that Brandon had harbored "intense anger" for Larry, which magnified and telescoped after lunch to "a point of rage. A burning pinpoint, a bull's-eye."
>
> (p. 71)

Brandon felt disgust toward Leticia but disgust failed Brandon. The emotion is supposed to label something as bad and quickly establish distance from it. It is meant to allow us to say, I have cleansed myself of that bad experience. But disgust was not up to the task of stanching self-loathing in Brandon. For him, Larry's transition into Letitia, who then flirted a bit with Brandon, meant that a girly boy or a sick, odd boy was interested in him, which meant that profound questions existed about his own being: was he a boy's boy, a manly boy? Was he a weirdo, a sick, lost guy like Larry or was he the tough guy he aimed to be? These questions caught fire. He had to turn to hate, and to violence. He had to kill Leticia in order to eradicate his doubts. He could not protect himself with mere labeling and symbolic extrusion by way of language and imagery. So he did not settle for spitting out words of disgust at Leticia, or taunting her; he took a gun to school and murdered her.

Clare Sears (2015) speaks of "problem bodies" that have no acceptable place in public space and she reminds us that Marjorie Garber "argued that the persistent popular appeal of transvestism stems from its extraordinary power to indicate 'category crises,' or moments of turmoil when the naturalness of binary classifications is called into question" (p. 8). Sears examines cross-dressing laws in San Francisco, instituted in the mid nineteenth century. Her comments show us the legal equivalence of intercategorical bodies and disgusting refuse. She states:

The gatekeeper emotion: disgust **41**

Laws that targeted problem bodies appeared in the "Offensive Trades and Nuisances" chapter of the municipal codebook. This body of law defined the atypical human body as an unsightly public nuisance, akin to sewage, trash, and slaughterhouses that operated within city limits. As such it positioned problem bodies on the margins of humanness – not as some *body* whose actions created public disorder but as some *thing* whose existence constituted urban blight.

(p. 10)

Sears's remarks illustrate how the distinction between moral and other disgusts tends to collapse as a person is experienced as a thing or a set of sensory impressions such as smell or sight. Sears says the problem bodies were "on the margins of humanness." Disgust often renders the human inhuman.

Native Americans talk of *two-spirit* people, who are variously named within different cultures. Rather than conceiving of the transgender individual as someone made vile by his or her status as alien or intercategorical, some tribes form a new category for those in-between (Williams, 1986). The fact that members of this category are seen at times as special or sacred suggests a retained awareness of their liminal status in relation to the more ordinary categories of male and female and turns our attention to the *fascinating* nature of the intercategorical. What stands in the margins can disturb but it can also entice. Had Brandon lived in a society that had integrated the idea of a two-spirit person as respected and intriguing, Leticia's friendliness might not have offended Brandon's self-regard. A society's management of categories that include and exclude undergirds each individual's sensitivities.

The impact on a society of deep questioning of gender (or other core categories) must not be underestimated. Such querying is profoundly liberating to some, but wholly unsettling to others. In the US, in 2016, we saw the unexpected political popularity of Donald Trump, who spoke to those for whom the sharp division of genders was experienced as reassuring and necessary, people who felt displaced and devalued as the category, "male," was giving up some of its gleam. Important to Trump's image was the traditionally feminine, largely silent and ancillary woman at his side. His macho image made him vulnerable to amused sniggering when he began to talk about "softening" in the context of his formerly stringent, hard-line immigration policy. Apparently sensitive to the derisive, obviously sexualized teasing about his "softening," he reframed his policy evolution, saying it might be "a hardening." Once in office, an early action of his Justice Department was to rescind an Obama-era civil rights ruling that required schools to allow transgender students to use the bathroom of their choice. States were now permitted to force such students to conform behaviorally to their biologically apparent gender.

Disgust is an anxious emotion of self-protection but also an organizing, simplifying, and self-bolstering emotion. If I am a man made anxious seeing another man becoming a woman, perhaps I am uneasy because I don't want to be reminded that I once was a little boy who expected to have breasts like Mommy, or because I fear the threat that age poses to my masculinity – now in decline – or because

42 The gatekeeper emotion: disgust

I feel some identity confusion in the face of another's radical self-identity change. Whatever the reason for my discomfort with the intercategorical state or the cross-categorical transit, disgust offers a forceful repudiation of the stimulus for dysphoria and achieves palpable distancing that is psychic but refers in reassuring fashion to the geometry of physical proximity and distance. I have created the psychic equivalent of throwing up and walking away from the mess.

Life uncontained

Not all intercategorical experience is disgusting, though it tends to make us uneasy. Is there something more that can be added to our formulation that would better account for what triggers disgust? How must we conceive of things in order to feel disgust toward them?

Disgust associated with proliferation and abundant growth is an area well-explored and described by William Ian Miller (1997). Miller talks of out-of-control growth and reproduction as the essential disgust stimulus. He points us toward what he calls "thick, greasy life" and observes:

> What disgusts, startlingly, is the capacity for life, and not just because life implies its correlative death and decay: for it is decay that seems to engender life. Images of decay imperceptibly slide into images of fertility. . . . The having lived and the living unite to make up the organic world of generative rot. . . . The gooey mud, the scummy pond are life soup, fecundity itself . . .
>
> (p. 42)

If we view it narrowly, the too much life thesis does not hold up very well. It founders here and there, but especially on the shoals of political, intellectual, and moral disgust, which form a large category of revulsion reactions. And yet, it seems to capture something essential about the characteristics we find in many disgust triggers.

Let me take as a test case the image of someone who checks into a hotel room and finds the bureaus and lamps covered with a thick coat of dust. The dust is not alive (unless we are thinking microscopically), so what is disgusting about it? Mary Douglas (1966) would say it is leftover matter or material out of place, that it is marginal stuff that has no identity of its own. It also has interpersonal meaning. It is a sign of neglect that might be taken personally as an indication I am of no importance and not worth a clean-up. It has as well physical characteristics that might disturb a person. It spreads out over everything, adheres at will, and tends to accumulate over time.

Miller's (1997) thesis allows for things that are *lifelike*, not literally alive, and thus captures a great many more disgust stimuli, including the dust that spreads, sticks, and makes its way into places uninvited. For a fully inclusive descriptor of disgust stimuli, we need to expand the category all the way to *whatever I imbue with life*. Now our category includes people and organic stuff, but also ideas and things

The gatekeeper emotion: disgust **43**

in the world that I see as mobile, energetic, or emotional. So whatever I infuse with life such that it might threaten me and I want to curtail contact might be a strong characterization of what disgusts.

If it is not organic life per se that threatens, what is it about the lifelike or life-imbued that is threatening? In part, it is the sense of *intentionality*. What is alive has a will and a purpose, an intention of its own that is not *my* aim. Its purpose may threaten or conflict with my own. Slime wants to ooze. Dust wants to spread and stick. Political ideas want to dominate and influence. It is the willfulness of life that troubles me. Neither horror, nor awe, nor fascination requires intentionality in its stimulus.

Life on a human scale is more likely to disgust than grand, cosmic life. Slime will disgust but a tsunami – though it may feel alive with intentionality – will horrify. If the stimulus seems like it might have a bodily impact, it is most likely to disgust. If it is not going to stay over there, but is coming over here, where my body is, the odds of disgust increase. Life on a human scale repels most because disgust is about protecting me, my little human, from you or from what would threaten not only my physical integrity but also my concept, the idea of me. I will return to this notion shortly but first want to ask, how do the category violations discussed earlier integrate with the life hypothesis?

Category breaches bring things to life. They enliven ideas and images, which begin to vibrate with vitality in the mind. If I encounter a man dressed like a woman, or a waiter serves me vichyssoise with a clump of hair in it, or I see a person bursting out of his pants or a woman moving so sluggishly that she seems half-dead, these moments of category disturbance rivet my attention. They kindle emotion and thought. They have power. They have come alive. Again, the life may be imbued, not simply perceived, but one way or the other it is present in the moment. Category breach is one of a number of forms of liveliness.

The ultimate threat of the lifelike is its capacity to impact my sense of *self-integrity*. I sense the possibility of harm to my self-with-a-body. I must protect this ever-changing, insubstantial yet essential self from the danger posed by the approach and possible invasion of something lifelike on a human scale. I must not let my self-with-body be ruined or lose coherence. In an earlier treatment of this subject, I commented:

> The best generalization I can produce with regard to what disgusts us is that disgust is an emotional option when nature, or any other force, acts to dwarf us as individuals – which may mean overwhelming us with a ferment of life close at hand or destroying life willy-nilly as if the individual signifies nothing, or letting life ooze from its packages, again saying that the containment of life in a particular, demarcated form, such as we judge ourselves to be, has been rendered vulnerable. Whatever lacks a containing set of boundaries of its own and yet is like us, in its organicity, would be most able to invade and overtake our boundaries. . . . Life that is aged and close to death, or diseased, or badly damaged – even socially, as from poverty or

44 The gatekeeper emotion: disgust

> interpersonal oafishness – also threatens us with the possibility we could become like that. The more we feel that something dangerous to us has the potential to *enter* us the more likely disgust will occur.
>
> (Miller, 2004, pp. 55–56)

In the passage above, I emphasized the idea of life *uncontained*, an idea that combines the notion of liveliness and that of category. What is alive and not kept in place by a container – whether physical or conceptual – can come my way, push against my boundaries, try to enter and become me. And because it is lifelike and thus *like* me, it is particularly apt to enter or adhere and to confuse the vital self–nonself category. Stuff that is not assigned its own container or has burst that frame, and stuff that is charged with life, or is lifelike, and of human scale, is most likely to threaten my boundary. Think of slime, a substance discussed brilliantly by Sartre (1966). Slime has no conceptual home – it is neither solid nor liquid. And it is full of actual life or the semblance of life. If we conceive of it as having intention – as a living being might – and that aim is to cling and to enter the skin, then the threat is greater still. The key concepts here are the lifelike and intentional, the role of category boundaries, and the threat to my self-integrity. These elements define "badness" in the moment of encounter with the slime. In other words, when disgust says, this is bad, these elements tell us what badness means.

As another example of disgust at the inorganic but lifelike, imagine someone disgusted by the excesses of Las Vegas: the lights, glitz, and conspicuous wealth. Here we see disgust at something material that humans have conceived, and which speaks of human desires and intent. Disgust would be an unlikely reaction without human energy behind the creation. We move, here, into the sphere of political disgust, which involves human energy used for destructive purposes. To capture political disgust with the "life soup" or "life uncontained" idea of disgust, we have to understand that someone else's politics come alive and take on power for me if I see their ideas as threatening. I can fend off the intrusion and force of their thoughts by condemning those ideas as revolting and feeling disgust.

Leach's (1964) category-violating, dog-eating example of disgust is not obviously suggestive of proliferative life. But if I am a dog-loving person or just an American or Englishman with clear ideas about what should be consumed, the thought of dog in my bowl comes at me with the force of life. Feeling the power of the idea of what is in the bowl, I turn to disgust for protection from an image or to preclude an event such as taking a mouthful. Any idea that threatens to taint or damage *what* we are or the *fact* that we are in some stable way ourselves might disgust us.

Excesses of stimulation are another source of disgust because they produce too much of a noxious form of life within the self. In the world of human transaction, there can be too much smell, too much noise, too much touch as well as too much proximity or access. All of these circumstances are capable of stirring disgust. Frederick Douglass (2010) leaned heavily on the concept of disgust over behavioral excess in discussing the strategy of slaveholders who encouraged days of drunkenness in their slaves. He saw how the slaves would disgust themselves through intoxication and associated, dissolute behavior. He understood disgust's power to drive a person back toward moderation, even if that meant doing the slaveholder's bidding. To maintain the self in physically and psychically intact state was preferable to freedom. The intoxicating substance and the dissipated behavior that threatened the intact self-state both became disgusting. William Ian Miller (1997) might call the experience one of "surfeit":

> [T]he slaveholders like to have their slaves spend those [holiday] days just in such a manner as to make them as glad of their ending as of their beginning. Their object seems to be, to disgust their slaves with freedom, by plunging them into the lowest depths of dissipation. For instance, the slaveholders not only like to see the slave drink of his own accord, but will adopt various plans to make him drunk. One plan is, to make bets on their slaves, as to who can drink the most whisky without getting drunk, and in this way they succeed in getting whole multitudes to drink to excess. Thus, when the slave asks for virtuous freedom, the cunning slaveholder, knowing his ignorance, cheats him with a dose of vicious dissipation, artfully labelled with the name of liberty. . . . So, when the holidays ended, we staggered up from the filth of our wallowing, took a long breath, and marched to the field, – feeling, upon the whole, rather glad to go, from what our master had deceived us into a belief was freedom, back to the arms of slavery. . . . The mode here adopted to disgust the slave with freedom, but allowing him to see only the abuse of it, is carried out in other things.
>
> (p. 69)

To become extremely drunk is not just to feel physically ill with headache or nausea; it also entails a disturbance in clarity of mind, in the sense of effective agency, and possibly in self-respect. The alcohol and the drunken state become repulsive due to their association with those experiences.

Morality and the alien; perceived and attributed difference

We have touched on instances of disgust over perceived immorality in the social-political sphere but the topic deserves closer attention. Haidt (2013) separates moral disgust from other types and uses a "vertical scale" to understand it. The vertical scale defines the human inclination to array experience such that animal and monstrous things are at the bottom and what is pure and spiritual is at the top. The lower on the scale a behavior or characteristic lies, the more likely the observer will feel moral disgust. Haidt states,

> Our idea was that moral disgust is felt whenever we see or hear about people whose behavior shows them to be low on this vertical dimension. People

46 The gatekeeper emotion: disgust

feel degraded when they think about such things. just as they feel elevated by hearing about virtuous actions.

(p. 103)

Douglas (1966) similarly referred to a scale, saying "For us sacred things and places are to be protected from defilement. Holiness and impurity are at opposite poles" (p. 7). Other anthropologists have questioned this scale by noting that sacredness and impurity sometimes coexist in taboo objects (Leach, 1964, pp. 37–38). A distinction between Douglas and Haidt (2013) is that Douglas talks about the state of impurity, or pollution, but not about the emotion, disgust. Disgust might at times be a response to impurity, but it is not the only possible reaction. Fear of the damaging power of the unclean is another likely response. Douglas is more concerned about how societies structure themselves to protect against vulnerability to the polluted than with particular emotions that individuals may feel when coming into contact with the impure, though the latter is at times implied. The same can be said of Geurts (2002) in her study of dirty money and birth dirt among Ghana's Anlo-Ewe people. She explains that,

There was a kind of dirt or soiled state that could not be washed out of either human beings or money, and the presence of this filth ultimately represented a morally compromised condition. . . . not simply in relation to physical hygiene but to the moral and social status of the individual as well.

(p. 133)

I have reservations about morality scales in disgust research for a number of reasons. First, it often becomes essentially impossible to tease apart responses to the physical from moral disgust. Second, human meaning-making is such that sorting out what should be high or low on the scale also becomes problematic. Many animal characteristics are admired, others are reviled. Some are abhorred in one context and venerated in another. Animalistic behavior seen as cute in a baby is viewed as repulsive in an adult. Sexual contact, which is animal, can be either disgusting or sacred. Saintliness and purity themselves can become objects of disgust if we see them as forced, self-righteous, or prissy. Few reliable rules determine what goes where on the scale. At best, one can say that if I, personally, believe it to be worthless or bad, it goes low on my scale. If I construe it to be admirable, it is the star crowning my tree; oftentimes, but not always, my individual view may reflect a cultural stance. The logic of moral disgust becomes tautological: something is low and therefore disgusting if I find it abased and disgusting. Simply put, disgust becomes moral when it focuses on my personal sense – or my group's belief – that certain human behavior is abhorrent.

I have used the alternatives "worthless or bad" to describe what may disgust us. Worthlessness may make something disgusting, but the disgust only gains a moral dimension when the thing is both bad and, further, when the badness is attributed to human action. Spoiled cheese is worthless and might be experienced as

The gatekeeper emotion: disgust **47**

disgusting, but bad political behavior is morally reprehensible because of the human agency involved.

Disgust is a self-protective emotion, but what is it about immoral behavior in another that threatens a person and evokes disgust? Moral disgust speaks to our profound embeddedness in our interpersonal worlds and our rootedness as well in our natural environment. Things that disrupt what we believe to be the correct order of things matter. They shake us, they trouble us, they frighten us, especially with respect to our ideas about our future and the prospects for our progeny and our planet. *Myself* – with respect to disgust sensitivity – can be a narrow concept or an expansive one that includes family, community, and natural world. When reacting with moral disgust, often a broad self-concept is in play.

Earlier I noted that a personal moral order cannot be assumed to place universal human rights at the top of the scale alongside God and the angels, so let us consider some voices of moral disgust that remind us that morality is subjective and variable and often is used in the service of violence or is allied with sadism. Like moral disgust that conforms to common religious ethics, moral disgust in the employ of aggression positions the other as alien and not familiar or kin to me. Moral disgust can signify the perception of alienness in others, but also the *attribution* of that status due either to lapses in my capacity for empathy or to active defensive processes, especially projective identification.

In his astute book, *Portrait of the Anti-Semite*, Jean-Paul Sartre (1948) examines the moral disgust the anti-Semite feels for the Jew:

An aversion is felt for the Jew, just as with some people an aversion is felt for a Chinaman or a Negro. And it is not from the body that such a revulsion springs, since you can very well love a Jewess if you know nothing of her origin, rather it passes into the body from the mind: it is something to which heart and mind are committed, but in such a profound and total fashion that it extends to the physiological, as is the case with hysteria.

(p. 8)

Sartre shows us aversion moving from the mind, or passions, to the body. Often, when disgust justifies violence, we see this sequence of experiences.

Both Sartre (1948) and Frederick Douglass (2010) – discussing US slavery and antipathy toward Blacks – talk about a vertical dimension to experience, of the type Haidt (2013) describes, but they could not be clearer in arguing for the self-serving construction such moral scales may entail. One man's morality is another man's rationalization of sadism. Thus we have examples of personally-motivated attribution of alien status. Sartre's essay, published just after the Nazi scourge of Europe, elucidates the corruptibility of conscience:

The anti-Semite flees responsibility as he flees his own conscience: and having elected to harden his personality in a mineral permanence, he bases his moral outlook on a scale of petrified values. Whatever he does, he knows that he

48 The gatekeeper emotion: disgust

will remain at the top of the ladder: while the Jew, whatever *he* does, can never mount above the first rung.

(p. 22)

The scale is morally self-serving. All that matters to its arrangement is *us* versus *them*. Douglass, as discussed by Martin (1984) shows us the use – in moral scale formation – of a perniciously-distorted portrayal of physical differences that keeps the black person at the bottom of the scale:

> Douglass contended that even when white portraits were compared with black portraits, both the portraits and the comparisons were anti-Negro. So as to exaggerate the differences between them, the best or "highest type" of white portrait would be juxtaposed against the worst or "lowest type" of black portrait, thus praising the alleged white physical ideal as beautiful and scorning the alleged black physical ideal as ugly. Douglass observed that: the European face is drawn in harmony with the highest ideas of beauty, dignity, and intellect. Features regular and brow after the Websterian mold. The Negro, on the other hand, appears with features distorted, lips exaggerated, forehead depressed – and the noble expression of the countenance made to harmonize with the popular idea of Negro imbecility and degradation. For a Negro to accept this racist, yet prevalent, sense of human physical aesthetics, Douglass implied, would be self-denigrating and conducive to self-hatred.
>
> (pp. 120–121)

As portrayed by Martin (1984), Douglass also details the cluster of debased characteristics regularly associated with black skin, thus maintaining a racially hierarchic social order:

> The deeply embedded Western cultural associations of blackness with sin, evil, lewdness, pathology, dirt, excrement, and darkness insinuated that human blackness as a personality or character trait was despicable. These negative cultural connotations combined with the debasement endured by free and slave blacks to promulgate black complexion as a badge of human inferiority. They also functioned as a justification for white supremacy along with black slavery and dehumanization.
>
> (pp. 119–120)

Also relevant to tendentious moral codes that promote the view of the black man as alien, repulsive, and not deserving human treatment was Douglass's (1999) 1854 speech, "The Claims of the Negro Ethnologically Considered," which addressed arguments that the Negro is not a man:

> Yet something like this folly is seen in the arguments directed against the humanity of the Negro. His faculties and powers, uneducated and

The gatekeeper emotion: disgust **49**

unimproved, have been contrasted with those of the highest cultivation, and the world has then been called upon to behold the immense and amazing difference between the man admitted, and the man disputed.

(pp. 283–284)

Oppressors force the victims of prejudice into degraded positions, then characterize them as vile due to behavior they cannot avoid. Their debased status validates not only revulsion toward them, but violence, including murder. Martin (1984) says of Douglass:

> As early as 1841, he had understood whites to be the source of the problem, the critical human agents behind black suffering and degradation. He thus bitterly chided them: "You degrade us, and then ask why we are degraded – you shut our mouths, and then ask why we don't speak – you close your colleges and seminaries against us, and then ask why we don't know more."
>
> (p. 112)

Douglass is also quoted as saying that, " 'degeneracy, . . . the weakness of the Negro . . . [is their] best apology for robbing him of his liberty, crippling his energies, shutting him out from the light of knowledge, and making him a beast of burden' " (Martin, p. 118).

We may think of disgust as a minor irritant in daily life, but interpersonal disgust and the attribution of alien status can be a force of monstrous power. In the name of moral disgust, genocides have been perpetrated. Heinrich Himmler's (1946) 1943 speech uses the classic language of disgust to rationalize the extermination of human beings. We should note his use of a moral hierarchy or scale, with purity and cleanliness where Haidt (2013) says it belongs, at the top. We can notice as well his imagery of excess or life uncontained:

> We have – I would say, as very consistent National Socialists, taken the question of blood as our starting point. We were the first really to solve the problem of blood by action, and in this connection, by problem of blood, we of course do not mean antisemitism. Antisemitism is exactly the same as delousing. Getting rid of lice is not a question of ideology. It is a matter of cleanliness.
>
> (pp. 572–574)

As we read about various inter-group conflicts rooted in rigid societal hierarchies, we learn that disgust plays a remarkably predictable role. Disgust-related characterizations of the oppressed are standard fare in these scenarios. One comes to see that in some instances, disgust is a fully felt emotion that will arise in the presence of the degraded and denounced other, but often it seems to represent a coding language used within the oppressor group that justifies violence and dominance and produces solidarity and shared identity. Actual feelings of disgust toward the

50 The gatekeeper emotion: disgust

victimized may or may not be present. The *labeling* of someone as disgusting may be more important than any felt experience of disgust. Thus one talks about Jews or Tutsis as cockroaches without necessarily feeling the upset that would make one avoid physical proximity with them.

The distinction between coding things as disgusting and feeling disgust is important because coding need not lie on the bed of insecurity and discomfort. We may characterize as disgusting something or someone we want to dominate or destroy, perhaps in pursuit of power or wealth, or driven by sadism or the belief we have been wronged. The one labeled disgusting may be a tool to a desired end and may or may not threaten us as does the person or circumstance that evokes a true feeling of disgust.

Developmental stages and disgust

Psychoanalysis directs us to certain disgust reactions that arise commonly in the course of development. In looking at these disgust situations, we should keep in mind that normative development varies somewhat from society to society, but that the common elements of disgust triggers – life uncontained and, often, category violations – should be regularly present across cultures.

Some things stir disgust in most all of us. Those common disgusts should turn our attention to the cultural practices that shape human development and to normative physical maturation and its psychological impact. As we enjoy and cope with growing bodies and minds, we have common encounters. Shared forms of disgust result.

Some of the near-inevitable disgusts we develop as we move through life stages include disgust over: (1) piggishness and gluttony, (2) those who are indifferent to dirt or wallow in it, (3) intrusions into our bodies or beings, (4) indiscriminate sexual behavior (which likely incorporates elements of gluttony and dirtiness), and (5) deterioration and decay.

In the earliest months of life, we meet the world largely through the senses, especially through the taste and feel of what enters the mouth. The infant is licensed to take in as hungrily as he or she wants, using the mouth, skin, or another modality. Essentially no restraint is placed on absorptive experience. Disgust precursors may appear in the form of early reactions to unwelcome contacts. W.I. Miller (1997, p. 55) remarked on his children showing a disgust-like face at four months of age, in response to a hair in the mouth.

Soon enough, parents – representing their cultures – begin to introduce restrictions that shape disgust experience. The word "enough" gains significance, as does the notion, "too much." First, restraint may be a matter of protecting health, or of hope that sanity can prevail in a household rocked by infantile needs but, in time, curbing impulse becomes the stuff of character. A person must know when enough is enough. One must not grab for more than one's due. One must say "please" before attempting to acquire something. The price of unsuccessful

The gatekeeper emotion: disgust **51**

incorporation of these lessons is piggishness. An infant who is primitive is shame-free, but when the undercarriage for control has matured, to remain primitive is to be crude, coarse, or animalistic. These words belong in the disgust lexicon. When the self is judged to be piggish, shame may follow or self-disgust if one takes a more aggressive, judgmental stance and bifurcates the self-experience into judge and adjudicated. Education about piggishness helps mold individuals so they can live in a group in which resources must be shared. Groups function better, with less violence, when people can show restraint in what they take and can help to moderate others.

When individuals incorporate the family norm that says, do not be a pig, they take on a communal use of disgust that, once developed, will persist even in the face of conflicting cultural norms such as, *look out for number one* or, at a national level, *America first*. Psychoanalysts, starting with Freud (1905), have called the internal opposition to piggishness a reaction-formation, and the idea has stood the test of many decades of clinical work. Such reaction-formation is simply an internal unfriendliness to the impulse to indulge piggishness and that opposition is experienced in the form of disgust, which can be directed at another or at oneself. Implied is that the impulse remains lively; we simply contain it by establishing the countervailing thrust of conscience. The modulation of piggishness may begin in connection with oral demands but it continues even into adolescence and gains associations along the way with other forms of behavior seen as crude or primitive. The disgust education of a child helps the child to learn and honor categories that are highly valued within his or her family and culture. Parents have many ways of saying, be a human being and not a pig, but say it they do.

It is worth noting that, in infancy, skin sensation is also important to comfort and pleasure. Skin contacts figure in disgust reactions, for example, when we touch something sticky or slimy, although this imagery seems less ubiquitous in disgust than oral imagery is. Moral instruction around touching what is repulsive certainly occurs, alongside instruction around piggishness. The contagion aspect of disgust is central to education about not contacting what is repulsive and children who have developed some capacity for self-control are expected to limit what they touch, including parts of their own bodies. Poor control over touching merges with the bowel dirtiness concerns of what has classically been called the anal phase of development. A worthy human being is not supposed to touch what is dirty and this idea extends to mental contact with dirty ideas. The leftover or the out of place (Douglas, 1966) – especially when it is alive or lifelike – often are avoided. The child's wish not to ingest or touch, for her own reasons, based on her own intuition of what is unappealing, interacts with education about what is disgusting.

In the psychoanalytically-termed anal phase, the child encounters wishes, fears, and fantasies around bowel activity and management. We teach the young child to put distance between herself and her feces and to take pleasure in self-control. This distance-taking soon ushers in the experience of disgust around bathroom matters, but alongside the disgust is fascination. The child wants to know what comes from within her, made by her. The child is taught to disavow her feces but

52 The gatekeeper emotion: disgust

knows their power. That child laughs when she uses that power, when she shouts out the forbidden words to get the grown-ups scowling, or stirs them to jump up and chastise her.

Eventually the growing child chooses sides, generally aligning – in pride or submission – with the adults, adopting the scowl, the pinched nose, the deodorizing sprays, the belief that dirtiness belongs with greed as another piggish behavior linked to life unmodulated, and leaving fascination to the youngest or for secret moments, interludes of sexual freedom, or jokes. Miller's (1997) "life soup" thesis becomes relevant with respect to the composition of the self. The child must not himself or herself *be* unregulated life or life uncontained or she will not be fully human, she will be disgusting. The category, humanity, is relevant to disgust both when we make another alien and disgusting and when we struggle with self-directed disgust that questions whether we ourselves are fully human or are, perhaps, animalistic or monstrous.

Negotiating interpersonal closeness and distance is a developmental process that begins in early infancy and continues into adulthood. Anzieu's (1989) discussion of "the skin ego" speaks to the early establishment of an experience of being a bounded self, separated by skin from all else that is nonself. The body in its skin serves as an analogue for the bounded self that exists experientially and without constant or obvious reference to the flesh. We feel separate not only because of our delineated bodies but because our mentation and perception is private and uniquely our own. We learn that our thoughts are not accessible to others. Our feelings can be secret as well. The way food affects our palate or color affects our aesthetic sense is special to us. Others' violations of our self-boundary, whether physical or emotional, often lead to disgust as we attempt to reassert our separateness and agency or to refuse excessive stimulation. A child pinched affectionately on the cheek by an adult not well known or trusted may react with disgust rather than the pleasure the adult might expect. The adult who wants to know too much about what one is thinking or feeling may elicit disgust, as sometimes seen in child therapy with children worried about whether they can withstand intrusion. A teen whose mother insisted on using a needle to do "surgery" on her acne felt disgust toward the mother for her intrusion.

Puberty is charged with feelings and impulses directed toward our own bodies and selves and toward other bodies and beings. Disgust figures in the traversing of puberty but the movement is from disgust to openness and acceptance; we reverse the course of the earlier stages, which move from engagement to restraint. Most come into puberty heavily armed with disgust reactions that protect them from feeling identified with anything too physical. They have learned the lessons of the oral and anal traversals and may have absorbed as well how to modulate inter-personal intimacy with disgust. Many greet the idea of adults who stick penises into vaginas or anuses, moan and sigh, nibble and suck with an enormous yuck reaction that is the fruit of all they have learned about how bodies, impulses, and intimacy ought to be contained. Thus armed, they are confronted with shape-shifting

The gatekeeper emotion: disgust **53**

bodies with new growths and altered contours, and they are buffeted by sudden surges of desire that, if indulged, plunge them into the messy physicality they learned to bridle as they restrained their early piggishness. How are they to integrate such immoderation and still be human?

Body change itself easily stimulates disgust because revulsion tends to protect the status quo if that has brought pleasure and security. So the little girl whose sleek, compact body has pleased her may not welcome the appearance of scraggly hairs on her private parts, which show up like dirt or contaminants, betrayals of what she has known and loved. They are no better than flies in one's cereal. The body's odor changes and its broad contours as well, and odd desires for messy and boundary-breaching entwinement with other bodies materialize. One client remembered sharp irritation with the male pediatrician who seemed to take some (in her mind, creepy and intrusive) pleasure in the changes in her young body, to which she had more than a little ambivalence. She saw her loved body as helpless to forestall alterations that seemed gross in their hairier, smellier aspects, and this man who had no business looking was indisputably disgusting in her estimation. She may have held him and his keen eyes responsible for the perpetration of this category-bursting outrage called puberty. The presence of disgust rather than shame spoke to the unintegrated nature of the changes. The new body lived in a region somewhere between self and nonself.

A girl whose experiences with a sexy, confident mother have been good ones may experience less disgust traversing puberty because she will move forward with excitement even in the face of uncertainty. Lacking that, this same client felt disgusted by Barbie dolls with their pointed, plastic breasts. She had no interest in their tiny, useless feet rigidly arched to receive plastic high heels. She even found Coca-Cola disgusting. What were those weird bubbles doing in her mouth? Signifying growing older, leaving behind childhood, clearly they were up to no good. She got relief learning that a fully adult friend of her parents always requested milk with his dinner, even at adults-only parties.

The pressure of sexual desire and the presence of sexually at-ease adults or appealing teens helps a child to suspend some of the childhood disgust reactions and open himself or herself to intense bodily experience that is part of adolescence. If the restraint on the earlier physicality of orality and anality has not been too harsh, and allows for an admixture of good cheer about indulgence, that too will help. Without these influences, the sexual adult will become a slut, cad, or animal who joins with the piggishly greedy and the wallower in dirt as another image of repulsively-unbridled instincts.

The idea of joining bodies, of suspending separateness in order to enter another's body or allow penetration, also easily triggers disgust, the gatekeeping emotion, in adolescence. Young people confront as well the idea that they – their bodies, their impulses – will be disgusting to a potential partner, who has himself or herself been reared on various aversions. A girl who has learned early that good girls are tidy, has not only to confront the smells and sights of menstruation, but also of

54 The gatekeeper emotion: disgust

vaginal secretions and perspiration. The body and the self are profoundly integrated, so if my body smells bad to you, then I am disgusting.

Also crucial in the mix is the ability to share one's emotional core, to develop trust in another, so that one can risk being dirty, messy, or wild without feeling intolerably disgusting; perhaps one even enjoys this license and feels more a wildcat than a pig. The minute distrust of a partner's honesty, affection, or intentions ruffles the relationship, disgust likely spikes. I train disgust on your body in order to keep you away from me, so that you cannot direct shaming energy my way.

Development does not stop with adolescence, and disgust continues to be relevant to change. Josephs (2016) described what he thought might be a normative return of disgust in later adulthood, when the press of youthful sexuality has diminished. He talks of looking back on early adult sexual adventure "with shame and regret rather than nostalgia" (p. 412). His conjecture deserves our attention, since the shame he discusses easily mingles with self-revulsion. One might surmise that later in adulthood the preference for protecting oneself from emotional vulnerability trumps the urgency of physical and emotional intimacy; disgust is available to help us in that endeavor.

In later life, deteriorative changes in the body easily trigger shame or self-disgust as well as disgust toward aged others. Menopausal night sweats, urinary incontinence, wrinkles, spots, vaginal dryness, impotence, all these experiences challenge our abilities to accept imperfectly "dirty," deteriorated, or uncontrolled bodies. The impulses to dissociate from one's body or another's body compete with tolerance and a sense of belonging to a community larger than oneself, an inclination bolstered by identifications with loved elders in possession of aged, imperfect bodies. At best, old age returns us to earliest animal awareness of elements such as softness, warmth, sustaining touch, and embrace rather than disturbing our ambitions for the hourglass figure, the peaches and cream complexion or the six-pack abs. But at worst, it leaves us in an unappealing stew of aversion and self-disgust.

A skilled novelist, Michelle de Kretser (2003), describes a Sri Lankan woman, Maud, who must contend with the ignominies of menopause:

> This sweat was a further indignity: it poured down her flanks, broke out on her forehead, gathered in the intimate creases of her flesh. She would wake in the night to find a soaking sheet twisted about her hips.

> From one day to the next her body became repellent to her. She became grateful for isolation, certain that she stank. Between breakfast and lunch she had doused a dozen handkerchiefs in eau de cologne and wiped herself down. She squandered a whole vial of orange water, upending it in her bath. The monsoon arrived and the weather cooled by three perceptible degrees, and still the clothes she put on when she rose were musky with sweat by eleven.

(p. 159)

The gatekeeper emotion: disgust **55**

In thinking about this character, I found myself wondering why some would emphasize shame in situations that, for another, bring self-disgust. Shame keeps the self whole. Generally, I am ashamed of "myself," the whole of me, and the "I" who is judging is also judged. Disgust more effectively bifurcates the self and gives us one who is repelled and one who is the awful object of repulsion. Maud was an aggressive character, and known to be heartless toward others. It seemed consistent with her character that she would take aim at herself in disgust more readily than she would shrivel in shame. The self-disgust attempts to say, this repulsiveness is not me; I don't recognize it, it is other. A client, John, spontaneously pondered why he felt disgust toward his body rather than shame. He felt that the self-disgust was aggressive. He hated that he had the physiognomy and expressions of his profoundly disappointing and disreputable father. The more he spoke of his disgust toward his body, the more his feelings about his lineage emerged. He spoke of one "polluted" person – his mother – joining with a second "polluted" person to create him. He recalled with abhorrence his mother asserting that he came "from my body." He felt "infested" by his parents and described a chronic pain in the lower abdomen that felt like disease. He thought it might become a cancer. He reeled out disgust words to try to capture his feelings for his mother: vile, loathsome, repugnant, abhorrent, repulsive. The belly pain seemed to connect him to her by way of memories of her pregnancies and of her anorexia. His need to attack every image he held of his parents and to separate himself from the two of them seemed likely to explain the uncompromising disgust he directed at his own body. The differential use of shame and self-disgust is worthy of research attention.

Oscar Wilde's (2015/1890) *The Picture of Dorian Gray* portrays a man willing to trade away everything he has or will have in exchange for a perpetually youthful countenance. In lieu of his own aging, a beautiful self-portrait in his possession begins to show age and also the stigmata of his dissolute behavior. He anticipates how age will be reflected on the canvas and in that foretelling we learn how repulsive he believes normal aging to be:

> Hour by hour, and week by week, the thing upon the canvas was growing old. It might escape the hideousness of sin, but the hideousness of age was in store for it. The cheeks would become hollow or flaccid. Yellow crow's feet would creep round the fading eyes and make them horrible. The hair would lose its brightness, the mouth would gape or droop, would be foolish or gross, as the mouths of old men are. There would be the wrinkled throat, the cold, blue-veined hands, the twisted body, that he remembered in the grandfather who had been so stern to him in his boyhood.
>
> (p. 798)

The passage is interesting in its reference to the grandfather who raised Dorian, an orphaned boy. The grandfather was unloving and unlovable. Had he offered a

56 The gatekeeper emotion: disgust

different vision of old age or been a more congenial elder with whom to identify, Dorian's disgust with that future might well have been mitigated. One woman I know who had plastic surgery had seen too much of her hated mother's aging face in the maturing of her own visage. She wanted "my own face back." Another woman saw the lines and sags in her aging face as "objectively" unattractive, but her face had become so reminiscent of her beloved father in his old age that she softened her attitude toward herself.

Disgust in the fabric of lives

Sensitivities that lead to disgust are deeply embedded in personality. These sensitivities promote active measures that limit our exposure to what disgusts us. Often, these actions operate as quiet background processes that influence which human and material environments we avoid and which we welcome. Disgust speaks loudly when we cannot control our contact with those things that repel us. A person rides a bus and someone with rotten teeth sits down beside her; she must remain in her seat for the duration of the trip. A partner chosen under the influence of infatuation displays obnoxious qualities hitherto unnoticed and a man feels trapped in his marital relationship. If an unwanted exposure can be easily curtailed, disgust is a momentary problem. When contact must be sustained (or is neurotically pursued), disgust generates high tension, often in relation to another person.

When disgust appears prominently in a no-exit situation, it is time to examine that disgust in order to see how it is operating and whether it represents a mental health problem. Is it protecting a person from closer contact that would be damaging? Is it expressing a deeply held value? In these cases, we might honor its message and see the disgust as an incitement toward action. Alternatively, disgust may represent avoidance of intimacy that has been rendered risky due to earlier life trauma. I think of one woman who married late and struggled with sexual aversion toward her husband. She had chosen this man by marrying him, but her heart had not fully embraced her choice. She had suffered traumatic abandonment by her father and intimacy with a man was fraught with danger. Disgust needs to be viewed in context, be that context developmental, cultural, political, or familial. In this familial context, analysis of disgust and efforts to modify it became important.

Another disgust reaction had a developmental context that suggested it was not highly problematic and perhaps not worth psychotherapeutic change efforts. An adolescent client spoke at length of her mother's disgustingness. She chewed with her mouth open. She left her hairbrush on the kitchen counter. She talked too loudly in public. To look into the depth of these occasional disgust reactions might have led to glimpses of reaction-formations or anxiety about her own capacities to be clean enough to be acceptable to others. I listened to them though with awareness that this young woman was eager to move away from her parents and to embrace travel or college. I commented, "It sounds like you are about ready to move out of the house." Were she an older person trying to foster more positive feelings toward

The gatekeeper emotion: disgust **57**

a partner in order to sustain the relationship, we might have tackled the disgust as a problem and explored how she could open herself to a broader range of contacts—including germs, messiness, and loss of personal space—without having to push away so hard in disgust. A more accepting and inclusive stance might have helped her under those circumstances. But she was 17 and was preparing to move on to an age-appropriate life outside the family. In this context, her brief eruptions of disgust served like an engine launching her from mother earth.

At any point in development, difficult circumstances can impact our readiness to feel disgust. Toxic physical or emotional stimulation can stir intensified interpersonal disgust that seeds later psychopathology, perhaps later disgust-proneness. Situations also can arise that call for high levels of disgust as part of adaptation to a difficult moment. These may or may not leave heavy marks on the personality.

When disgust appears interpersonally, it is valuable to note which of the modes discussed in Chapter 1 is in use. Is the person sharing emotion, imposing emotion, or targeting another with feelings? These modes will play out in psychotherapy as emotion is disclosed to the therapist, forced on the therapist, or directed at the therapist. For example, John communicated that he wanted me to hear and empathize with how readily he became disgusted with his coworkers. He wished I would understand how these feelings caused him conflict with others and wanted me to reflect on why he readily felt them. His primary intentions were that I understand his pain and also that I join my ego with his and help him address a daunting interpersonal problem. At other times, however, he communicated that were I to stake out a different position from his regarding a person he found disgusting, he would be angry at me and feel alienated. Under those circumstances, he would tease me with mild sadism and suggest that I would pay a price for maintaining distance from his emotion. On rare occasions – usually softened by joking – he would suggest that I was myself behaving in a disgusting way, for example, by going on vacation with my family when he would be left alone and forlorn. What was wrong with me that I didn't offer to take him along? When I was becoming to him a disgusting alien, he needed help in allowing and expressing directly his hostile emotion. He found such expression unsettling to our relationship and likely to elicit a counterpunch of disgust on my part.

We can observe a continuum of disgust-proneness ranging from the acutely sensitive to the highly resistant or insensitive. Those most prone to disgust go through life on alert for repulsive encounters. They labor particularly when the environment is new and unfamiliar, and areas of disgustingness have not yet been detected or addressed, for example, through disinfection. Such a person might be most comfortable at home, where the cleaning has been done by known and trusted hands. The farther from home he or she goes, the greater the risk of disgusting encounters. The person distrusts the unknown with its broad potential to threaten security or to expose him or her to displays of unsettling impulses or identifications. So the oft-disgusted person lives cautiously and tries to limit encounters with what feels foreign. In some cases, phobias appear and may target things felt to be disgusting,

58 The gatekeeper emotion: disgust

often what has motility and thus obvious invasive power, for example, insects or rodents. This person finds his disgust disturbing and he wants to avoid it. Others actually court moderate levels of disgust and enjoy the intensity of the "eew" moment, for example, in tasting an unfamiliar food such as a grasshopper.

At the opposite end of the continuum we have the person who seems never to experience disgust. She looks with indifference at people who lie and steal, who urinate in the street, or dig in their nostrils on the bus. Perhaps her own behavior, too, fails to respect common limits regarding comportment, so she disgusts others (but feels no shame or self-disgust). Some might see this rare person as primitive, as lacking in taste, culture, sophistication, and values. Some would direct opprobrium her way or wonder what is wrong with her. Disgust helps us to form a tableau of what we find acceptable and what we reject. It helps us define core categories such as adult behavior, sophistication, and respectability, even humanness. When children behave badly, parents sometimes reprimand them, "Have you no shame?" but they might as well ask, "Have you no disgust?" Shame and disgust are hand in glove when it comes to corralling improper behavior (Miller, 1985, 1996). Generally people have acute sensitivity to whether they might be disgusting others with their behavior, and they want to avoid that outcome or, occasionally, to use it aggressively to say, look how I can upset you. A commercial for a home deodorizer played on human anxiety about being disgusting by suggesting that a person's environment might be more malodorous and offensive than he can know, because he has gone "nose blind" to his own smells (so he had better buy the deodorizing product and protect himself from embarrassment).

Between the two poles of disgust-proneness lie people of intermediate sensitivity and those with islands of imperviousness and zones of reactivity. Since we tend to judge others in relation to ourselves, if I have a generally high tolerance for disgust around physical matters, I may regard the more sensitive person as prissy and she may view me as slovenly or unsanitary. I may be tolerant around dirt and body products but fanatical around what I judge to be material over-indulgence of rich children, or weak business ethics, both of which I find repellant. Thus the patterns of disgust in the mid-range are many and varied and help to generate the permutations of human personality.

I want to examine three protective functions of disgust, any of which might pertain to a moment's disgust or a lifetime of the emotion. More than one of these dynamics can exist in a single emotional moment. In considering individuals, we will be looking at highly personalized disgust triggers, but the universal is nested within the idiosyncratic. In looking at life stories, our interest in symbolization and defenses will be great, since these processes shape a situation according to a person's needs and wishes, which exist in the light of his or her unique history. Defenses will operate in relation to experiences that bear the core components of disgust, for example, a woman might use reaction-formation disgust to fend off attraction but will do so by defining a man who flirts with her as alien or as deviating from her idea of what it means to be masculine, and so she wants him far from her body and mind. She experiences the category stress typical of disgust as well

The gatekeeper emotion: disgust **59**

as the sense that the stimulus is dangerously alive, in a way she labels as bad. In this example, the defensive need colors perception and thus creates a disgusting being that can be rejected.

Three protective functions of disgust include:

1. reducing vulnerability to powerful, destructive others that could infect and damage us;
2. limiting our guilt, anxiety, or shame about impulses and actions;
3. distancing ourselves from people or things that represent imagery of an unacceptably damaged, weak, abnormal, or destroyed self.

Reducing vulnerability to powerful, destructive others that could infect and damage us

Recall the elephantiasis story from Chapter 1 in which the young girl (as remembered by the adult) feels subjected by her teacher to a film about sick people who both disgust and fascinate her. The viewing leaves her angry at and appalled by her teacher and by the narrator of the film, both of whom are seen as perpetrating harm against vulnerable people (those who are sick and the children watching the film). In discussing this story earlier, I neglected certain questions. A primary unstated question is, why did this experience make such an enormous impression on the girl and remain toxic for the woman she became? We lack history about the narrator, but nevertheless can entertain a number of possibilities.

Salient aspects of the narrative were, first, the overall abandoned, lonely, sad, poor conditions of the people. These people were lost and left. They were in an abject state. Second, the people had very peculiar, damaged, distorted limbs that drew close attention – both disgust and fascination – from the girl. She makes a strong mental connection between the overall desolation of the people and their bizarre bodies. The bodies are the proximal disgust stimuli. They fit the disgust pattern of violating a natural and reassuring category, that of normal physical form. They also suggest life unbounded because they are swollen and appear to be infected by a disease, which intimates destructive growth.

We need as well to consider that fascination may have preceded the disgust and stirred guilt in the girl. Why was she peering so intently at these distorted limbs? Might she be hurting these poor people? In this view, the girl herself is the merciless teacher and narrator, but she has transferred her guilt to them. Her disgust argues, I am innocent, and victimized as well. I am not the perpetrator here.

The threat to the girl is in the possession of an ugly body, but also in the derelict condition of those burdened by such flesh. She could be like they are. She feels their feelings and knows their disgraced, ruined state. Might this disgusting-body status have a particular, emblematic meaning for the girl that is not revealed in her narrative but explains the power of the moment? She might have a sick parent whose body strikes her as damaged, whose plight seems that of abandonment. She might herself feel deserted and devalued, as a body and being. She might

60 The gatekeeper emotion: disgust

associate the swollen limbs with something that troubled her eyes. Perhaps she saw a swollen penis or pendulous breast and found it peculiar and frightening, but had no way to discuss what she had viewed. If so, she might have put aside the image only to have it recur by way of the enlarged, hard limbs of those with a disease that sounds like "elephants." The word itself might add meaning to what her eyes have seen.

Looking at more proximate causes for her distress, we need to consider the current situation in which the young woman, not the child, finds herself. She is in a classroom – the site of the original suffering. She is being asked to complete a task that holds no obvious reward for her. Perhaps she feels coerced by instructor and researcher and this current tension participates in eliciting a memory of forced engagement.

In the elephantiasis story, we see disgust both characterizing an experience and attempting to modify it. The disgust says "this experience is bad – I want it to end" and it also restricts and contains it, says it is this, not that. It is a swollen leg of an African not a sick mother's leg or a distended breast. It is a bad experience forced on sick people by a film maker and forced on me by a teacher. It is not (or is it?) a fascinating thing I love watching because it is like nothing I've seen and it is happening to them, not to me, and it is oddly exciting.

The elephantiasis narrative shows disgust responding to an unexpected stimulus – diseased limbs – that has impressed itself upon a person and needs containing. The trajectory is predominately from the outside event to the inside state. In other instances, we see disgust beginning with a person's need to reject someone or something. That need tailors perception and gives rise to the characterization of something or someone as disgusting. An example would be the person threatened by intimacy who perceives all potential lovers as disgusting. The disgust evolves from a prior need, in this case one for interpersonal distance. In each instance, disgust can be considered a tool, with particular form and function, that operates in the development of experience. If I give you a basket, you might use it to carry peaches, while your brother uses it to carry acorns. Because it is a basket, it has a somewhat-defined form, which means that its utility has limits; neither you nor your brother will use it to carry water.

A second example of utilizing disgust to reduce the invasive and emotionally disorienting power of the other is also an example of an individual dealing with what Atlas and Benjamin (2015) refer to as "too muchness," W.I. Miller (1997) calls "surfeit" and I have discussed as "excess." John, introduced earlier, presented with chronic, low level nausea that was a cognitively-unelaborated emotion, which came and went inexplicably. He had a number of specific memories of acute disgust linked to highly disturbing, intrusive behaviors by his mother. One such memory concerned his mother regularly coming into the bathroom unbidden when he, a teenager, was in the bath. She then insisted on washing his hair. The disgust was an attempt to characterize and reject intolerable aspects of the situation, including unwanted sexual stimulation and physical and psychic intrusion. The experience was a massive threat to his sense of being a normal teenager and, additionally,

The gatekeeper emotion: disgust **61**

exposed him to shame (later, self-disgust) about his body because he saw himself through the scrutinizing eyes of an often-sadistic parent.

For this young man, disgust inhered in his memories and was quickly reproduced in current day relationships with any woman who was powerful in his life and thus threatening, including women whose sexual attractiveness stirred him. The disgust seemed like an emergency mechanism for keeping him out of intimate situations that might recreate the dangers of his relationship with an emotionally ill and overwhelming mother. In addition to sharp disgust, he experienced the free-floating nausea that could seem "psychic" to him rather than bodily in origin, but was difficult to elaborate cognitively. The nausea may have related in some way to his mother's eating disorder, which led her to vomit and to offer up food to the family that he found revolting.

This young man learned to use disgust aggressively in ways that fiercely denied vulnerability and merged with contempt. It took little for him to characterize another person as "a piece of shit" or "a vile cretin." Any perceived slight would suffice. In these situations, narcissistic rage flared and the disgust was both the face of his fury and a protection of his self-regard. The entwining of universal and idiosyncratic disgusts was evident in this man. His mother's behavior would be considered excessively stimulating and invasive by most any teenager and it violated the category, teen, by treating him like a young child. But the particularity of his feelings and the evolving, defensive use of disgust spoke to a life story that was uniquely his.

Atlas and Benjamin (2015) discuss the case of Leo, an individual who uses disgust to convey hatred of the unsatisfying and painfully over- and under-stimulating other, who is experienced through the lens of the infantile self–mother relationship. Leo cannot attempt to fill unmet needs, because his desires will lead, he feels, to toxic interactions. The authors say of clients like Leo, "These patients live with a constant fear that appears very early in their analysis, the fear that they will be again seduced, attach and left dysregulated and distressed" (p. 10).

Signs of vitality in the therapist – especially indications that the therapist is *feeling something* and is thus an independent agent with her own body and mind – elicit disgust in Leo. The logic of his disgust seems to be, if you are alive you will overwhelm me. Her vitality disturbs the sense of a properly-boundaried, good enough self. The authors say of Leo:

> [He] interrupted his analyst by scolding: "Stop that fucking feeling." He added: "I can't stand it when you suddenly sound moved. Don't be offended, it has a physical effect on me; it's uncomfortable, even disgusting." The patient has been in analysis for five years, and his analyst is well acquainted with his hypervigilant responses to feeling, his continual demand that she not "dramatize things," sense them without making a sensation. He fears her potential hyperarousal at a level of physiological response, disgust.
>
> (p. 10)

62 The gatekeeper emotion: disgust

They summarize Leo's therapy:

> He brings a violent sexuality and part-objects into the room. The primitive aggressiveness and invasiveness of his fantasies feel assaultive: he speaks of "repulsive breasts," "a disgusting, stinking vagina," and "an unsatisfying dick." "I had sex with her," he tells me, describing a recent encounter. "She shouted, and her shout did not connect with her body. She's my fuck-buddy. Her vagina feels like metal, and I go in and out."
>
> (p. 13)

Like John, disturbed in the bath, Leo shows us the sadistic use of disgust as an attack on the other that asserts the other's total worthlessness and protects the self from vulnerability to disturbing forms of stimulation. He is terrified of a woman's humanity and wants her to be "metal," so that he can go in and out without anything of hers adhering to him. Disgust often says another is not human enough, is alien, but Leo's disgust says the person is too human, and thus intolerable. For him, humanity is not a precious category but a foul one. A woman cannot have human feelings and a body without overwhelming him, therefore, disgust is requisite. In discussing this case, Atlas and Benjamin focus on the mother whose *absence* leads to internal overstimulation by distress, but one would wonder as well about the distressingly-present mother, even if she were there only in a child's imagination.

Another patient of mine, reported earlier (Miller, 1986), showed a similar dread of a partner's emotions as "too much" and thus disgusting. The disgust he and Atlas's and Benjamin's patient feels demonstrates *life uncontained* in the interpersonal sphere. Lively qualities and behaviors of the other person flow too freely and powerfully toward the self, elicit profound negative associations, and overwhelm. The other person can be seen as category-bursting with respect to the self category because the self is devastated by the contact:

> I want to be able to have a very close relationship with someone without having my whole life fall apart – without my not being able even to take care of myself, not to feed myself, not to give myself sleep because I'm in love with someone, because I'm being intimate with someone. [Therapist asks what happens when he tries to eat]. . . . All the food tasted – it tasted terrible. None of it appealed to me – sweet things were *too* sweet. They made me feel like throwing up. And starchy things were *too* starchy. It made me feel like it's too much . . . I'm gonna get it out.
>
> (p. 302)

He talks more about his girlfriend:

> The thing that I think overwhelms me about her is her problems. . . . It's her needs. Like when she's strong, when she says to me all these things about

The gatekeeper emotion: disgust **63**

me and tries to bring me up I feel alright about the relationship. I don't feel like I'm drowning. But after I saw her today, I just wanted to vomit. I just wanted to throw up. [Therapist: What was it?] She was falling apart and when she was falling apart all she was was just needs – all she was was OH, OH I NEED. I NEED. I NEED. And I tried to help her – I tried to say, okay, calm down. I tried to help her, I tried to give of myself – I tried to be strong and she didn't give me anything back. I mean like in fact she sort of just left me hanging there.

(p. 305)

The young man may well be confusing his own great needs with his girlfriend's, but his experience is of urgency intruding on him from outside, which he must reject violently through disgust. Life uncontained is present as is the perceived invasiveness characteristic of disgust stimuli. Category stress is evident in his inability to see the young woman as a partner rather than one for whom he must care like an infant; she inhabits an intercategorical position. His girlfriend's needs affect him so deeply that they besiege his body as well as his mind. They emotionally and physically sicken him, so that her intrusion disturbs the self category. *Sharing* the emotion with his therapist and *targeting* the girlfriend with the emotion are his modes of interaction.

A clinician told of responding with disgust-like emotion to a woman patient who insisted the therapist become, in concrete ways, her "mommy." The therapist said, in a presented paper:

As her outpouring of emails flowed – some tender, some coy, some demanding – I started to feel like I was suffocating in a sticky blend of breast milk and baby spit-up, and that Athena was hoping to adhere me to her with this pungent and viscous glue. Athena's demands felt annoyingly manipulative, so far beyond any reasonable expectation of my time, and yet I was becoming viscerally aware of how real these needs felt to her. It was not a game.

(Davies, 2017)

The therapist responds to the threat that her own adult, differentiated, professional self will be damaged – in category-bursting fashion – by unwanted intrusion by this giant baby. She generates a rich blend of images that convey smell (baby spit-up) and touch (stickiness), as well as symbols of infantile life (breast milk): the composite points to disgust at the patient's invasion. We might wonder as well whether the disgust signifies the need to turn off empathy for intensely infantile demands. Too much compassion for such neediness can bring anxiety if it evokes one's own desires or elicits a feeling that the bearer-of-needs is in deep trouble because she will never be satisfied and perhaps never helped to feel whole. If the job of helping belongs to the therapist, the weight of such demands can be

64 The gatekeeper emotion: disgust

enormous. Disgust aims to quickly erect a wall against the patient's needs, any corresponding longings of the therapist, and whatever fears may exist regarding the patient's future, given her insatiable state.

Limiting our guilt, anxiety, or shame about impulses and actions

In Chapter 1, I introduced the massive disgust of a woman whose waiter revolted her with "white liquid" on his lips, though he brought her "delicious" food. Her spontaneous associations were all to other disgusting things associated with the mouth or with eating:

> I cannot stand toothpaste or seeing a person brush his/her teeth with foamy toothpaste.
> It nauseates me.
> I don't use toothpaste.
> I also can't stand seeing a person chew gum or blow gum bubbles.
> My stomach is turning over just thinking about it.
> And the thought of people swallowing semen?

The preponderance of eating images suggests the possibility of a persistent reaction-formation against oral wishes. Edith Jacobson (1964) responded to Freud's emphasis on genital level reaction-formation with the proposition that oral reaction-formation is a source of disgust. Presumably, both types of reaction-formation are possible and bespeak impulses denied through disgust.

In US discussions of transgender policy, the idea of allowing people free access to any public bathroom incited an uproar of outrage and opposition. The former Arkansas governor, Mike Huckabee, spoke to the rampant concern. *Politico* (Gass, 2015) reported him to have said:

> I wish that somebody would have told me in high school that I could have felt like a woman when it came time to take showers in P.E. I'm pretty sure I would have found my feminine side, and said, "Coach, I think I'd rather shower with the girls today."

Huckabee engaged his subject matter with humor, but others expressed genuine anger and disgust in response to the bathroom controversy. Those most concerned about transgender people using the "wrong" bathroom (usually, transgender men using the women's bathroom) may be frightened by their own wishes. A number of varieties of impulse likely are at issue. One type emerges in Mike Huckabee's joke: the desire of a man to look at naked women. Note that the imagined, high school aged Huckabee has gone from the toilet to the shower, where much would be on display. The former governor is not particularly intimidated by his wishes – he is willing to reveal them and laugh. But some would be very frightened by

The gatekeeper emotion: disgust **65**

voyeuristic impulses and would need to project them onto some other man who is, disgustingly, pretending to be a woman in order to get a look at the naked ladies.

Desires to touch in ways society forbids, or to attack and harm, are other impulses that might trouble a person. We must also consider the yearning to join and identify. The man who finds himself deeply disgusted by a transgender person's option to go into a women's bathroom may envy that person's opportunity to be close to women, perhaps to express kinship with them. Something in him wants to say, I am a woman, too. Almost all men begin their lives in intimate association with women and many may have felt their bodies to be like those of the women they loved. They may have dealt with disappointment, or shame, as they – early in life – came to learn they must separate from these women, go with the men, lead lives without breasts or babies (Fast, 1984; Benjamin, 1995). To see another man take leave of his masculinity and march unpunished into the room meant only for women thus has the potential to stir sadness, even grief and envy, all of which complex emotions can be circumvented through disgust at those who would make that trip.

Disgust works to deny or forestall impulses on which we dare not act. It can also rationalize acting on desires that would be forbidden, were disgust not present as a rationale for the behavior. Violence, especially sadistic aggression, is often the otherwise forbidden action. The dynamic of disgust rationalizing violence has impacted sweeping populations of people. Stunning examples occurred during the Third Reich and also in periods of institutionalized slavery or repression. Primo Levi (1989) discussed the transport of Jews to concentration camps in empty train cars, with no food, water, ventilation, seating, or even a chamber pot, and he noted a sinister use of disgust to rationalize violence:

> The convoy was stopped two or three times in the open countryside, the doors of the freight cars were opened, and the prisoners were allowed to get off – but not to walk away from the tracks or to go off on their own. The doors were opened another time, but during a stop in an Austrian railroad station. The SS escort did not hide their amusement at the sight of men and women squatting wherever they could, on the platforms and in the middle of the tracks, and the German passengers openly expressed their disgust: people like this deserve their fate, just look how they behave. These are not *Menschen*, human beings, but animals; it's clear as the light of day.
>
> (pp. 125–126)

Levi goes on to consider how such humiliation, which renders the Jews disgusting, served German purposes:

> Certainly, this was one of the fundamental features of Hitlerism not only inside the Lagers; and it seems to me that the best comment on it is summed

66 The gatekeeper emotion: disgust

up in these two remarks taken from a long interview by Gitta Sereny with the already mentioned Stangl, ex-commandment of Treblinka.

(Levi, 1989, p.135)

"Considering that you were going to kill them all ... what was the point of the humiliations, the cruelties?" the writer asks Stangl, imprisoned for life in the Düsseldorf jail, and he replies: "To condition those who were to be the material executors of the operations. To make it possible for them to do what they were doing." In other words: before dying the victim must be degraded, so that the murderer will be less burdened by guilt. This is an explanation not devoid of logic but it shouts to heaven: it is the sole usefulness of useless violence.

(Levi, 1989, pp. 125–126)

Nazi propaganda gave birth to the repulsive Jew. Outrageous deprivations forced the Jew into compliance with his loathesome portrayal, thus the ground was laid for the Jew's extermination. Sartre (1948) tells us:

[B]y Nazi propaganda, on the obscene pages of Streicher's *Stürmer*, the Jew is described as a hairy parasite, fat, with crooked legs, a beaked nose, flapping ears, good only at harming others. German he is not, by axiom; indeed, his presence is sufficient to contaminate public baths and even park benches.

(pp. 128–129)

Sartre has understood that behind such societally "cleansing" activities or acts of putting people in their "proper" places are human yearnings hungering to be satisfied. I speak now of sadistic impulses to debase and harm others, and to exploit them sexually. Demeaned characterizations have value in setting up projective identifications, which means that someone with a great interest in some impulse state but a sense as well of its reprobate nature, will stamp someone else, some awful *other* or *alien*, with that status, then maintain an abiding interest in the one who now contains and displays, he believes, the awful, but terribly exciting, quality. Sexual impulses frequently are projected in this fashion and lead to fascination with the carrier of the wish, who is condemned, hated, reviled, even killed, while remaining of great interest.

Sartre (1948) and others have seen that the degradation of people is used to unleash and exempt from guilt the most sadistic of impulses. Sartre describes a classic projective identification when showing how the anti-Semite's endless contemplation of Jewish "evil" allows him to envisage all the things that excite him. Among them are hypersexuality, avarice, criminality, secrecy, and money:

But Evil, on the other hand, is something he can contemplate untiringly, something for which he has not only the intuition but, one would say, the taste as well. With an energy touching on obsession, he returns again and

The gatekeeper emotion: disgust **67**

again to anecdotes of obscene or criminal actions, which excite him and satisfy his perverse leanings: but since, at the same time, he attributes them to the same infamous Jews on whom he pours his scorn, he gluts his passion without compromising himself.

(pp. 37–38)

Similar psychodynamics exist around other genocides and around slavery, an institution economically beneficial to some that depends on the slave-trader or slave-owner's ability to justify brutal exploitation. Such misuse of persons is abetted by rendering them as alien, as intercategorical insect-humans, or as refuse. We tend to believe it is normal and natural, even desirable, for us to clean up trash or exterminate insects. To the extent we can persuade ourselves that some persons are not in fact human but are a form of dirt, alien life, or oddly amalgamated creature, violence is rationalized.

When groups within society use disgust and degradation to indulge forbidden impulses and to justify violence, the disgust also operates to consolidate a feeling of belonging to a superior group. It becomes an assertion of identity that says, we are the disgusted ones, the ones spitting at the Jews, Blacks, or Gypsies, the ones entertaining ourselves and building *esprit de corps* by telling each other stories of their disgraceful behavior and revolting physicality. *Esprit de corps* can also emerge in disgust-consolidated groups that are concerned less with impulse repudiation and more with the loud expression of hostility toward those who defy the group's values. I think here of the rampant sharing of disgust among those disturbed by the 2016 US election of Donald Trump as president.

Distancing ourselves from people or things that represent imagery of an unacceptably damaged, weak, abnormal, or destroyed self

I turn my attention now to disavowed identification. The mode of interaction on display is the targeting of others with disgust:

> The couple sat before me. Sixty-something. Married a dozen years. She, wearing shorts and a tee shirt, giggling like a pre-teen. He reaching over to squeeze her knee, touching sequentially the half-dozen large jewels with which she had bedecked herself. Then, a light touch to her thigh, a tickle on her arm. He grinned, gave her a mock leer, vocalized, "hoo-hoo" lustily. He referred to her – addressing me – as "my stunning lady," commented on her flirtations, how she'd come to him naked and surprised him while he bent over the plumbing, wore decorative pasties on her nipples and nothing more, delighted him. My god, I thought. You are not that attractive, not young, not beautiful, not graceful by any means. They were making eyes at each other, she giggling still, he grinning. I should have been tickled by their sexuality finally burgeoning after years of our joint labor. Instead, I was

68 The gatekeeper emotion: disgust

disgusted. I could have been unengaged, mild in my pleasure, amused, satisfied with work well done. But no, I was disgusted. And guilty as I recognized the hostility of the emotion.

I had to ask myself, why this collapse of maternal enthusiasm for growth? I came upon their indignity as my initial explanation. I targeted their clumsy seduction, their lack of sophistication, subtlety, modesty, their shamelessness, age-inappropriateness. I didn't recognize this reaction as the familiar category crisis of disgust, which occurred here as old age mimicked youth and left its rightful station. I did see the more idiosyncratic roots, which included awareness that in my childhood world this couple would have been targeted: silly, childish, ridiculous, wearing their hearts on their sleeves. They had made themselves entirely too vulnerable; I couldn't abide it. They were me, an adolescent self, adoring openly an older man I'd fallen for, incurring the delighted ridicule of sister and father, the guardians of judgment (and category integrity). Were I to join this couple in their delight, I would again be vulnerable to harsh adjudication. Better then to be judge, high commissioner, hurler of thunderbolts of contempt, and grunts of disgust. Either would suffice to keep them from touching me and communicating their contagious indignity. To all that, add a dollop of envy because they had found some enchantment with each other and were parading it in front of me; I was nothing more than audience, appreciative or otherwise.

As a second example of disgust used to distance oneself from unacceptable self-images, I think of an experience volunteering at a local grade school. I frequently worked with two mischievous second grade boys, both of whom, each in his own way, was bubbling with fears and wishes that emerged in macho talk and action. The chatter of each boy often tarred the other with words that connoted worthlessness, such as the word, stupid (or stoopid, in this case). Another word much used was poop. Stupid and poop both signified worthlessness, although poop was disgusting and stoopid meant worthless but did not so obviously connote disgust. One day though the boys used the words in more or less equivalent ways by writing them down and then attempting physically to touch each other with the written words. I was struck by the concrete physicality of their play. If I touch this bad word to you, pin it on you, you become the bad thing. Because disgustingness is contagious, all one needs to do with something repellant is to touch it and you will become sickening yourself. We can see the relationship between contagion and touch: what is on the skin of someone or something easily enters and becomes them. The game the boys played was animated by the thrill of trying to get the bad word to adhere to the other child, and trying to evade the other's attempt to pin it on you.

As another example of disgust protecting against negative self-imagery, I think of a woman who told me the story of her adolescent daughter who found the mother's housekeeping intolerably sub-par, declared many parts of the house repulsive, and railed against the mother for making it impossible for the girl to bring friends to the house. The idea of a filthy house disturbed the daughter's idea

The gatekeeper emotion: disgust **69**

of what belonged where: dirt and disorder did not suit a house. In contrast with the story of the 30 cats, this tale did not have a grossly dirty reality underpinning it. The mother did seem to accumulate clutter, but the kitchen, for example, was not unsanitary, just disorderly, and at a level that would not impress visitors as disgraceful. Thus the daughter was sent into category crisis of the marginality type by a situation that would not agitate most. This young girl had a rigid character that maintained core categories more anxiously than many. Also important was her concern about her own social acceptability; she seemed to be externalizing a feared defect onto the mother, as adolescents do. Mom, not me, is unpresentable. If it weren't for Mom, I would have friends and bring them home. I'm not afraid of my peers, I'm disgusted by my mom, as they, too, will be. Because she had been close to her mother, and was identified with her, Mom's deficits would all the more readily transmit through contagion.

Also at issue for this young woman, I suspected, was a developmental issue around independence from her mother. Like most of us, she wanted to be successful in adulthood, but she feared being on her own and grieved the loss of intense childhood intimacy with Mom. To feel continual disgust with her mother – whatever its focus – was to say, mantra-like, *I do not want you, I do not want you, I do not want you*. In this way, she disavowed the longings that might threaten. She used disgust as a reaction-formation that blocked the development of yearning.

We often see disgust respond to unexpected confrontation with a powerful stimulus, but here we have a person *prepared* to feel disgust, ready to feel it time and again before she even encounters an actual dirty refrigerator or floor, when the meeting is only in her head. The threats we have discussed – as determinative of disgust – are real and vivid, even overwhelming to her, but they are largely internally constructed. Her eyes alone see the countertop as repulsively filthy, or the floor as revoltingly sticky. Obscured is the greater jeopardy she might experience should she surrender her disgust. Without it, she would have to face her fear of bringing friends home. Without it, her longings to stay a child at her mother's side – a hunger that cannot be fulfilled – might emerge. No matter how earnestly her mother sweeps and scrubs, the house remains dirty and disgusting, because the daughter needs it to be so. *Modally*, her disgust is not shared emotion, but is emotion triggered by another, who is its target.

In a contrasting case, one woman, Mindy, essentially *refused* to feel disgust where others in her family did. She had several familial models of people with low disgust thresholds – people quick to locate, condemn, and retreat from ickiness in the world, with its odd creatures, substances, and smells. As a younger child of an overburdened mother of borderline personality organization, she herself was often classified as belonging to the world of yucky and expendable, excess stuff. She developed an unusually high disgust threshold and an attraction to circumstances from which the disgust-prone members of her family recoiled. She liked to muck about in puddles as a child and wetlands as an adult, and seldom felt disgust at creatures, biological processes, or cutting edge art forms or ideas. How did that happen? Some of it may have been in her genetic package but I think, as well,

70 The gatekeeper emotion: disgust

that she identified with the devalued mess and was not about to allow it to be fully debased. No, she would discern treasures in that mess, call it an abundance, a creative mother lode, and aggressively protect its right to be. Any dirty, wild creature she could get her hands on was a source of wonder, any drooling dog or crazily flapping bird that happened into the house and needed corralling was a gift. In other moments, she could be shame sensitive but tried to protect a core of good-self feeling through refusing to let her status as unwanted, messy, extra child root too deeply.

Mindy was happy in the fields and swamps and unallied with the family members who found dirt and sloppy places disgusting. Disgust, however, held a prominent place in her life, along with contempt, because she passed harsh judgment against those who were acquisitive of material goods saying, in effect, you, not me, are the repellent ones. Her disgust and contempt were aggressive, outspoken, and attempted to control others' indulgences in purchases. She herself saved money, for reasons she didn't understand, and refrained from expenditures. Her self-denial ranged from practical items to clothing, even at times to social relationships. Later in life, as she matured and benefited from therapy, she became less fearful of certain of her own impulses. Gradually, she gained contact with intensely envious feelings probably rooted in desires for parental attention and love but taking the shape of demands for possessions. She who had expressed such disgust over others' material desires became aware of the internal demand to be the one most richly gifted with goods and money. She recognized that her insistence on saving money had served both to flaunt her lack of material desires and to secure for herself the means to indulge such desires, should she ever wish to do so. She found her aggressively acquisitive impulses reprehensible, once they were revealed, but recognized their genuineness and depth and the relationship they held to her disgust and contempt toward others. She who had indulged only in free things— art, experience, nature—wanted the goods that form the basis for an economy that rewards some and deprives others. She demanded to be the one rewarded, not the one denied. She wanted to have the most and to see others suffering from frustration and envy. She also aimed, through disgust toward others, to negate the injury felt when she had been the object of disgust as the dirty, unwanted, later-born child.

As another example of disgust protecting self-regard, I introduce a research narrative (Miller, 1986), collected in 1974, which concerns a disappointing purchase of a stereo turntable. The audio equipment, which arrived broken, appears to have been a powerful self-representation.

> I had decided to make a rather large purchase of a turntable for my stereo.
> First Disgusting Event: Upon returning to town, the opening of my package revealed my toy to be damaged. Such comments as 'What a piece of shit' and other expletive deleted remarks were results of Disgusting Event #1.

The gatekeeper emotion: disgust **71**

Second Disgusting Event: Seeing that I had purchased the turntable from an audio chain (who happened to have an in-town location), I rushed to the store with the hope of exchanging the turntable in mind. Once there, I was greeted by a techniquely ignorant salesman who, being too lazy to fill out transfer forms, said he was unable to help me and suggested I drive back to Toledo to the original audio outlet. So much for Disgusting Event #3.

Particular characteristics of the salesman which stood out in my mind were his appearance: dressed quite nicely in order to assure potential customers of his "Businesslike manner", and his often-stereotyped "wide smile" which rapidly disappeared once the nature of my problem was learned. Also our salesman was most willing to interrupt our discussion in order to run over and greet other prospective suckers who had entered the store.

[Your disgust was trying to say?] Statement: "This guy was generally all fucked up and his business practice made me puke."

The young man's disgust at the broken turntable signals his need to dissociate from something damaged. His encounter with the flawed equipment occurred when he was entertaining a fantasy of acquiring something special. The wonderful item would enhance his self-regard. Instead, he gets a piece of shit. He seems to want the reader to share his disgust, in order to validate his view that the defects in the situation belong to the salesman and the stereo equipment. He links this garbage with the male salesperson who will not set things right for him. His disgust migrates from the turntable to the salesman. Verbal aggression toward the seller seems to be an effort to relieve the young man of frustration and humiliation. The salesman becomes worthless and is reviled using moral disgust: "his business practice made me puke."

A specific fantasy about the salesperson enlivens the narrative. The seller is trolling for suckers. The young man wants help from the salesman who has the power to restore his trust, optimism, and pride, but the man has no interest in helping the youth. His smile is false. It aims only to lure potential dupes and is not what a smile should be: a sign of availability and warm intentions. The salesman is both a bad father, who cannot help the young man feel proud and complete, and a bad mother, who promises caring, but instead exploits and abandons.

I offer one more example of a person who used disgust to attempt to wall off parts of the self that were unacceptable to her. Like Mindy, she had an interestingly complex relationship to messes. She was a midwife who gloried in bringing new babies into the world and, in that context, she was unperturbed by messy physicality. But situations that bid her to make contact with feelings of hurt, vulnerability, and narcissistic rage made her feel she was a mess. She would become acutely uncomfortable and want to leave a therapy session feeling that nothing good could come from wading into such yucky feelings. They made her "want to vomit" and made her physically nauseated. She did not describe shame over her feelings, but her disgust was accompanied by embarrassment that another person would see her in such an emotionally messed up state. She also became angry at the exposure of

72 The gatekeeper emotion: disgust

such vulnerability and wanted to curtail it as quickly as possible. For this woman, love of newborn babies conveyed self-love and love of humanity. But newborn emotions evoked self-judging and self-abandonment. She responded to her inner emotional mess with what Kristeva (1982) calls abjection. As with Mindy, a nuanced pattern of embracing in love and rejecting, through disgust, represented this woman's expressions of self-love and self-loathing.

The topic to follow is horror, which treads some of the same ground as disgust, but brings its own unique concerns and composition.

3

THE BREAKDOWN EMOTION

Horror

> What manner of man is this, or what manner of creature is it in the semblance of man? I feel the dread of this horrible place overpowering me; I am in fear – in awful fear – and there is no escape for me; I am encompassed about with terrors that I dare not think of. . . .
>
> *Dracula* (Stoker, 2013, p. 55)

We have seen that disgust depends on the experience of a bounded self, which takes shape from living with a body enveloped in skin (Anzieu, 1989). Disgust conveys that something may disturb me by entering me and polluting my self or body, and thus it implicates my self-regard. Disgust also entails the belief that I can label something outside myself as bad and increase my power in relation to it.

Horror is a special type of fear. It follows when the core supportive structures of a person's world have degraded. Essential supports may be outside or inside the self and body envelope. In a state of horror, these foundations no longer hold; change has taken place so that a man becomes an insect, a happy face turns to a creepy clown smile, or a town the landmarks of which have defined *home* collapses into heaps of rubble. An awful idea or memory may grab me from within and create horror that dissolves a placid mood.

In horror, what is unsettling is not contained by extrusive images of a tongue that pushes out offending matter or a hand that wipes clean the skin. Instead, the disturbance overtakes us in a way that agitates us to the core. Contemplating horror, we see how slippery the inside–outside distinction can be. To perceive is to bring inside; perceiving softens the self–other boundary. If I see something as horrible, horror has entered me. The disturbance impacts the body and psychic self and cannot be circumscribed as it would be in disgust.

The action life of disgust is muscular, expulsive, and quick. The action life of horror is absorptive and slow. I must see what is there. I must understand. I will

74 The breakdown emotion: horror

take my time in learning and in trying to test my sanity and stability in the face of threat. Uncertainty, unfamiliarity, and intensity attend the experience and prolong my attention to the state of upheaval, though if I cower in the face of it, I may shut my eyes and try to turn away.

Disgust involves judgment – of myself, of what I face that disgusts me. Horror has no concern with measurement and rating. It wants to know what the thing is, and how I can endure it. It wants to say how unbearable this is, not whether it is good or bad.

The uncanny

Freud's (1919) investigation of the uncanny was the first psychoanalytic look at horror-related states. Horror and the uncanny are distinguishable concepts, though both entail an altered view of how our world is constituted and involve questions about the nature of reality. Freud's uncanny puts a person in contact with an unsettling and peculiar mix of the unexpected and the predictable. Horror, in contrast, is the registration of a deep disturbance in my universe such that I feel that my outer or inner world is no longer safe and may not sustain me. The uncanny may elicit an additional response of horror but need not do so. Freud himself struggled with the relationship of the uncanny to horror and said of the uncanny:

> It is undoubtedly related to what is frightening—to what arouses dread and horror; equally certainly, too, the word is not always used in a clearly definable sense, so that it tends to coincide with what excites fear in general. Yet we may expect that a special core of feeling is present which justifies the use of a special conceptual term. One is curious to know what this common core is which allows us to distinguish as "uncanny" certain things which lie within the field of what is frightening.
>
> (p. 219)

Freud goes on to refer to an "uncanny impression" (p. 220) and further states that "the uncanny is that class of the frightening which leads back to what is known of old and long familiar" (p. 220).

Freud's (1919) uncanny rests on an encounter with something familiar that had been repressed, as in the case of castration anxiety, or had been developmentally surmounted, as with the belief that our thoughts are omnipotent. He states that "an uncanny effect is often and easily produced when the distinction between imagination and reality is effaced, as when something that we have hitherto regarded as imaginary appears before us in reality" (p. 244). His uncanny is an intercategorical experience that treads the line between reality and imagination and unsettles our ability to differentiate the two. It represents an occurrence of what is in one respect expected, but in another regard surprising. Freud gives as an example the experience of wishing someone dead just before that person actually falls dead; the belief in omnipotent wishes is fleetingly reinstated. He stresses the relationship between the magical moment and earlier states of mind that have been largely abandoned or repressed, but any odd, unanticipated shift in the construction of our reality – which causes us to question our perceptions and to interrogate reality itself – can evoke the uncanny sensation of strangeness.

Analyses of horror often refer back to Freud's article on the uncanny, but such references generate some degree of confusion since Freud's uncanny is not the equivalent of horror. The two categories overlap only if moments of experience meet the criteria for both. In looking at horror, I will carry forward several core concepts from earlier chapters: self and its boundary, category-breaching as a stimulus for emotion, and humanity as a key category.

The inhuman being

The category, humanity, is of particular importance in understanding horror. Alteration in human forms and behaviors is a common cause of horror and includes both the damaged or distorted human and the intercategorical status of someone part-human and part-nonhuman. Even ordinary life forms can evoke horror if they elicit the feeling they are distortions of what is human. An enlarged, animated picture of an insect that shows it eating or cleaning its mouth parts, might evoke horror if the insect seems humanlike but not human, thus it strikes us as a troubling perversion of the human. Because the insect is armored and lacks the soft character of human bodies, it seems to occupy a troubling intercategorical space somewhere between the normal human and the machine. An actual machine will on occasion evoke horror if it seems disconcertingly lifelike. The exception would be the human-like machine, the robot, that a person has created. Our design of the robot, control over it, and ability to make it friendly to our desires will mitigate horror.

Human relations are at the core of our safety and security. For a person to lose humanity is horrible and for a dangerous non-person to invade our concept of humanity is horrible as well. Whether such images elicit disgust, horror, or both will depend in large part on self-boundary and scale. If something is experienced as fully entering and overtaking the self, horror is a likely response. If the being or thing is conceived as containable and as threatening the self from outside, so that I can label and reject it as bad, disgust is likely. Possessing human scale also disposes us toward an experience of disgust. A tornado might elicit horror but a gnarled hand extended in my direction might evoke either horror or disgust, depending on particulars of the image.

Any human form that shows a disturbance in expressive capabilities or desires has potential to elicit horror. The clown is well known to disturb some people, even if not obviously sinister. The clown distorts normal expressiveness, for example, by showing a painted, permanent smile that lacks the ordinary responsiveness of a living grin. The smile is designed by nature to be a fairly reliable indicator of benign intent but a fixed smile can hide all varieties of purpose. Here is one of the research participants portraying her horror of clowns:

76 The breakdown emotion: horror

> I've never been a fan of horror movies. I am known to have bad dreams. So when my best friend asked me to watch the movie "It" with her, I hesitated. I am already scared of clowns. Its something about them that makes my skin crawl. And the eerie way that the clown smiled in the movie creeped me out even more. Throughout the movie, I was shaken with fear. I had never been so terrified in my life. Everything little thing made me jump. The clowns laugh was the worse. It made me feel little shocks in my body. The scene where the clown was hiding under the little girls bed was the most horrifying. I used to have horrible nightmares about clowns as a child after a trip to the circus gone wrong Everything about the movie scared me and I do not think I will be watching the sequel.

Several research narratives featured an abnormally *blank* human face as a component in a horror scene. The blank face signifies one of two things: either the human empathy on which we depend, or the facial legibility we require, is absent. We find ourselves with an unreliable, possibly dangerous creature, with whom we cannot identify and whom we cannot trust. A young woman research subject illustrates these dynamics well:

> A time where I felt horror was when witnessing an animal being slaughtered. I was looking for my necklace in a woods-like clearing by a creek in my neighborhood. The person who hunted it down had this expressionless look on their face; not blinking, but almost as if in a trance. He was hacking and hacking away at the deer as if it had wronged him in some way and he was getting revenge. I had never seen someone look so enraged and I ran back to safety in fear that if he saw me I would be next.

The girl reads fury in the man's actions, but her horror turns not just on his violence but on his opaque countenance. What does it mean to be hacking furiously at a body while one's face registers nothing? This odd combination is even more menacing than violence linked with a furious face.

A blank face can also signify that the person himself or herself has been *rendered* inhuman by some force that might afflict and degenerate the bystander as well because it is afoot in the world. Like electricity or magnetism, horror acts on the observer. As one can be electrified, one can be horrified. To be horrified is to be transformed, perhaps transfixed, by a dark force so that all natural, fluid expression may fall from one's face. The girl looking at the movie about elephant-iasis victims (Chapters 1 and 2) seems to fear she will become a casualty herself. She states, "These people were very sad looking, and the ones that were not wore very blank expressionless faces." Something has happened to these people to extinguish their humanity. The blank face also invites our projections and threat-laced transferences.

Zombies often have blank faces that convey the destruction of a human core. They are felt to have power to alter and degrade another's humanity. The nature

The breakdown emotion: horror **77**

of horror is to disrespect boundary. Horror does not remain outside, but enters and – once within – twists and deforms the interior so that the sane, human essence that was present is warped or annihilated. Whether imposed by zombies or others, blank or piercing staring can elicit anxiety as it raises questions about the mental process behind the fixed gaze as well as questions about damaging, invasive power. Is the staring person whole and human within? Is he attempting to violate the private space of the one at whom he stares? A psychiatry instructor (personal communication) told the story of feeling an overpowering need to stand up and flee an interview with a schizophrenic patient who was staring ceaselessly at him.

The emotionally misleading, thus indecipherable, is a variation on the blank face. *The Trial*, Franz Kafka's (1998/1935) story of a universal man, Josef K., can be glossed from the perspective of horror over the blank or misleading, mystifying face. The protagonist – called K. throughout, effacing his identity – stands accused by the government of an unspecified crime. Despite K.'s repeated efforts to understand why he is inculpated and what will befall him due to the allegation, he cannot fathom the accusation because the communications of those with whom he interacts are indecipherable. The world in which he lives has become emotionally illegible to him.

K.'s confounding experience emerges in this passage:

> No, as K. had seen himself, officials, and relatively high ones at that, came to him, offered information willingly that was clear or at least easily interpreted, discussed the recent progress of the trial, indeed in some cases even allowed themselves to be convinced, gladly taking on the other's point of view. Of course one didn't dare trust them too far with respect to this latter trait; no matter how decisively they state their new intent, which is favorable to the defense, they may well go straight to their office and issue a decision for the next day that conveys the exact opposite, and is perhaps even more severe with respect to the defendant than that which they had at first intended, and which they claimed to have entirely abandoned. Of course there was no way to protect oneself against that, for what was said in private conversation was exactly that, a private conversation with no public consequences. . . .
>
> (pp. 116–117)

The passage was excerpted from a paragraph eleven pages in length. The absence of paragraph breaks says something about the world K. inhabits. Familiar structure is absent. Right is not set apart from wrong, nor truth from fiction, intention from action. K. is not starting in terror like the woman imagining the evil clown under the bed, but his world is nonetheless fully disarranged. K.'s universe is quietly horrible. I have said that when horror comes, the world around us loses its ordinariness but, ironically, the horror of K.'s life is that insanity is masked in what – tonally and emotionally – bears the trappings of the quotidian. No one is yelling. No blood flows. The world is meekly insane and that quality of understatement

78 The breakdown emotion: horror

is itself a component of the craziness because why should the disappearance of all that we need, in order to comprehend life, be hushed in nature? K.'s placidly horrible world is a freakishly unintelligible face. It suggests as well a person who cannot see *his* face, so that he becomes no one, simply K.

A woman mentally and physically abused offered another example of the horribly untrustworthy face. She told the story of her abuser sitting beside her on the couch, cheerfully enjoying TV with the family while slipping his hand under a blanket to masturbate her. He became a monster to her, an individual whose relaxed face was a horrible denial of his inner reality. The hand silently molesting her was his real face.

The person turned monstrous is another variant of the inhuman human. Like the blank-faced person, the individual with malign emotion or with an atypical, unfamiliar face or form that suggests unreliability, will horrify. Novelist Michelle de Kretser (2003) shows us the power of a monstrous infant to horrify. The child is innocent and has not acted to harm anyone, but our reliance on familiar form is great within a category, humanness, that is of vast importance to us.

> They had a child, a boy with a large lolling head. In their sister house in the hills the nuns had a special wing for unfortunates. It was sheer charity on their part to take the baby. Yet Padma could not reconcile herself to the loss. She turned sullen. Sirisena saw suddenly how coarse she was. She picked a louse from her scalp and squashed it between her thumbnails.
>
> (p. 155)

Regarding the regularity of the human form, it takes next to nothing to horrify us. If our focus is the head, the center of human emotion, it requires, in this case, two words: large, lolling. Grieved, the mother herself becomes a monster, one who treads the line between horrifying and disgusting.

Damage to our humanity is another form of monstrosity that horrifies us. A patient told a story of sitting beside a gape-mouthed, blank-eyed man, who seemed demented, at a celebration of life for a friend who had himself died from Lewy body dementia. Her emotion flickered between disgust and horror: disgust when her attention was trained on the idea he might touch her and something physical that could communicate his disease might contact her; horror at the empty eyes and at the *idea* of him, which was the thought of any human so deteriorated and the notion that such damage might befall her, a loved one, or anyone in the human community. The disgust feelings focused on the physical, but she did not actually believe anything materially dangerous would transmit from him to her. The fear of such a contagion contained her belief that she needed protection from the man's inhuman condition.

Below are two narratives that research subjects offered as examples of disgust, but they show the conflation of disgust with horror over the inhuman human. Both of them portray a malevolent person's spirit suffusing the moment and making

The breakdown emotion: horror **79**

it awful in a holistic way. The stories involve terrible damage to bodies, in these cases animal bodies, which can elicit blends of disgust and horror. They also entail broad concepts of guilt and innocence and the collapse of trust in an important human relationship. Images of an inappropriately smiling face are present as well.

> When I was younger, my grandfather used to take me out with him hunting. I was never really good at it. I would always get queasy. There was one specific day I remember. My grandfather and I went out to hunt deer. I was 17 at the time. When he placed the shotgun in my hand and told me where to shot, I got a little nervous. I fired and I hit something. It was a deer. I immediately felt so much disgust rising up in my chest. It hit me hard because I had never taken a life. Just the thought itself was enough to disgust me. My grandfather walked up to the deer to check if he was still breathing. He wasn't. I started coughing and gagging everywhere. There was so much blood everywhere and I smelt like death. It disgusted me that my grandfather was so happy. He loaded the deer up on his truck and we were on our way. I never went hunting again. Death is too disgusting for me. Especially to witness it up close or to be the one to cause it.

The young man talks primarily about disgust – at death and at his grandfather. But the unspoken, deeper feeling about his grandfather is horror because he has proven himself a bad and untrustworthy spirit. Disgust is an emergency effort to control an emotionally overwhelming situation by judging his grandfather as morally bad and by focusing on the physical particulars of the moment – the flowing blood, the smell – rather than the horrible totality. Images of the breaching of the physical envelope of the body often conflate disgust and horror. The two emotions become essentially indistinguishable in the moment.

The second narrative again aggregates bodily disgust, moral disgust, and horror. It, too, belongs within the category of horror over an inhuman human.

> I remember the day I felt the most digust. I had a friend who had some weird hobbies like catching bugs and animals and pretending he was an animal hunter. One day he took his hobvies a little too far for my comfort. We were playing in his backyard and a rabbit peeped out of the fence. It stuck its head through one of the whole but got stuck trying to push through. My friend decided to "help" the rabbit but instead rabbed the rsbbit by the head and twisted its neck, as the rabit resisted, until its neck snapped all the way around. He then pulled the rabit all the way through the hold and used his pocketknife to cut off its foot and said now he will have good luck forever. I was so disgusted I threw up and never hung out with him again.

In each case, the narrator has a close association with a person he sees as violent and callous, even sadistic. His disgust says he wants to create and guard a strong

80 The breakdown emotion: horror

separation between himself and that troubling person; the barrier protects him from the person's malevolence and defends his identity by saying, I am not like this bad person. His horror represents his absorption of and weakness confronting what exists in his human environment. When a person travels too far from normal humanity he or she becomes, categorically, an alien. To be alien means that you exist at so great a distance from me that I cannot identify with you or make sense of you.

Trauma often involves rethinking the human world. Faith in the decency of others is shattered and cannot be reconstituted. Human beings have become monsters. A survivor of the Rwandan genocide describes her mother's murder and the permanent impact on her view of humanity (Hatzfeld, 2006):

> I know, myself, that when you have seen your mama cut so wickedly, and suffer so slowly you become forever less trusting toward people, and not just the *interahamwe*. I mean that someone who has seen atrocious suffering for so long can never again live among others as before, because this person will remain on guard, suspicious of people, even if they have done nothing. I am saying that Mama's death brought me the most sorrow, but that her overlong agony did me the most damage, and that now this can never be fixed.
>
> I also know, for the future, that a man can become unspeakably vicious in no time. I do not believe in the end of genocides. I do not believe those who say that we have seen the worst of atrocities for the last time. When a genocide has been committed, another one can come, no matter when, no matter where, in Rwanda or anyplace, if the root cause is still there and still unknown.
>
> (p. 29)

We see the typical, foundational aspects of interpersonal trauma: loss of trust in all people and lasting spiritual damage. The cruelty, the heartlessness, the deformation of the human being leads to days of horror and their abiding effect, trauma. Trauma can occur without horror. Simple terror may precipitate it, as may experiences bathed in numbed emotion, but horror is a common antecedent of trauma. When horror has traumatized, it often persists in troubling memory or spawns new horrors that belong to the unsafe world in which one now abides.

Malign spirits

The malign spirit that renders the world unsafe, and thus horrible, may associate with the human, or the supernatural, or it may have an undefined source. The wicked spirit suggests an element in the universe that we do not understand and cannot control, which puts us in danger. Evil spirits may feel uncontained and, as such, mimic the atmospheric quality of horror, which is not about the packaged mess on the door step, but concerns what is dispersed and permeating.

The breakdown emotion: horror **81**

We see the horror of an injurious spirit used to advantage in an ad to encourage immunization against shingles by the drug Zostavax. The camera focuses on an older woman getting ready to jump into a swimming pool. Her scant clothing and readiness to immerse herself increase her vulnerability. The mock-friendly narrator states:

> "Impressive, Linda, it seems age isn't slowing you down. But your immune system weakens as you get older, increasing the risk for me, the shingles virus, I've been lurking inside you since you had chicken pox, I could surface any time as a painful, blistering rash – one in three people get me in their lifetime Linda, will it be you?"

The ad effectively seeds anxiety through the classic horror trope of a body off-guard and exposed to invasion by an ill-intentioned force that cannot be seen or controlled. More horrible still is the idea that the enemy is already within. It is "lurking" and biding its time until the host weakens, as it inevitably will, through age. At that unspecifiable point in time, the disease agent will make its move and begin to transform and ruin the body. The false friendliness of the narrative voice and the repeated mock-intimate use of the woman's name is itself a horror element of the deceptive-face variety.

The following narrative again shows an untrustworthy spirit in action. The incomprehensible nature of the force adds to its power in destabilizing the person. The spirit does not fit any familiar category and cannot be combatted through understanding or simple action:

> We had just sold our house in North Carolina and had moved into a three-bedroom apartment. The place had a claustrophobic feel, much like living in a vacuum. Strange disturbances started soon after we moved in and always happened at night after my children were in bed. Knocks would occur on the wall between my son's bedroom and the living room, quiet at first then growing progressively louder. My son, who was three, was always in bed asleep. After several nights of knocking, the smoke detector would scream out after midnight, for no-known reason. After a few weeks, whatever was in the apartment turned on my clock radio. Static blared, waking me up at 2 am. I could see it in the bedroom, a dark thin figure pacing by the mattress, but I was unable to move. It seemed to be there for hours. I spoke to my husband, who was traveling for his job (active duty Marine), about what was happening. I went to our local church and spoke to a priest. I burned sage, recited prayers, and splashed holy water. I thought my children were immune, clueless about what was going on in the apartment, until one day my son and I were picking up my daughter, who was six, from school, when he asked me how much longer we had to stay there. I told him not long, but added, why do you ask? He said, "Because I don't like the thing that crawls into my bed, it's sticky." We packed up and left two days later.

82 The breakdown emotion: horror

The creature's ability to undermine safety rests in part on its nameless, unknowable nature and its indeterminate intentions, as well as its mystifying physical and behavioral character.

Phobias that horrify can be examples of malign spirit contained and circumscribed by defined imagery. The spider that makes a person's heart race is no ordinary spider. It is ominous and awful. Its treachery is not confined to the corner of the room like a typical spider sitting idly on the wall. It overtakes the whole room because it might jump, it might hurl itself through the air and land in your hair or your mouth, get right inside you or sink its teeth into you. Never mind that spiders don't have teeth. This spider has weapons galore.

Phobias exist at the junction of horror and terror. They are keyed-up, nervous states of extreme fear, which we call terror, but the broad reach of the mind in limning the enormity of the threat is best called horror. While terror tends to sharpen and narrow focus on the feared object, horror is absorptive as it ponders the world that has been overtaken by disorder or evil. A woman I know told me that the inside pattern of certain tulips "gave her the creeps" and she had to turn the flowers away so she could not see the insides. I asked about "the creeps" and she said it was a mix of fear and horror. She thought the black insides looked "primordial" and might be reminiscent of a spider web or a flying bat. Tigers with real teeth and predatory intent terrify; bold, sensual patterns inside tulips can permeate the mind and emotions in an idiosyncratically potent way that horrifies.

The person suffering from a phobia often can isolate her horror and confine it to one thing so that she believes she can avoid panic by eluding her spider. She may use disgust to characterize and contain the stimulus further. However, she is never too far from the knowledge that she lives in a world in which spiders are ever possible, indoors or out, night or day. And she knows that if she encounters that spider, the horror and terror will overwhelm her, as water floods through a breached dam. Safety abides only in avoidance – mastery is not possible.

Ethnographies of nonindustrialized, less educated societies are replete with testimony about the everyday impact of evil spirits (Sobo, 1996). Seldom do the investigators discuss the particular emotions that come from engagement with malign spirits. My impression though is that horror is by no means an inevitable reaction to such encounters. Instead, behaviors meant to protect against the evil arise; behavioral management frequently seems to supplant horror when evil spirits are daily fare within a culture. Research into this area would be of interest.

The invaded, altered self

Horror often follows from the idea that something has happened to my self so that I am severely altered in a way that makes me unable to live in comfort, competence, and human relatedness. From a categorical perspective, horror over what deforms the self is a category-bursting experience, with the relevant class being self. The earlier example of a woman reacting to dementia can also be glossed from the perspective of the altered self. The woman's horror was a fear of what

The breakdown emotion: horror **83**

could befall her as she aged. She might lose her humanity and become a half-human, unrecognizable creature.

Oscar Wilde's (2015/1890) *The Picture of Dorian Gray* engages a number of horror tropes. Prime among them is the altered or damaged self. Dorian Gray is an attractive and appealing young man who so deeply fears aging that he utters the wish to stay forever young while allowing a beautiful portrait of himself to bear the stigmata of old age. His desire is somehow granted and the portrait over time turns hideous as it shows both his aging and signs of the debauchery that his deal with the Devil has licensed. The portrait is a distillation of the twin disturbances, sin and age. The story shows us the subtle nature of concepts of the intact, normal person. To remain forever young when we are designed to age is a perversion and breeds horror. Rivers are not meant to stop their flow, nor are human beings meant to cease aging and possess limitless youth and beauty. Dorian Gray's inability to accept that human beings are not gods and must wither and die sets up the destruction of his physical image and his spirit; the latter becomes more and more stressed, frantic, and decadent. What happens to his self and body and, indeed, his soul is horrible. Part of the tension in the narrative derives from the moments in which Dorian must move the screen from his portrait and confront the grotesque image of himself.

Some forms of mental illness are horror-associated for the ill individual or the onlooker because of powerful images and experiences of ruin to the self. The stigmatization of mental illness surely rests in part on our horror that the self is being ravaged in a fashion outside a person's control, whether or not that damage is visible to others. Severe depression and anxiety, as well as psychosis, all involve changes in the core self-experience that suggest the self overtaken by forces the person cannot regulate, so that he or she feels, *I am not myself.* One becomes a monster to one's own eyes and simultaneously feels the horror of inability to stop painful, decompensatory processes such as rampant anxiety, ferocious depression, obsessive rumination, cognitive disarray, or wavering discernment of reality. Not infrequently, the uncontrollable pain of mood disorders takes the form of cognitively-unelaborated feeling that is largely mystifying, or is explained through weak conjecture about what might be causing it. Perplexity adds to the sense of invasion, sometimes by a malign spirit. Imagining such alterations taking place within another, but not knowing their precise contours, can cause horror in considering that other person. Often what is veiled from sight, but suspected to be dismal or sinister, is awful to us. Dorian Gray's suffering is as great before the curtain is moved aside as it is after the picture is revealed.

Raised devoutly Catholic, Timothy experienced acute adolescent conflict about his surge in sexual desire, which was rendered more unacceptable to him by its homosexual nature. He began to conceive of himself in horrific terms. He was an animal or a monster; he deviated from core categories of humanness and goodness and could not bear for anyone to know his secrets. Superego activity was so relentless that it drove quasi-psychotic beliefs about the devastating impact masturbation or sexual fantasy would have on his social functioning. If he expressed his sexuality in any way, he would be transformed into a social cripple who could barely speak

84 The breakdown emotion: horror

or walk in public. Timothy was Dr Frankenstein's creation: socially isolated and monstrous. His inability to control obsessive thoughts and a variety of compulsions contributed further to the belief that he was defective. While his beliefs about damage occasioned by masturbation or sexual fantasy were entirely irrational, they did not deviate so greatly from cultural constructions about blindness, damnation, or castration resulting from self-stimulation.

A young woman experienced crippling anxiety that she could not understand or control, despite dedicated work in therapy and efforts to utilize strategies she learned online. She felt tormented by the anxiety itself but also by a horrifying sense she was a sick, damaged person and would remain so ever after. SSRI medication mitigated the physical anxiety but, for some time, she remained horrified that she was ill in a fundamental way.

The unsustaining environment

When the physical world that sustains life cannot be trusted, horror follows. In recent years, projected effects of global warming have led to feelings of horror in those who fully imagine these occurrences and feel a sense of threat. Apocalyptic books such as Cormac McCarthy's (2006) *The Road* or Doris Lessing's (1999) *Mara and Dann* kindle horror by evoking fantasy of life without normal sustenance or existence beset by cataclysmic natural forces, such as ruthless storms or gigantic, predatory insects. These texts remind us of our ultimate dependence on the natural world, a topic little discussed within psychoanalysis but prominently featured within horror literature and film. Our emotions have evolved to capture and manage our relations with nature as well as our intimacy with other human and nonhuman beings.

We see what disgusts us as in some way wanting or aiming to approach us closely, touch us, or come inside us, and to make us foul like it is. It has intentionality. Such intentionality is not required for horror. Climate change lacks an aim and won't disgust, but will horrify. The same is true of a tsunami. Random occurrences will not disgust but definitely can horrify precisely because they don't take our needs or wishes into account and may mindlessly overwhelm us. Being nothing and of no account in the face of merciless forces is a common horror scenario.

Though horrifying forces in our outer or inner worlds may lack intentionality or aim, requisite for horror is a fearsome *character, essence*, or *identity* that defines the thing encountered. Losing my balance so that I come close to taking a bad fall will only terrify me unless my thoughts turn to the frightening nature of what might have befallen me. The more I elaborate these thoughts to limn an awful future, the more likely that horror will enter my mind. A quick fall alerts my nervous system but has no character or essence. A fall delineated in fantasy has a menacing character or nature. Once such a disposition has been defined, intentionality, too, is common, thus intentionality is a frequent but non-essential element in horror. If intentionality enters, we have a confrontation between two beings with my being poised to encounter a threatening, perhaps alien other.

The breakdown emotion: horror **85**

A collapsing *social* environment can produce horror, even absent images of malicious humans. Interviews with residents of Chicago focused heavily on losses and threats associated with rampant gun violence. They revealed the horror of a chronically perilous environment. The interviewees' attention was not on the hostile intent of those wielding weapons, but on the constant risk to inhabitants, often from stray bullets. Again, the distinction between terror and horror relies on the presence or absence of a defining character to the threat. In this case, horror followed from an omnipresent, menacing, though aimless disintegration of social security.

Disturbance within a family structure is a variation on the theme of the un-supportive environment. In an astute book on Gothic horror literature, William Day (1985) discussed incest as a violation of the concept of family. In the presence of incest, all the key role distinctions that constitute a normal family have disappeared. Lines carefully drawn have been erased so that we live in intercategorical space: "Incest transforms the stable pattern of relationships into a sexual free-for-all, in which fathers become husbands, sisters become wives, and each person is, potentially, any other person's lover" (p. 120).

Ellie Wiesel (1960) shared a Holocaust memory that portrayed a son whose attachment to his father is devastated by starvation and exhaustion. The father's life and his feelings have come to mean nothing to the son, with tragic consequences. The scene contains a number of horror elements including the theme of the human turned monstrous. The destruction of family attachments is more horrible than the physical violence. The father calls out to his son:

> "Meir. Meir, my boy! Don't you recognize me? I'm your father . . . you're hurting me . . . you're killing your father! I've got some bread . . . for you too . . . for you too. . . ."
> He collapsed. His fist was still clenched around a small piece. He tried to carry it to his mouth. But the other one threw himself upon him and snatched it. The old man again whispered something, let out a rattle, and died amid the general indifference.
>
> (p. 106)

We see that "recognition" has as much to do with recalling the meaning of "family" as with facial recall. The father reminds the son of the emotionally significant category, family, but the meaning of the word has disintegrated for the son. The blank face makes an oblique appearance in the Wiesel passage in the form of the "general indifference" with which the killing close at hand is viewed.

Death of a deeply loved individual is a form of exposure to an unsustaining environment. After such a loss, the remaining world is so depleted of life's essentials that it becomes a place of horror. The person feels, I am living where I cannot bear to live, in a world absent all I need. Such grief is the psychic equivalent of subsisting in a village blasted by a typhoon or a house with no food. A research participant tells a story of foreseen losses:

86 The breakdown emotion: horror

> When my wife went into labor it was the best day ever. We were so prepared to bring a child in this world. But when we were at the hospital waiting on the baby to come, the doctor told us he had bad news. I couldn't understand anything he was saying as my heart was beating so fast. He was saying that there were some complications. My world was spinning. I thought I was going to lose my son and wife. During the labor my wife lost so much blood for a second they thought she might not make it. She had to have an emergency C section and I watched the whole thing in horror. She was in the hospital for weeks after having him. It was a horrible experience. Losing someone you love is very heartbreaking. Just the mere thought of it breaks my heart.

His anticipation is horror rather than terror alone because the eventuality he imagines is full of meaning. It has a defined and disquieting character.

Instability and uncertainty

Change often brings delight, but may usher in horror as well. Whether change is internal or environmental, it results in novel forms in relation to which we must establish de novo, *am I still safe*? Often horror ensues from *seeing anew* what we thought we understood but now reconceive. Both the story of the rabbit-killing friend and of the grandfather who loved hunting exemplify perceiving an important relationship in a fresh light that highlights its treachery. In these instances, the horror came from behaviors that revealed the once-loved individual as pernicious and possessed of a dark spirit. In other cases, seeing anew may depend more on the complex history of an individual's internal landscape. Imagine a mother whose young son has been conceived through rape. Despite this history, the mother easily bonds to the infant and adores him, but when toddler-age defiance and temper flare, this behavior evokes for her images of the overpowering man who assaulted her. Suddenly, she looks "inside" the boy and sees his father in him. The child becomes profoundly altered for her and unlovable. The example demonstrates the frequent dependence of horror on psychodynamically complex sources, including projection and, in this case, transference. Because others' insides always remain in some ways opaque to us, distortions are a constant factor in human life.

Uncertainty also makes us vulnerable to horror. We know instinctively that our worlds are fragile, can be swept away by a mother turned icy or a father suddenly cruel, and we fear such eventualities. Children forever interrogate their parents – directly or obliquely – will you still love me if I am X, Y, or Z? Though destined to fail, they try to ferret out every possible contingency of life with parents who cannot be entirely known or fully know them and who, being human, are subject to change. Life is further complicated by our difficulty thoroughly comprehending or controlling *ourselves*. We are erratic, unknowable selves living among changeable, opaque others. The child struggles to fathom his or her own range of being, and the parent's as well, and hopes to believe that the sustaining dyad will hold, no matter what waivers within either party.

Carnage

Lacking intact bodies, we do not survive. Without others' bodies, we are bereft and likely do not flourish. Disgust often joins with horror in the context of carnage, a word redolent of flesh. Carnage brings us strong and sensorily-rich impressions of body contents spilling out from torn skin, and apprehension of an unbalanced and baleful world. The sensory elements powerfully trigger disgust; the idea of breach of a critical container – skin – also rouses disgust, which is trying to reinforce that frayed boundary. A man with PTSD experienced this flashback:

> A sickly sweet smell of melted flesh. The wave surges bringing the odour of vomit and bowels. Smack! It hits me again. A sea of red; human carnage on all sides. Screams for and from the dying. I don't even know I'm screaming until my throat dies on me, but still I scream silently.
>
> (Tyrrell, 2015, p. 4)

Were they isolated, the smell of melted flesh and the odor of vomit and bowels might arouse only disgust, which would work to insist on a boundary between the offending odors and the self. But the scene in its totality – the awareness of death, pain, torn bodies, and terror invade and overwhelm the narrator and draw him into the realm of horror. The image of bodies ripped open so that one's material foundation fails is particularly horrifying. The man screams in horror, not in disgust. The rent body images are the most disturbing of intercategorical encounters. They show us that category breaches figure in both disgust and horror.

Disturbed moral order

Unlike disgust, horror does not concern itself with judging. Its aim is not to say, this is bad and I want that fact known. Horror rests on chaos and distress, on disturbance of sanity and balance, not on judgment. Though uncondemning, horror responds to a perceived immoral world by establishing, I am unsafe here, and by asserting, this is painful for me to experience. A research narrative offered the following story as an example of horror. As often is the case, we see in it the intertwining of horror and the more judgmental state, disgust:

> I had a neighbor of mine who we grew up together and were good friends but he had one problem, he often felt the urge of looking down on other people and especially people the minority groups. I have never had any problem with anyone on whatever basis so I was disgusted when my neighbor assaulted a man unprovoked but only on the basis of his race. We did not choose to become who we are and for that reason, I felt that was wrong.
>
> Sometimes I am just overwhelmed by the kind of people that we live in because I believe in life, everyone deserve equal opportunities. One thing that disgusts me in life is racism. People should not be judged on the basis

88 The breakdown emotion: horror

of their race, gender of even religion because we are all the same in the eyes of God. In addition to this, one cannot single handedly claim to be superior because I often feel the judge to ask, on what are you basing that on?

To live in a morally disordered world renders us insecure, just as physical chaos would. This type of horror response is easily seen during periods of political upheaval when people believe that their own, deeply-held values are losing influence in the public domain.

Social and sexual deviance and destruction of the family

Daphne du Maurier's *Rebecca*, copyrighted in 1938, offers us a fictional view of one historical era's beliefs in the devastating impact on family life of atypical gender behavior and of strongly implied lesbianism. In her story, both disgust and horror play a role, but the larger position goes to horror as the emotion that registers the collapse of the family.

Rebecca portrays complex and ambivalent views regarding female autonomy, as it expresses itself within a family structure. The plot and characterization point toward dire consequences of breaching conventional norms of feminine docility and heterosexuality. The story is that of a young, insecure, orphaned woman who is wedded by an older man, Maxim, whose first wife, Rebecca, has died in a boating accident. The young woman feels overshadowed by the deceased wife, who is portrayed by all who knew her as remarkably gifted, capable, and independent. The young narrator assumes that her husband still adores and mourns his lost wife, however, we in time learn that he despised her, that she was unfaithful and unloving, and that he in fact murdered her.

Central to the horror in *Rebecca* is the figure of an older woman, Mrs Danvers, head of the estate's housekeeping staff. Mrs Danvers is a sinister individual, whose face appears like a glowering skull, who adored Rebecca and detests the narrator's assumption of Rebecca's role and title, "Mrs de Winter." Mrs Danvers' devotion to the deceased Rebecca appears in the text in highly sexualized terms. The picture of a lesbian attraction is unmistakable. Mrs Danvers is called "Danny" by Rebecca and the masculine name further adds to the suggestion of improper gender role. Also important in the book's imagery is Rebecca's hint to her husband that she may be pregnant, paired with the revelations that her body is growing a cancer, not a child, and, additionally, she has a malformation of the uterus that renders her sterile.

Relieved of her idealization of Rebecca, the narrator grows stronger. Knowing that Rebecca's memory need not be feared, "I was not young any more. I was not shy. I was not afraid" (p. 267). She has come into her own as an individual and a sexual woman: "I was free now to be with Maxim, to touch him, and hold him, and love him" (p. 267). But Maxim grieves his loss of the poor, adrift, innocent child-bride and says, "I was looking at you. . . . It's gone forever, that funny, young, lost look that I loved. It won't come back again. I killed that too, when I told

The breakdown emotion: horror **89**

you about Rebecca" (p. 281). Maxim despised the headstrong Rebecca and is displeased that his young wife is growing up. Indeed, he begins to weaken as his bride strengthens, as if they cannot be on equal footing.

The narrative evokes fear and aggression toward the independent Rebecca, who is heartless, unnatural, and sterile – indeed, horrifying. It also arouses horror toward Danny, the murderous woman whose erotic passion defies nature, just as her mistress's hunger for adventure and autonomy flouted "normal" marital bonds. Thus horror centers on the threats to conventional domesticity and sexuality.

Also evocative of horror is the nature imagery that opens and concludes the book and plays the role of objective correlative to the interpersonal story told. The nature tableaus vivify the idea of unregulated, unnatural sexual passion:

> I saw that the garden had obeyed the jungle law, even as the woods had done. The rhododendrons stood fifty feet high, twisted and entwined with bracken, and they had entered into alien marriage with a host of nameless shrubs, poor, bastard things that clung about their roots as though conscious of their spurious origin. A lilac had mated with a copper beech, and to bind them yet more closely to one another the malevolent ivy, always an enemy to grace, had thrown her tendrils about the pair and made them prisoners. Ivy held prior place in this lost garden, the long strands crept across the lawns, and soon would encroach upon the house itself.
>
> (p. 2)

The imagery of perverse sexual union emerges through descriptions of nature over-running the ordered gardens of the house after it has been burned by the enraged Danny. The plants are monstrous in their untamed growth and in their bizarre matings. Danny is a creature of untempered emotion, not reason, who can contain neither her sobs of grief nor her deadly fury. The story opens and closes with the imagery of nature's wild response after Danny's fury has spent itself in fire:

> The woods, always a menace even in the past, had triumphed in the end. They crowded, dark and uncontrolled, to the borders of the drive. The beeches with white, naked limbs leant close to one another, their branches intermingled in a strange embrace, making a vault above my head like the archway of a church.
>
> (p. 1)

We see in *Rebecca* that part of the danger in atypical matings is the disturbance of procreation, that great cast into the unknown that both inspires and terrifies us until we learn what we have produced. These "alien marriages" are believed, within the text, to produce "bastard things."

Disregard for conventional family structure intertwines with the Oedipal theme of a young girl, barely a woman, who marries an older man in the wake of his

90 The breakdown emotion: horror

murdering his wife. The mismatch in their partnership joins forces with the unnatural women – Rebecca and Danny – to unloose great destruction. Du Maurier approaches her theme with mixed emotion about the role of women. In the end, the protagonist gains strength but her life is veiled in sadness and lived in constricted circumstances, both occasioned by her husband's enfeebling.

Like the Wiesel reminiscence about the son who no longer knows his father, *Rebecca* shows us horror that can occur when a foundational category, such as family or gender, is distorted so that we inhabit the land of marginal or intercategorical space.

Intercategorical and marginal space, power, and danger

Early in Superbowl 2016, a Geiko ad ran featuring a creature that combined a baby, a puppy, and a monkey. The idea was to represent "three awesome things" in one, the combination of which yielded something even more awesome. I found the image disturbing, not awe-inspiring. Thinking the television network might just have offered me a gift of data on reactions to intercategorical experience, I checked the Twitter feed on the ad and found a flood of disgust reactions, but also expressions of horror at the unnatural mating that confounded ordinary classification.

Mary Douglas (1966) considers the power we find at the body's margins:

> To have been in the margins is to have been in contact with danger, to have been at a source of power. It is consistent with the ideas about form and formlessness to treat initiands coming out of seclusion as if they were themselves charged with power, hot, dangerous, requiring insulation and a time for cooling down.
>
> (p. 98)

The marginal is distinguished from the intercategorical in hugging the border of one entity rather than positioning, conceptually, between two defined states. Douglas makes the important point that the body self should not be assumed to be primary in relation to the societal self; it is not invariably elemental to our sense of order, therefore, just as a configuration seen in the world can symbolize something about the self or body, a pattern seen or stamped on the body or a posture assumed by it can symbolize something about our social world. As the tattoo artist knows, the skin may be a canvas on which one writes about the world. Body margins are intrinsically meaningful, but so are boundaries within the outer world, for example, the border separating family from stranger or earth from sky.

Anthropologists' explorations of the universal power of marginal or intercategorical status enrich our understanding of the ways in which the human mind may either flee liminal space or linger there. A fire consuming a house may horrify

The breakdown emotion: horror **91**

but the power associated with destruction of familiar, constricting form may also captivate as it consumes a known order. For the person who sees the violence of hot tempers and a destroyed family in the towering flames, the fire takes on added dimensions of meaning.

In many tales of horror, the margin most at issue is that between the surviving self and the destroyed self. Frosh (2013) explores the state in which the self gives up some of its definition, yet survives:

> But fright does other things too. Applied to the thrill-seeking tendency, it is clearly a way of waking ourselves up out of a lethargy produced by living too much in the same. Running into danger not only tests our limits; it is also a way of loosening the self – losing the self – perhaps in order to give up normal constraints, or perhaps to bypass the inhibiting self-scrutiny that makes us too human, too self-conscious. The shiver produced by ghost stories, the shock of horror films, the giddiness of wild fairground rides, the 'adrenaline rush' of battle: these things all shake up the boundaries of the self so that we become more alive, less individuated and self-conscious.
>
> (p. 18)

As personal boundary, self-image, and self-regard cease to occupy us, leaving only the attention to survival, we become one with the encountered force. The dynamism of the river becomes the churn of our emotion. Our horror, terror, or thrill mirrors the roiling of the water.

Those who move between worlds, who frequent the electrified margins, are sometimes called witches. Leach (1964) knows this terrain and describes it well:

> For example, anyone familiar with the literature will readily perceive that English witchcraft beliefs depended upon a confusion of precisely the categories to which I have here drawn attention. Witches were credited with a power to assume animal form and with possessing spirit familiars. The familiar might take the form of any animal but was most likely to appear as a dog, a cat, or a toad. Some familiars had no counterpart in natural history; one was described as having "paws like a bear but in bulk not fully as big as a coney." The ambiguity of such creatures was taken as evidence of their super-natural qualities.
>
> (p. 53)

When witches are out and about, the ordinary rules of reality do not apply. Such novelty can create wonder, but also horror, which we feel when the world behaves eccentrically in ways that imperil us. The research narrative below was offered as an example of horror. Part of its interest lies in the ambiguous cast to the magical moments a 25-year-old man experiences. They menace and delight. His world is inhabited by a spirit that frightens but does not seem malign:

92 The breakdown emotion: horror

This is real life incident

Actually I am living alone now. A small home for rent. I moved to there before 6 months. At that time I always wake up at 6 AM. First 1 week was good. Got good sleep. But in one day morning when I waked up, I heard a female voice. It said "I will come back". Voice is not in horror mode. But in simple and nice sound. I actually got wondered and frightened because I was alone. Then how that female sound heard? No idea. After that I searched every room. Nothing found. After that I got little fear inside me. But after that day no other horror things happened there. Actually who was that female? I have 3 guesses. May be some my illusion. Because I was in half sleep.

My 2nd guess is that is may be an holy angel. To protect me When I sleep :) When I waked up she went and said she will come back when I sleep again in dark. And 3rd thought is scary. May be that a female ghost. Honestly I really missed that voice.

This is real. Not any fake. Is this good?

Though this young man appears not to be a native English speaker, he grasps the subtleties of the word, horror. He shows us that bright magic and dark magic may keep company, as may the sacred and the profane.

The margins may belong to witches and magicians, who combine categories or shift shapes, but they belong as well to artists, those among us who are drawn to the powerful places where ordinary categories converge and chafe. In a 1922 letter to his friend, Max Brod, examining the vocation of the writer of fiction, Kafka (2013) said:

But what is it to be a writer? Writing is a sweet, wonderful reward, but its price? During the night, the answer was transparently clear to me: it is the reward for service to the devil. This descent to the dark powers, this unbinding of spirits by nature bound, dubious embraces and whatever else may go on below, of which one no longer knows anything above ground, when in the sunlight one writes stories. Perhaps there is another kind of writing. I only know this one. . . .

(p. 84)

The artist finds his or her attention drawn to places that often go unseen: the sites where familiar forms unravel, where death situates, and birth as well, processes equally transformative. The artist's creation of a new form says, I have seen something in my mind's eye and now will create a material or experiential event that speaks to another human being who, in turn, will see, and respond.

In reading testimony of both perpetrators and survivors of the Rwandan genocide, I was struck at times by the eloquence of the testimony (Hatzfeld, 2006, 2008), the beauty of the language itself. Was it just a matter of selection, on the part of the book's author, of the most evocative of phrases, or did something in the experience itself promote a reach for articulacy. I noticed in myself an odd and

The breakdown emotion: horror **93**

somewhat disturbing love of the language, of its force and sensitivity. To describe horror beautifully is a peculiar yoking, so why did I value the words so? Just because poetry is precious? Perhaps the words were beautifying the horror, humanizing the blasted landscape for me, turning black coal into diamond? I think rather that I had entered the realm of twin powers – the power of destruction and of creation – and was awed by that pairing, by that concurrence of two realms of power, as a person might be while witnessing a nuclear explosion. The creation was imbued with the might of the destruction and vice versa.

The poet, Mary Oliver, is drawn to moments of twinning that contain, in one breath, beauty and violence, wildness and domesticity, quickening and death, compassion and aversion. The coupling of apparently contradictory things contests prosaic boundaries and leaves the moment demanding our attention, though it may horrify and repel us as well. We can see such a play of emotions in Oliver's poem, *The Sea Mouse*. It asks us to feel – synchronously – wonder, pity, disgust, and horror at the sea mouse that is "delicate and revolting." It has us narrow our focus to the tiny and broaden it to the grand, all the while seeing each as of a piece with the other:

The Sea Mouse

What lay this morning
on the wet sand
was so ugly
I sighed with a kind of horror as I lifted it

into my hand
and looked under the soaked mat of what was almost fur,
but wasn't, and found
the face that has no eyes, and recognized

the sea mouse—
toothless, legless, earless too,
it had been flung out of the stormy sea
and dropped

into the world's outer weather, and clearly it was
done for, I studied
what was not even a fist
of gray corduroy;

I looked in vain
for elbows and wrists;
I counted
the thirty segments, with which

it had rippled its mouse-like dance
over the sea's black floor—not on

94 The breakdown emotion: horror

feet, which it did not have, but on
tiny buds tipped with bristles,

like paintbrushes—
to find and swallow
the least pulse, and so stay alive, and feel—
however a worm feels it—satisfaction.

Before me
the sea still heaved, and the heavens were dark,
the storm unfinished,
and whatever was still alive

stirred in the awful cup of its power,
though it breathe like fire, though it love
the lung of its own life.
Little mat, little blot, little crawler,

it lay in my hand
all delicate and revolting.
With the tip of my finger
I stroked it,

tenderly, little darling, little dancer,
little pilgrim,
gray pouch slowly
filling with death.

(pp. 41–42)

Oliver bids us enter a world of disgust and horror with her imagery of a creature that defies human conception of what a whole and healthy life-form should be. It is toothless, legless, earless, no more than a fistful of corduroy. And yet it struggles for life and in that way is marvelous. Of the storm that cast ashore the hideous-marvelous creature, Oliver tells us "the storm unfinished, whatever was still alive stirred in the awful cup of its power." Power resides in a storm but abides as well in the mind, heart, and pen of the artist who perceives and creates, in her way, that tempest, and places it before us on the page, so that we, too, conceive it, all of us a bit godly in our fashioning. She balances us between life and death, showing us that both can fill and empower. In this poem, Oliver takes us to the cusp of awe, which shares ground at times with horror, as in the grand storm that is equal parts creation and calamity.

Writing *The Metamorphosis*, Kafka (2013) grasped the danger and power of an intercategorical condition, which allowed him to explore many aspects of horror including the altered self and the unsustaining world of a failing family. The story begins, "When Gregor Samsa woke up one morning from unsettling dreams, he found himself changed in his bed into a monstrous vermin" (p. 3). Surely, this story is one of horror. How could a man who wakes to find himself transfigured into a

The breakdown emotion: horror **95**

giant beetle not be horrified? And if that vermin retains human consciousness and conflates two categories that belong at opposite poles of creation, horror indeed.

While the odd and unstable pairing of bug and human awareness makes Gregor horrible, the text elevates our notion of Gregor over that of lowly insect and thus, in one respect, diminishes our horror. When the ignorant cleaning lady addresses him naively as "you old dung-beetle," the reader, who has been spending time in Gregor's very human consciousness, is surprised, and unsettled (Corngold, 1972). We have been busy at the category border constructing a new concept – that of the beetle who has human cognizance – but the woman's comment has stolen away the identity-fluid, category-breaching, neither-nor, both-and Gregor we were starting to conceptualize and accommodate.

Much of the drama in this story is the struggle over whether and how we, the readers, can fashion a space for this creature who is in all respects wrong; can we succeed in forming and naturalizing a brand-new category? The story is also a family's tale and offers a perspective on how such a grouping might respond to any rebirth that seems unnatural, for example, a gender change. Will Gregor's family confine him to his room, feed him garbage, yet show him some tolerance and tenderness, perhaps en route to finding a way to make their peace with him? The Samsa family explores these differing options and we walk the edge of horror as we contemplate Gregor's loss of their support. At one point the narrator tells us:

> Gregor's serious wound, from which he suffered for over a month – the apple remained imbedded in his flesh as a visible souvenir since no one dared remove it – seemed to have reminded even his father that Gregor was a member of the family, in spite of his present pathetic and repulsive shape, who could not be treated as an enemy; that, on the contrary, it was the commandment of family duty to swallow their disgust and endure him, endure him and nothing more.
>
> (p. 44)

The apple is awkwardly lodged in flesh and cannot be removed, just as Gregor himself is embedded in his family. They are trying to "swallow their disgust" which means they incorporate the idea of this new Gregor. While doing so, they absorb boarders, representatives of the larger society, and all begin to enjoy the beautiful violin music Gregor's sister creates. Gregor emerges from his room and tries to join the family and the boarders and to become part of the community. The boarders see him and at first are more fascinated than repulsed. There seems hope that a new community might form, one that includes Gregor. But the boarders will not accept Gregor. With this rejection by the larger community, the family is done with their efforts to integrate Gregor. They have concluded their attempts to overcome horror at his condition; he is no longer a member of the family and we have moved onto the terrain of horror at the loss of a sustaining environment. The sister declares him a monster – an aberrant, intolerable creature – of whom they must be rid. He is now fully alien.

96 The breakdown emotion: horror

The story belongs to the family, but also to Gregor, through whose consciousness we know the world. When Gregor awakens to find himself grossly altered, he is not instantly horrified. How is that possible? Perhaps it is because his inner self feels as yet intact. He is in a beetle body but has not become a beetle. He is very much himself and is attempting to manage his situation with his customary approaches to problem-solving. He imagines his malady will be fleeting; it will be wieldy. Because he is calm, we, the readers, can remain placid and not accede too quickly to horror; we can wonder if horror is requisite at all. It is heartening to see Gregor make a case for himself – despite his ugliness and vermin corpus. We see him wrestle with whether to insist on his rights, his inclusion, or to give up and accept that he is beyond the pale of humanity. His fate depends on his family's struggle. Will they decide that his hideousness is theirs – they are, after all, family? They do not. His sister withdraws her love and her prior ambivalent ministrations and declares he must go. The father asks what can they do? and the reader knows the question's answer: vermin can be killed – the law assigns no penalty for such an action. But the family has no need literally to murder Gregor. The decision of their hearts becomes his directive and he, on his own, withers and dies.

Before his bodily atrophy begins, Gregor hears his sister's speech:

> "It has to go," cried his sister. "That's the only answer, Father. You just have to try to get rid of the idea that it's Gregor. Believing it for so long, that is our real misfortune. But how can it be Gregor? If it were Gregor, he would have realized long ago that it isn't possible for human beings to live with such a creature, and he would have gone away of his own free will."
>
> (p. 57)

His sister has destroyed him by disavowing him and failing to recognize that he exists. The beetle is suddenly "it" – a creature, not human, not Gregor. She believes, ironically, that if the beetle *were* Gregor, he would know himself to be a monster (not Gregor) and go away. So he must die (which he does, proving he *is* Gregor and knows he must save his family) so that the family can re-coalesce in comfort and carry on (which they do). In the end, the monster – the creature who defies familiar reality – cannot be tolerated. He had remained horrible to the human family, who knew how to level disgust at him and extrude him. Unincorporatable, he had to die.

The Metamorphosis speaks to the fragility of self, to the illusion we are unitary and stable and move through the world a firm and fixed being, deserving a single name and category, that we never awaken as a beetle or a slug, never feel like the vermin in the house. But indeed we are not anywhere near so cohesive as that and we rely greatly on an accommodating and mirroring world for our security.

Developmental

Horror rests on the experience of being trapped within an intolerable reality, whether it is internal (a pain-filled mind) or external (wartime violence) or whether

The breakdown emotion: horror **97**

that distinction is moot. Thus horror requires only the capacity for this variety of suffering and can be imagined to exist very early in life, though we have no way to establish such anguished states with certainty.

Psychoanalysts have conjectured a great deal about very early experiences of psychic suffering that have the hallmarks of horror. For example, Melanie Klein's (1955/1986) portrayals of infant interactions with the bad breast portray the infant in a world of persecution and filled with hatred toward the hurtful mother. In her study of body modification practices, Lemma (2010) discusses both Klein's and Kristeva's visions of the maternal body as horrifying to the infant and she introduces cases of adult body modification that seem to depend on early experiences of needing to escape such a maternal presence. Parsing Kristeva, Lemma talks of the formation of the self through the process of abjection:

> Julia Kristeva's notion of abjection is central to understanding the meaning of the maternal body and adds to Klein's important contribution by specifying why the maternal body can be experienced as "horrific". . . . Kristeva evocatively depicts the dread of the maternal body and hence the fear of falling back into the mother's body. . . . Unlike Lacan who argues that the baby starts to differentiate himself from the mother during the mirror phase, Kristeva suggests that this separation occurs much earlier . . . when the baby begins to expel from himself what he finds unpalatable. This is the process she calls abjection, that is, a rejecting or jettisoning of what is other to oneself so as to create borders of an ultimately always tenuous "I". The abject is what we spit out, almost violently, from the self.
>
> (pp. 95–95)

Major challenges attend efforts to reconstruct infantile experience based on adult pathology (Stern, 1985) or on creative work such as horror films (Creed, 1993; Schneider, 2004). Adult responsiveness to images of horrific mothering or generation of such imagery need not mean that each person thus reactive has passed through a developmental period prominently featuring horrific maternal experience. As imaginative beings with minds that naturally seek to explore borders between known and unknown, good and bad, and minds that probe hyperbole and excess, we may be drawn in horror and fascination to what we have not previously experienced or have only sporadically known. The person who responds with a shudder of horror to the Hansel and Gretel image of a wicked witch who aims to fatten, then boil and eat captured children does not have the same history as the person preoccupied with this story. Even with the person haunted by an image, we ought not too quickly to assume infantile roots unless we have evidence in ego function of such a history. While we may agree with Creed (1993) that "Virtually all horror texts represent the monstrous-feminine in relation to Kristeva's notion of maternal authority . . ." (p. 13), we can accept generalizations about horror films or texts while maintaining caution about the developmental inferences we draw.

98 The breakdown emotion: horror

Later efforts to master infantile pain may interweave with innate human curiosity regarding what lies over the border of normality. Thus the monstrous-feminine that Creed (1993) notes as ubiquitous in horror texts may relate to more than the monstrousness of the archaic mother (which Creed opposes, in somewhat traditional gender-categorization, to the "law of the father"). The growing, older child excited and alarmed by Hansel and Gretel pushing the wicked witch into the oven may be reworking early encounters with the abhorrent mother but may as well be looking for imagery powerful enough to contain his or her abundant aggression around restrictions on autonomy or insults to self-regard, or may be anxious to explore life's awful and marvelous possibilities.

Also important in conjecture about infantile experience is the awareness that later childhood and adult experience of trauma can lead to emotion and imagery that easily is read as infantile. A woman client was subjected to highly erratic and aggressive mothering and to years of sexual abuse by a boyfriend of the mother. She was symptomatic with indescribably painful and horrific feeling states and fantasy, as well as prolonged fugue states, chronic suicidality, and self-harm. In many areas though, her ego functioning and relatedness were excellent. Though themes of monstrous parenting were omnipresent in our work, the trauma she sustained – especially the sexual abuse – was such that it was not possible to assert that the themes were infantile in origin. She was physically confined with a person who psychically and bodily penetrated her with energy and objects she found to be dirty, dangerous, and sinister. She was invaded by someone who would be considered an inhuman human, in the terms of my earlier discussion, whose smile and eyes were not to be trusted, who had the power to degrade her body and being into something ruined and shameful and also to injure and perhaps kill her bodily self. In horrific circumstancs, deciphering what is infantile in origin can be very challenging.

The prevalence of blank-face images in horror narratives suggests that the mother who presents a vacant face when a loving face is wanted or expected might be a source of childhood horror if the experience is unrelieved, the breach unrepaired, or the child is especially vulnerable. Similarly, mismatch between behavior and emotional display may be horrifying, as in the case of the teacher who behaves hurtfully while wearing an opaque or smiling countenance. Passing experiences of this sort must be common to many children and may begin to develop the category, horror, that later life experience – including that of books and films – will expand. Harry Stack Sullivan conjectured that infants are likely to experience horror as well as "awe, loathing, or dread" (Spezzano, 1993) when a mother is overwhelmed by anxiety and tries to shut down the infant emotionally.

Children's vivid imaginings and their youthful uncertainties about how visually to process complex environments of light and dark, shadow and movement leave them vulnerable to horrifying imagery of monsters and robbers that invade familiar spaces and can destroy them and those upon whom they depend. Psychoanalytic thinking has heavily emphasized the early mother-child dyad as fertile ground for horror, but infants are sensitive to other environmental impressions including noise,

The breakdown emotion: horror **99**

light, color, and temperature from early on and great inner disturbance representing early forms of horror may follow from noxious stimuli related to these dimensions of life. A young child might be horrified if a mother's lovely face becomes distorted by hate or injury but also if the child's familiar sleeping room is filled with piles of huge, unstable boxes.

Later in childhood, the young person's world becomes more complex and ideationally rich and he or she attaches to views of the other as having an inner space or a moral center. This complexity leads to new types of horror less linked to physical and facial appearance. The older child might be horrified if Mom shop-lifts a piece of jewelry because he then questions, who is this mom? Is she the nice person I thought she was or has she changed or been hiding her true self? The horror here concerns nothing immediately harmful to the child but involves ideas about how a parent should act. The older child holds beliefs about acceptable behavior. These values are learned from parents but also from the culture, so he or she now has expectations of what constitutes a good mom or nice neighborhood. One adolescent told a story of feeling horrified to learn from an article on beauty that her eyes were too far apart. Her own aesthetic sense had not lead her to this flaw, but the information, once absorbed, became a dreadful thing about herself that could never be escaped, and had, she felt, grave consequences. She would be regarded as unattractive and shunned rather than loved and sought.

Horror has links to body injury, thus may be part of the child's imaginal landscape whenever he witnesses or learns about damage that can befall his own or others' bodies. Physical damage is associated with emotionally disturbing notions including impermanence, unbearable pain, or deformity that makes a person a monster. Visions of castration or other forms of body injury may be triggered by normative developmental forces or by a special event such as an operation.

The body changes associated with puberty will bring horror for some children since a strong attachment will have formed to the pre-pubertal body as a source of many pleasures and, generally, many loving interactions with parents. The pubic hairs suddenly snaking along previously smooth, clean skin may bring either horror or disgust. New odors and secretions can be greeted similarly. Reactions depend on what the child has felt about the adult maternal or paternal body. The more those bodies have been judged to be admirable and loving, the easier the accept-ance of one's own transformation. But even in the best of circumstances, changes may be disturbing. Whether disgust, horror, or both are triggered under these circumstances will depend on the child's nature and defensive strategies. The child inclined to marshal aggressive energy may use disgust. The disgust may be self-disgust or other-directed disgust, depending on whether the child has integrated the new body-element as *self*. The child inclined toward a passive experience of invasion may be more disposed toward horror. Though not our focus here, shame may also be in the emotional mix.

Old age and physical decline are strongly associated with horror, as I have already noted. One's own aging can perturb two core categories, that of self and that of humanity. Change is continual in life but is bearable, at times welcome, if seen as

100 The breakdown emotion: horror

growth or maturation. The alterations associated with old age are in many societies viewed as deteriorations and losses. Transformations in others may be similarly viewed. Major decline, especially of cognitive capacity, shakes our sense that the altered person remains human. That shift in perspective brings loss, anxiety, and guilt over the devaluing of another, as components of the horror experience.

Any emotion will have occasional defensive value and horror is no exception. For example, I might be troubled by recognition of my own unethical behavior and refocus my attention on another's malfeasance, which I insist is horrifying. Expressions of horror can also appear as part of a reaction-formation against attraction to sadism. Horror does not play nearly as prominent a role in defense as disgust does. Much more common are defenses directed *against* horror.

Defending against horror

We know that the foundations of horror and those of trauma overlap considerably. In many instances, horror is transient or is the limited horror of watching a film or hearing the nightly news. In these cases, trauma likely does not result though lasting and cumulative stress may occur. When trauma does ensue, various forms of dissociation that attempt to attenuate or eliminate horror feelings commonly are seen.

Reading interviews with perpetrators of the brutal Rwandan genocide (Hatzfeld, 2008), I was struck by the absence of horror where it would be expected. The perpetrators' ability to defeat horror allowed the carnage to proceed. One could hear in their testimony the anlage of horror, but the emotion was largely aborted. To feel no horror over one's brutality toward others is to dehumanize, so that identification with the victims as other human beings is absent within the moment of action. Later, horror may dawn, but it applies no brake to one's behavior. We can listen first to a voice of horror-free murder. The topic set for discussion with the interviewer, Jean Hatzfeld, was the comparison between field work and the work of killing:

> Adalbert: We roasted thick meat in the morning, and we roasted more meat in the evening. Anybody who once had eaten meat only at weddings, he found himself stuffed with it day after day.
>
> Before, when we came home from the fields, we'd find almost nothing in the cooking pot, only our usual beans or sometimes even just cassava gruel. When we got back from the marshes [where murdering Tutsis], in the cabarets of Kibungo we snapped up roast chickens, haunches of cow, and drinks to remedy our fatigue. We found women or children everywhere offering them to us for reasonable prices. . . . We overflowed with life for this new job. We were not afraid of wearing ourselves out running around in the swamps. And if we turned lucky at work, we became happy. We abandoned the crops, the hoes, and the like. We talked no more among ourselves about farming. Worries let go of us.

(pp. 54–55)

The breakdown emotion: horror **101**

Rwandan testimony suggests that banishing horror through dissociation comes more easily to the perpetrator – himself physically safe and rewarded for violence – than to the victim. The man speaks of no distress, only satisfaction with his new "job," that of murder, for which he overflows with life.

Here is another individual, less content with a life of murdering. He registers disgust at some of the physical aspects of killing in the swamps, but horror is absent:

> Pancrace: In the beginning the Tutsis were many and frightened and not very active – that made our work easier. When we could not catch the most agile of them, we fell back on the puny ones. But in the end only the strong and sly ones were left, and it got too hard. They gathered in little groups, very well hidden. They were picking up all the tricks of the marsh game creatures. When we arrived, too often we would get all mired up for nothing. Even the hunters grew discouraged. Plus, the marshes were rotting with bodies softening in the slime. These were piling up, stinking more and more, and we had to take care not to step in them.
>
> (p. 55)

He feels disgust at the rotting bodies but makes no connection to his own behavior as morally repugnant. His report and Adalbert's are entirely dehumanized and show no registration of the humanity or suffering of the victims. They reflect only the hunters' discomforts or pleasures, present and past. The people Pancrace kills are just "marsh game creatures" who have their tricks for surviving. Other reporters communicate a massively excited blood lust, compounded with greed for looting, which also worked against awareness of victims' humanity and countered the development of horror:

> Adalbert: There were some who brutalized a lot because they killed overmuch. Their killings were delicious to them. They needed intoxication, like someone who calls louder and louder for a bottle.
>
> Animal death no longer gave them satisfaction, they felt frustrated when they simply struck down a Tutsi. They wanted seething excitement. They felt cheated when a Tutsi died without a word. Which is why they no longer struck at the mortal parts, wishing to savour the blows and relish the screams.
>
> (p. 121)

The groundwork for deadly dehumanization was laid by years of poverty, envy of the Tutsis, orders to kill given by esteemed superiors, group pressure, shaming over failure to kill, threat of punishment for not murdering, a highly excited "hunting" mentality, material and food reward for killing, generations of racism fed by Belgian colonial rule, and a long habit of degrading and depersonalizing talk about the potential victims.

In testimony about their first murders, the perpetrators often showed the potential for horror at their actions, but the horror is checked:

102 The breakdown emotion: horror

> Pio: I had killed chickens but never an animal the stoutness of a man, like a goat or a cow. The first person, I finished him off in a rush, not thinking anything of it, even though he was a neighbour, quite close on my hill.
>
> In truth, it came to me only afterwards: I had taken the life of a neighbour. I mean, at the fatal instant I did not see in him what he had been before; I struck someone who was no longer either close or strange to me, who wasn't exactly ordinary anymore. I'm saying like the people you meet every day. His features were indeed similar to those of the person I knew, but nothing firmly reminded me that I had lived beside him for a long time.
>
> I am not sure you can truly understand me. I knew him by sight, without knowing him. He was the first victim I killed; my vision and my thinking had grown clouded.
>
> (pp. 20–21)

Pio struggles to convey the extent of his dehumanization. In the aftermath of killing, his inhumanity is strange to him and he feels it will be beyond the understanding of his interlocutor.

In the next excerpt we see again the dehumanization and defeat of horror but we hear as well, in the final chilling lines, the potential for realization of the human consequences of one's actions. That recognition is the place of horror:

> Pancrace: I don't remember my first kill, because I did not identify that one person in the crowd. I just happened to start by killing several without seeing their faces. I mean, I was striking, and there was screaming, but it was on all sides, so it was a mixture of blows and cries coming in a tangle from everyone.
>
> Still, I do remember the first person who looked at me at the moment of the deadly blow. Now that was something. The eyes of someone you kill are immortal, if they face you at the fatal instant. They have a terrible black colour. They shake you more than the streams of blood and the death rattles, even in a great turmoil of dying. The eyes of the killed, for the killer, are his calamity if he looks into them. They are the blame of the person he kills.
>
> (pp. 18–19)

In looking earlier at the common, horror story references to blank eyes, I noted that such horror relates to the death of humanity that we associate with vacant eyes. In Pancrace's retelling of his life as a killer, the eyes, again, are the strongest communicator of human presence. When the victim's eyes meet his and say, *I am here*, his ability to dehumanize wavers. We see from these perpetrator testimonies that horror is not just an affliction, it is a capacity. To register horror in the face of human violence affirms our loving bonds with each other.

In the horror experience, we may not know what the troubling thing is or where exactly to locate it. It is likely to be dispersed – outside and inside, spread across space – and may be alive or lifelike in its mobility. Disgust can operate as

The breakdown emotion: horror **103**

a rescue operation in relation to horror. Because disgust isolates a problem and actively establishes distance, it offers some relief. Kristeva (1982) believes that disgust is used to rid oneself of the horrifying mother. Disgust says, this inner horror can be packaged and extruded so that I am free of it. In the disgust experience, even if the offending thing comes inside us – we swallow a mouthful of sour milk – our imagery of the offense keeps it contained. The badness is in the stomach and all our muscles will mobilize to expel it. We have body orifices that are like doors that can be shut; these openings are literal and imaginal barriers that come to life in disgust experience and can rescue us from horror.

Religions both employ and protect against horror. Images of Hell that religions have expounded concretize the horrified emotional state. Unrelieved exposure to a world of physical and psychic pain, a realm that cannot be restored to safety and comfort, cannot be rescued by the passing of time or the arrival of a friendly face, constitutes Hell. Packaging our personal horrors in the vault marked Hell can help us to contain and manage them. We can locate all horror in Hell and labor to protect ourselves from it; we hope to experience its opposite in Heaven. A young woman who had been severely, physically abused found relief in fundamentalist Christianity through which she could conceive of an avoidable hell.

In offering such powerful relief, religions exact a price. Wielders of punishing hellfire, they have authority to control our actions and impulses, even our thoughts. Religions have utilized horror for centuries to consolidate power in the church as the only source of protection from an intolerable fate some believe is otherwise inevitable. Many feel a need for such protection. Either they have suffered horror and desire to control its reoccurrence or they feel deserving of horrible punishment because they have done wrong.

In artistic depictions of Hell, violence against the human body is striking and hints at fury unleashed against those who enjoy the body, who are unfettered by religious or superego dictates. The price of such indulgence is clearly depicted in horrors inflicted on the body. The horrors perpetrated against Jesus's body are also central to the Christian world view and reinforce for the believer the ghastly possibilities of what the human body may suffer. Our potential agony in Hell and Jesus's hell on earth conflate as stimulating, cautionary tales of horror that may as well offer hiding places for sexual sadism.

In his analysis of Gothic literary themes, William Day (1985) explores the theme of humans damaged and turned monstrous because they are conceived unnaturally, without normal sexual joy, due to the repressive influence of culture and religion. He argues that violence is wreaked against the body and soul when one submits to a constraining culture. Thus we have religious arguments for horrifying hellfire occasioned by free expression of instinctuality and we have as well an argument for damage inflicted by unnatural *restraint* of instinctual joy. In order to gain prominence as institutions that protect us from horror, religions may generate the horror from which we need safeguard.

Addiction offers relief from horror by way of mind-altering substances or activities. We see in such dependence a passive-to-active defense that attempts to

104 The breakdown emotion: horror

eliminate a highly stressful state of tension by means of action. Ironically though, addictive activities often result in strained helplessness in relation to a powerful substance or a behavior, such as gambling, compulsive shopping, or collecting.

Horror tends to be read as an emergency that requires immediate action. That urgent state leads to radical defenses such as dissociation or addictive behavior. Though difficult to achieve, increased horror tolerance is a goal of treatment. Since trafficking in horror is stressful for the therapist, he or she needs to guard against impulses to flee into problem solving and advice giving. Profound grief is a horror state that easily elicits urges toward flight both in the bereft and in the caregiver. Nonproductive actions often attempt to relieve horror. Some may lead to addiction.

Both phobia and counterphobia have some degree of power to relieve horror. The phobia embodies horror, but in doing so, focuses and concentrates it, through symbolization, in a limited sphere, thus may protect against more disseminated states of emotional distress. Often clients will make occasional mention of an object of phobic attention without major focus on it as a life problem. But does the phobia contain an important communication about the inclination of that person's world to tilt toward a psychic space in which he or she is profoundly unsafe, threatened, and in the company or care of one who is alien and unloving? One client spoke only occasionally about her spider phobia and her need for her husband to manage any situation that might put her in contact with a spider. Her therapy centered on an overwhelming relationship with an emotionally chaotic mother to whom she felt bound by worry. To step away from the mother and cease worrying brought tremendous guilt and self-sabotaging behavior centered on restricting adult pleasure and personal effectiveness. Needing her husband to rescue her from spiders was part of a larger tapestry of regression. As she made headway in therapy and culti-vated a more adult relationship with her mother, the spiders in her world seemed smaller and more manageable and she was able to marshal courage, which brought pride, in managing them on her own. Counterphobic patterns have been well explored as efforts to deny and at the same time master fears that have elements of horror.

Nightmares

Like most practicing psychologists, I have listened to a great many dream reports. A strikingly large percentage of such reports are introduced by the dreamer saying he or she had a very "weird" dream. In reality, to say a dream is weird says merely that it is a dream, because the most ordinary of dreams is weird by daytime standards. Our dream realities have a different architecture than waking reality. Shape-shifting and transporting of consciousness from one locus to another is quite ordinary in dream life. A beetle with a human mind might not surprise us until we wake from the dream and pronounce it weird. Finding the feeling "myself" within another person or being physically absent from one's dream but psychically present might not excite the dreamer. Moving from one country to another without any means

The breakdown emotion: horror **105**

of transportation need not trouble us. Being five years old one minute and fifty the next might not cause concern either. All the violations of normal categorization that horrify us when awake and engaged within a quotidian world of stable persons, objects, and events do not reliably arouse such emotion for the sleeper. And yet, all our common emotions are alive in dreams, including horror, which operates so powerfully that it turns some dreams into nightmares. If the significance of intercategorical, boundary-challenging experience is much altered and reduced, what does horrify us in our dreams?

The best I can do on this subject is to offer an hypothesis, which is that the dreamscape is multilayered and includes a range of experiential possibilities. Those include times in which the rules of waking life do not apply but also instances in which those rules do pertain and their violation elicits the emotion such breaches would evoke in waking life. I give as an example a nightmarish dream I was told in which a man cuts off the head of his favorite dog, using a sharp knife. While doing so, he has no feeling of distress but instead a vague feeling he is doing something necessary. Later in the dream, he re-encounters the decapitated dog and experiences overpowering feelings of grief, guilt, and horror over what he has done, just as he might in waking life. We can look at the dream from a symbolic perspective. The man had just made a decision to end psychotherapy. Associations suggested that the decapitation stood for the relationship he had chosen to amputate and the shifting feeling within the dream represented two attitudes toward the termination: he was simultaneously doing what needed to be done, and committing a gruesome murder.

Whether for the purpose of symbolism or for some other reason, our dreaming mind allows us a greater range of responses than our waking interactions allow. If while waking we experienced huge instability in our attitudes toward an animal, a person, a line of traffic, or a belief, chaos would ensue. But within the container of dream life, such range is possible and remains safe, except in those cases when we feel shaken by overwhelming emotion. To have a dog that we one moment slaughter and the next moment mourn is possible and perhaps useful, if we are making a tapestry of symbols and emotional statements. Thus, odd transitions and juxtapositions need not bring a crisis, however, they retain the possibility of being problematic if such difficulty serves the dreamer's expressive need. If the dreamer wants to cut off a dog's head and feel unmoved, he can do that, and if he wants to look at the dog's head lying beside its body and feel horrified, he can do that as well. If he needs the man who is also a beetle to horrify him, he has that option, but horror is not required by the scenario.

Waking life is far less plastic than dream life in its respect for familiar categories. Comparatively speaking, things in daily life hold their meaning. Events can be commanding in dictating feelings. Reconsidering the horror story the research subject told about his childhood friend who murdered a rabbit, we see that the intentional wringing of the rabbit's neck will never be anything but horrifying to the boy. It speaks to a bad spirit that has permeated his world, and to a friend turned diabolical. To abandon that feeling, a massive alteration in perspective would

106 The breakdown emotion: horror

be required. Perhaps, as an adult, he might see the incident differently if he learned the abusing boy had himself been mistreated. But in the childhood moment, his feelings are fervent, distinct, and fixed. Compared to the dreamer whose decapitation of a dog can be a necessity one minute and a monstrosity the next, the waking person lives in a world that dictates more consistent relationships between emotion and event.

Awakening from nightmares points to those atypical occasions in which the sleeping mind is indeed disturbed, but the distress follows not from bizarreness (as defined by waking standards), but from the generation of overpowering negative emotions. Various factors might unleash those emotions. Perhaps the mind is entering sleep in some way prepared for nightmare, thus ready to generate anguish within a dream. The readiness might follow from too much daytime stress or disorder, or from drugs or other biochemically-altering events. Or the nightmare might erupt due to a calculus unfolding within the dream itself. For example, the dog-decapitator's mind might generate the beheading as an apt image of the necessary end to a therapy relationship. Later, he might become so stressed by the image's relationship to the actual, loved dog (or ambivalently-regarded therapy) that a more typical daytime logic takes over that says, It is horrible that I have killed and mutilated my dog. Some images and occurrences may be too challenging for the sleeping mind to contain, not because they are aberrant but because their daytime emotional significance – still active in some way during sleep – overwhelms the sleeper.

Horror in the fabric of lives

A woman client regularly described her marriage by reference to the horrible things her husband said and did to her and the horrible behavior of her in-laws. She used these descriptors in almost every session and said that her "mother-in-law is the most horrible thing that has ever happened to me, except for my husband." This woman had been exposed to more horror than most. She was brutally assaulted and nearly killed in adolescence but she seldom spoke of the attack or described it in emotional terms. The marriage and in-laws, however, were a focus of constant distress. She was particularly horrified by her in-laws' purchase, supported by her husband, of frilly clothing for her young daughter. Asked to flesh out her experience, she spoke of the "objectification" of the child through the purchase of fussy clothing. She saw the child as surrounded by "an explosion of ruffles" and had no sense that her horror might be an overreaction to the in-laws' behavior. I conjectured that, for her, objectification of a girl child was so linked to mortal vulnerability that the battle with the husband and in-laws had a life-and-death quality and the idea of bows and ruffles on clothing became a horror. I privately noted that her complaints, which were dramatic, and her resistance to proffered remedies, often left me with countertransference frustration that I once characterized for myself as feeling tied up and helpless, which brought to mind her assault. Her husband, too, used imagery reminiscent of her attack when describing the impact her horrified

The breakdown emotion: horror **107**

remonstrations had on their marriage. Because she repeatedly put herself in situations that led to her angrily complaining of horrifying constriction of her autonomy, I posited that the earlier trauma, with which she had had no help, left her defensively displacing the horridness of her circumstance onto a succession of other people to whom she bound herself. She then needed to escape their influence. The relatives who would force her child into clothes that would rob her of her autonomy and safety were part of that succession.

In this woman's life, catastrophic horror appeared to lead to a need to represent life's dangers through distortions of others' intentions and exaggerations of their limitations. She turned the husband and in-laws into ridiculous individuals who were beyond understanding, whose needs were absurd and could not possibly be met. They were aliens and she was right to dismiss them in horror and struggle against them.

John, discussed earlier, had a childhood marked by trauma and his inner world was further disordered by a brain injury suffered later in life. In therapy, he anxiously confessed about his fantasies of cannibalism and his offers to serve up "brain stew" for his friends to "enjoy." He had long kept these fantasies and jests secret, afraid that the disturbance they created internally would be intensified if I showed dismay in hearing about them. Ultimately, he wanted to reveal them, hoping I suspect that I could integrate them into my positive regard for him. That acceptance would help him see himself in less dreadful terms. Here was an example of a person horrified by the functioning of his own mind, who turned to the outer world hoping for an interpersonal experience that might mitigate his distress. He composed the horrific imagery – which grossly disturbed core categories such as edible–inedible – but felt horrified at himself as the author. He believed in those moments that he was a monster, an inhuman being.

I had known John for years, was deeply fond of him and not frightened by his excesses, so I had ways to absorb and understand his fantasies – we even laughed about them, which allowed his horror to subside. His horror turned less on the images themselves – which satisfied his sadism and relieved helplessness – than on the idea he was a monster and would be seen as such. Had he not shown some initial distress about his thoughts, I might indeed have felt some horror, because his indifference would have signified too great a lapse in human sensitivity. I also understood some of the narcissistic complexity in the backdrop of the brain stew image, given that he had experienced a life-altering injury to his brain. A passive-to-active element of turning horror about self-injury into hostile joking was apparent.

The two patients exhibited contrasting use of the horror each had amply experienced during a traumatic early life. The woman attached her horror to her husband and in-laws and attempted to diminish their legitimacy as interlocutors with meaningful thoughts and feelings. The man saw monstrosity within himself, though he imagined "feeding" that malign stew to others as a dark joke that would engage both himself and his banquet guests in the world of horrors.

4

THE IMBIBING EMOTION

Awe

The tour through disgust and horror might leave one thinking that human nature is nothing but the desire for security in the familiar, the safe, and the well-contained. But were that so, what would we make of Lewis and Clark, of Picasso, of Frederick Douglass? What of the child pulling open a seed pod to see what hides within or even the one who disdains coloring within the lines, wanting instead to create a wildness of purple and black? We spurn safety and rigid boundaries as much as we desire them.

The mother gazing at her baby's face, a child observing the bright beauty of an autumn leaf, a puppy's paw, a pink cloud sailing the sky – awe is the great, egalitarian gift of the universe. If horror says there is no home in this world for me, awe declares, look what an amazing home I have; how fortunate I am to have come into being and awareness in such a place. Awe is horror's opposite and antidote and yet, as we shall see, they sometimes mingle.

Awe is a spreading and generous emotion. The artist or scientist feels awe in creation, which stimulates his own second creation – that of art or insight – which stirs the awe of she who now perceives what man, in godly fashion, has made. In *October Maples, Portland*, poet Richard Wilbur (1988) gives us a defined moment, which, like the autumn light, is its own lasting light:

> It is a light of maples, and will go;
> But not before it washes eye and brain
> With such a tincture, such a sanguine glow
> As cannot fail to leave a lasting stain.
>
> (p. 198)

Awe leaves a lasting tincture. Often its focus is great beauty, which may be natural or man made, the elegance of an orchid or of a theorem.

110 The imbibing emotion: awe

Awe is a quiet emotion, a silent moment of perception, feeling, and thought, of reaching out and up, but moments of awe, however hushed, have immense sustaining power. In looking at research narratives, my greatest take-away has been an appreciation of just how crucial awe is to nourishing love of life and supporting perseverance through adversity. Awe is not just frosting on the cake of life. It is fundamental, especially for those who strive to achieve difficult aims that require withstanding hardship and for those whose lives are so challenging that simply enduring requires great strength. Awe figures in human survival and in human artistic and intellectual achievement. A man credits a moment of awe for the writing of a novel years later:

> The place that left the most indelible impression on me was a campsite near Grand Island, Nebraska. Somehow I got away from the group, and lay in a field of tall prairie grass. All I could see was grass and blue sky. I honestly think my ability to write "These Fair Days" came from that experience. I was genuinely awed by the prairie. Still am. The cover of "These Fair Days" is a photo taken at a state park on the Missouri/Kansas border, where I hike whenever I can.
>
> (James Meyer, author of *These Fair Days*,
> personal communication, 2017)

The phrase "I stood in awe" captures the way in which awe quiets a person physically and mentally, so that he or she becomes, simply, the act of receiving what is there. One is "in" awe. While feeling awe, one absorbs something of the world and is concurrently absorbed or "in" one's receptive state. Looking at awe, I will build again on language, though it remains a wobbly pedestal on which to steady one's thinking. Still, we must accept the guidance we get from language, which has evolved over a long period of interchange between instance and word.

Definitional

The term and terrain of the English word, awe, bear a relationship to many other words and territories, so it is necessary to stake out some reasonable geography for awe before proceeding. The aim is challenging because the soil beneath emotion words is built of shifting sands due to variable usage. Nonetheless, we can find some common ground in the contemporary use of the descriptor, awe, to make a good base for further discussion. I cannot consider all the words that in some way approach awe, because they are many. Some can be distinguished fairly readily, for example, admiration holds in common with awe the sense of something larger than normal, but it is a calmer, cooler emotion that does not position the object of one's attention at so exalted a level as awe does, nor suggest the excitement that attends awe or wonder. Admiration has additional features that wonder, for instance, lacks, including the positioning of another above the self and a rather particular implied assertion, *I look up to you*, when applied, as typically it is, to other

The imbibing emotion: awe **111**

people. Wonder and oceanic feelings have both received considerable attention – wonder in the philosophy literature and the oceanic within psychoanalysis. I will focus my comparisons on them.

Saarinen (2012) did an elegant job parsing the history and multiple meanings that have been attached to the idea of oceanic feelings. He examined comments by Rolland, Freud, and Ehrenzweig and concluded that a range of states rightly fall within this category. All share what he calls a *diver–ocean relationship* that speaks to a loosening of ego boundaries and to contact with what normally is not available to consciousness – due, he believes, to repression.

Freud (1930) had no personal experience of the oceanic but labored to understand what had been described to him by a dear friend, Rolland. He said, "If I have understood my friend rightly, he means . . . it is a feeling of an indissoluble bond, of being one with the external world as a whole" (p. 65). Freud supposed that oceanic feelings might be rooted in early feelings of unity with the external world. He suggested that some adults, like his friend, continue to have access to this early ego state in later life:

> [O]riginally the ego includes everything, later it separates off an external world from itself. Our present ego-feeling is, therefore, only a shrunken residue of a much more inclusive – indeed, an all-embracing – feeling which corresponded to a more intimate bond between the ego and the world about it. If we may assume that there are many people in whose mental life this primary ego-feeling has persisted to a greater or less degree, it would exist in them side by side with the narrower and more sharply demarcated ego-feeling of maturity, like a kind of counterpart to it. In that case, the ideational contents appropriate to it would be precisely those of limitlessness and of a bond with the universe – the same ideas with which my friend elucidated the "oceanic" feeling.
>
> (p. 68)

While Saarinen (2012) describes intermittent loosening of adult ego controls, which allows for contact with the repressed (the diver enters the ocean), Freud (1930) – attempting to account for his friend's near-constant awareness of the oceanic – describes *parallel* ego states. He does not posit repression as a dominant mechanism that keeps the oceanic out of reach for people like himself.

Saarinen's (2012) central metaphor for the analysis of oceanic feelings helps us distinguish oceanic feelings from awe. The diver goes down into the ocean of the unconscious or preconscious mind. He discovers what is in some respect already there but has been unaccessed, and by entering into this ocean, the subject finds himself merged with other living beings or with universal forces. The oceanic follows from experiencing what is a potential self-state, whereas awe rests on an encounter, often unexpected, with something more clearly not-self in relation to which one softens the feeling of boundary, in order to take it in.

112 The imbibing emotion: awe

In contrast with the oceanic, awe relies on a sense that the encountered is greater than the self, or on a comparison between the ordinary and the awesome. Oceanic states are fundamentally about expansion of self, whereas awe is primarily an appreciation of relative grandeur or vastness in what the self encounters. Because of this comparative stance, the awed person maintains a greater awareness of self-boundary than the individual in an oceanic state.

The trails of *wonder* and awe proceed together at times but separate on other occasions. Philip Fisher (1998) defines wonder as a state that strikes suddenly upon first exposure to something beyond expectation. This contact moves or transports us unbidden. He states:

> The sudden appearance of the rainbow, its rareness, its beauty are all part of this initial act of striking us, trapping and holding our attention by means of beauty and the unwilled response of wonder. The "Ah!" of wonder is unreflective and immediate. It comes from us almost fast enough to say that it, too, surprises us. We learn a second later that we are already in the state of wonder. . . . Wonder begins with something imposed on us for thought.
>
> (p. 40)

Fisher's (1998) descriptions show us the intersection of wonder and awe. Both states require an encounter with something extraordinary that makes a great impression and focuses our attention while we engage with the stimulus. In contrast with wonder, as defined by Fisher, awe can be negatively toned and can shade into fear and apprehension. Awe responds to power, which can be generative, destructive, or both, whereas wonder turns only on beauty and delight. Witnessing a nuclear mushroom cloud might well inspire awe; wonder would not capture the elements of the experience. In contrast, a stunningly starry night sky might be described by either wonder at its beauty or awe at its magnitude. Those moments of wonder that involve a sense of scale and an awareness of magnificence form a subset of awe.[1]

Keltner and Haidt (2003) are among the few within psychology to turn their attention to awe. They present a clear, researchable, and thoughtful formulation of a prototype of the emotion in which the crux of the feeling state is binary, and includes the recognition of vastness and also the felt need to shift one's cognitive frame as part of the encounter.

I agree with Keltner and Haidt (2003) that the registration of vastness is definitive of awe and forms one of its central chords. The word, grand, would apply as well. To the presence of vastness or grandeur I would add the experience of being moved by that vastness such that one feels astonished and dwarfed by its existence and aware of a power so great that it has frightening potential. Actual fear may or may not be present; fear is one of the common currents within awe and is considered by Keltner and Haidt as the "dread" subtype of awe. I also concur with Keltner and Haidt's second criterion – cognitive accommodation – if that

The imbibing emotion: awe **113**

condition can be satisfied by an adjustment as simple as adding to one's schema of what *exists* in the world the thing one is beholding. One sees a giant redwood and feels, I did not know such a thing existed. Cognitive adjustment is one of the core elements of awe if "it exists!" is recognized as such an accommodation.

Also important as a common aspect of awe is the wish or compulsion to sustain sensory and cognitive contact in order to absorb the experience and, in some instances, to begin a process of thinking about whys and hows of the awesome stimulus. Fisher (1998) talks of wonder as the beginning of thought and means to describe such an initiation of inquiry.

As with wonder, novelty sets the stage for awe, but regarding both states, we should remain aware that an encounter is not defined by the presence of the object alone but by the subject's readiness to perceive its qualities. A person in a deep depression might meet with an expansive and rare natural phenomenon and feel neither wonder nor awe. Similarly, one might experience and then experience anew something vast, so that even though I have seen such a sky before, I am in a different state of mind on second viewing, see it afresh, and am just as awestruck this time as the last.

Some psychoanalytic and psychological theories hold in common phylogenetic ideas about awe or related states serving a purpose in man's early encounters with powerful humans. In discussing taboo in "savages," Freud (1913) reviewed anthropological studies, especially Frazer, and he called our attention to the taboo nature of royal figures, who are dangerous to encounter. He spoke of "holy dred," which he offered as a definiton of the taboo. Keltner and Haidt (2003) suppose similarly that awe may have evolved as the emotional component of confrontations with powerful tribal figures. Keltner and Haidt do not share Freud's interest in the role of emotional ambivalence in interactions with the powerful.

Psychoanalysis has fallen short in recognizing human beings' embeddedness in a natural world that is more than the symbolization of maternal or paternal power and love. We have evolved on a particular planet within a specific galaxy, creatures of earthly landscapes and heavenly skies and these environments hold meaning for us, with respect to comfort, beauty, and danger. They inspire our horror and our awe. Thus while it is important to consider how certain preludes to awe might exist within our earliest human relations, we must consider as well awe's links to our physical milieu. Emotions that appreciate magnitude, such as awe and horror, respond as well to existentially powerful life occurrences including birth, puberty, aging, and death.

Core concepts and awe

Self-boundary

In a state of awe, people experience an openness to something in their surroundings or, occasionally, in their thoughts, that is associated with a feeling that might be described as, "I drink this in" – thus the designation, the imbibing emotion.

114 The imbibing emotion: awe

If asked to associate imagery with an awe experience, the images that come may be of fully open eyes and mouth and expansion of the self, as if the self were a container, perhaps an elastic one such as a balloon, that could be filled by something absorbed visually or through the mind. We are reminded that self-boundary is an experience, one that includes cognition and imagery. When in awe, we envision ourselves as open and absorptive.

With respect to self-boundary, the contrast between awe and disgust is great. When disgusted, we feel we are protecting our inner space against contamination. Self-fortification is conceived as a stiffening and outward thrust of a boundary.

Awe shows us the delight that can attend the relinquishment of boundary. Such surrender occurs when we feel safe. A research participant communicated her delight by talking of feeling overwhelmed "in a good way":

> I felt awe just the other evening when I visited the exquisitely beautiful yard of a local gardener (on a Garden Tour). This yard (acres in size) was the most gorgeous, well designed, well tended, varied, almost magical garden I've ever seen. I felt awe at the vision, resources, and sustained commitment that enable(d) him to carry out this project. The garden/yard spilled down a several-acre front yard and continued around the side and back of his house. The colors, varieties, fragrances, and variety of plants was breathtaking.
>
> What made this awesome? The scale, the beauty, the commitment of a single person to creating such a place of natural beauty. It was overwhelming in a good way, at a time in our society dominated by daily news of terror and horror.

To be overwhelmed is to be impressed by the grandeur of the garden but suggests as well a change in self-state that leaves the person feeling relatively small and fully open. The moment is given enriched meaning when the woman positions it as a delightful counterpoint to the pain of living in a violent world.

Category-breaching

One of the category concepts important to awe is that of the alien or not-me experience. In a state of disgust, we emphatically reject and label as bad what is alien. We may even render something alien in order to justify a rejection we seek to display. In contrast, awe turns with interest and appreciation to the alien and says, look at this marvelous thing, idea, or person; I want to continue to behold it, to be in its presence, to admire it, though I may fear it as well. Awe takes its time and sustains contact. Again, it contrasts with disgust but here we see some common ground with horror because horror, too, beholds the alien with interest. Horror remarks that the alien has entered the self, but does not choose, as awe does, to welcome it. In horror, the self experiences threat and may feel itself altered in the direction of alienness. Horror and awe can converge if I am focused on ambivalently-regarded power or if awe has a counterphobic element that insists,

The imbibing emotion: awe **115**

I am not afraid and overwhelmed by this person or occurrence, I feel only delight and awe.

The second of the category concepts relevant to awe is category-bursting. Unlike disgust and horror, awe welcomes the explosion of a category and says, how interesting and grand that something in the world has radically mutated and become, magically, something else. Such an act is full of energy. In awe, the energy perceived is fantastic and creative (though may be destructive as well). So if I behold all the dampness in my garden turned to crystals, after a sudden freeze, I am entranced by this energy of transformation. Or if I think about the big bang, the idea of such massive and creative reconfiguration inspires me. A number of research subjects told awe stories centered on the transformation birth entails. At times, the category that bursts is *myself*. If I give birth to a baby and now, suddenly, I am no longer a single person, but am a parent, I may welcome with awe this radical change in who I am.

One young man told a story about the transition from life to death. He emphasized the image of Heaven opening and taking in a soul. The man, age 20, absorbs the love and glory of God and is reassured at a time of loss. The moment is itself *about* an act of admission or absorption, into Heaven:

> The first time I ever caught myself being in awe, was at my Grandmothers funeral. Everything about that moment was amazing. Although, it hurts losing someone you love, I know she is in a better place. It was at her grave site when the feeling of awe took over me. As I looked up into the sky, wanting to say a prayer to the Lord, I could see the rays from the sun hiding behind the clouds. Where I'm from this is known as heaven opening up its gate. I felt like I was standing on holy ground. I felt it in my heart that my grandmother would make it to heaven and being there at her grave site and seeing heaven open up for her was astonishing. The fact that there were 100's of people there for her and everyone noticed heavens rays at the same time really out me in an amazing state of awe.

In category-bursting fashion, the sky in a rare moment became Heaven and his Grandmother became a soul who could transit from earth into heaven by way of a gate he had never before seen.

Awe is unique among the four emotions in training its attention on a perfect specimen of a category. What elicits awe is *best in class*. It is the most beautiful pearl I have ever seen, the most richly colored sunset, the most intelligent professor. Whereas disgust and horror concentrate attention on disturbing deviations from a valued category, awe dwells on the superlatives.

Humanity

Horror points to what deviates from humanness in ways that threaten my survival or my security. Inhumanity where humanity should prevail horrifies. When awe

116 The imbibing emotion: awe

trains its attention on the category, humanity, it is recognizing something previously not encountered, but welcome, something that is grand about the group to which I belong. A patient told me the story of a Congolese man who stood up to heavily-armed forces in order to protect orphaned gorillas in his care. The patient commented repeatedly that the heroic man said of himself, "I am not special." These words of humility left the story-teller in awe of the Congolese man, who did in fact seem special to him. The way the man occupied the ordinary category, humanity, left the patient in awe. Great humanity is an example of the "best in class" aspect of awe, but is worth special attention since "human" is among the most important of classes or categories.

Awe and horror

That which creates can also destroy, therefore, embedded within productive power is the recognition of injurious force. Where we see and feel might, but cannot be certain of its bent, creative and damaging energy, awe and horror, mingle and we feel tension and excitement.

In the poem, *Beside the Waterfall*, Oliver explores the co-occurrence of predation and beauty, violence and simplicity. She gathers them beneath the canopy of wildness and lets us know we cannot have an either–or world without paling our experience.

Beside the Waterfall

At dawn
    the big dog—
        Winston by name—
            reached down

into the leaves—tulips and willows mostly—
    beside the white
        waterfall,
            and dragged out,

into plain sight,
    a fawn;
        it was scarcely larger
            than a rabbit

and, thankfully,
    it was dead.
        Winston
            looked over the

delicate, spotted body and then
    deftly

The imbibing emotion: awe **117**

tackled
the beautiful flower-like head,

breaking it and
breaking it off and
swallowing it.
All the while this was happening

it was growing lighter.
When I called to him
Winston merely looked up.
Grizzled around the chin

and with kind eyes,
he, too, if you're willing,
had a face
like a flower; and then the red sun,

which had been rising all the while anyway,
broke
clear of the trees and dropped its wild, clawed light
over everything.

(pp. 6–7)

Oliver's poem highlights the energy of unlikely pairings, which, she reveals, are really not improbable but are as predictable as the sunrise. Her dog – blithe, unselfconscious, predatory – lifts his bloodied face to observe his mistress with kind eyes. The morning sun is blood red and drops light that is "wild, clawed." The dog's face is as much a flower as the fawn's. Violence mingles with delight and the narrator is awed. She asks the reader to join her in appreciating the bloodied dog "if you're willing."

In *Porcupine*, Oliver explores the concurrence of dazzling beauty and horrid danger, of longing to encounter such exquisiteness and relief in the escape from its barbs. The poem's vibrancy comes from the discomforting but natural pairing. The awe is enlivened by an element of horror:

Porcupine

Where
the porcupine is
I don't
know but I hope

it's high
up on some pine
bough in some
thick tree, maybe

almost done
to himself.
For years I have wanted to see
that slow rambler,

that thornbush.
I think, what love does to us
is a Gordian knot,
it's that complicated.

118 The imbibing emotion: awe

on the other side	I hug the dogs
of the swamp.	and their good luck,
The dogs have come	and put on their leashes,
running back, one of them	So dazzling she must be—
with a single quill	a plump, dark lady
in his moist nose.	wearing a gown of nails—
He's laughing,	white teeth tearing skin
not knowing what he has	from the thick tree.

(11)

She is dazzling and dangerous, sought and fled, a lady and a thornbush. She is dressed for the theater wearing a gown of nails and a smile of skin-ripping teeth. Oliver embraces the tension of apparent opposites, the drama of the edges, and she escorts us to these blustery and marvelous places. A common current, fear invigorates her awe. We are in intercategorical space. The category breach is not key to the generation of awe, as it is with disgust, but awe that rubs elbows with fear has complexity added.

Like Oliver, Holocaust writer, Jean Améry (1980), considers the ambiguous and shifting nature of power. Might is horrible no doubt when it lashes the flesh and spirit but is it awesome as well, the stuff of gods? Améry is describing a Nazi torturer's quest for total dominion over another's being and body:

> With heart and soul they went about their business, and the name of it was power, dominion over spirit and flesh, orgy of unchecked self-expansion. I also have not forgotten that there were moments when I felt a kind of wretched admiration for the agonizing sovereignty they exercised over me. For is not the one who can reduce a person so entirely to a body and a whimpering prey of death a god or, at least, a demigod?
>
> (p. 36)

In neo-Nazi movements and other exaltations of violence, we witness awe at the madmen of history, at those who can wipe out vast swathes of humanity with an enormous will and the machinery assembled to support it.

Horror is order exploded, and awe, more often, our gasp when faced with a remarkable construction. But frequently the two abide together because destroying an old organization is birthing one that is new. I am horrified by the cataclysm that is nuclear conflagration but awed, too, by the roiling cloud of fire, endlessly complex in its movement, its shaping and reshaping, its blasting clean while remaining single and coherent in form. It combusts as a great poem does, managing complicated motions while staying somehow whole, not torn asunder. The word, *awful*, with its embedded contradiction, alerts us to this twinship. In a story of madness – perhaps inspired by his own encroaching syphilitic psychosis – Guy de Maupassant (2015) described the fusion of horror and awe through a scene of a

The imbibing emotion: awe **119**

wildly burning house and said, "By now, the house was nothing more than a magnificent but horrible funeral pyre, an enormous pyre that was lighting up the earth and burning men to death . . ." (p. 316).

Several research participants explored the margin between horror and awe. One told of supernatural energy afoot in the world:

> There is this conspiracy theory that tends to front a theory on the existence of aliens. Sometime last year, my uncle visited and he spent most of the time detailing how he saw a flying saucer. Now the government has spent a considerable amount of time disapproving the conspiracy theory but if you heard my uncle speak, you would actually believe that he saw an alien come from the flying saucer. Up to today, I have never been able to tell if the story was true.
>
> The idea that we are not alone and that there is the existence of extra-terrestrial creatures that are most likely plotting to take over the earth is both scary and wonderful at the same time. I would definitely be impressed if I came across a flying saucer. The problem is I wouldn't want to see what comes out of it and above all, the whole idea of aliens is not so attractive. If you have seen the representation of aliens in movies, even you wouldn't want to come across one.

The young man loves the idea of something supernatural and novel, the stuff of wild imaginings. But he believes that a real encounter with an alien would be horrifying were that extraterrestrial akin to those depicted in films.

In speaking of horror, I noted that malign spirits or energies in the universe – whether human, supernatural, or magical – could be a source of horror. Awe, too, traffics in spirits and energies – both natural and magical – but the forces are creative and enliven us, so we open to them. Some people sense palpable energy in the world. Such perception may relate to their faith and the belief in deity. For others, no such energy exists. Only known, defined beings are felt to possess vitality.

Day (1985) explores Gothic fiction, in which the shared terrain of awe and horror is frequently surveyed. In fictions such as *Frankenstein* (2015/1897) and *The Picture of Dorian Gray* (2015/1890), an awesome conception turns horrible when the power unleashed is beyond the control of the one who has arrogantly conceived it. Day relies heavily on the notion of *enthrallment*, which seems to walk the border between awe and fascination. The individual who surrenders himself to enthrallment, in disregard for ordinary reality, runs the risk of an encounter with the horrible. Dorian Gray is enthralled by the idea of staying forever young, but the laws of reality balk at such grandiosity and punish him with horror. Victor Frankenstein, too, conceives of something godlike that reaches beyond what humans should contemplate. He is punished as well by horror. These are stories of hubris, of thinking that man can play God without paying a price. In them, awe runs aground on the banks of horror.

120 The imbibing emotion: awe

Life-sustaining awe

The research narratives that feature awe often show it to be life changing. Awe alters the person's broader conception of the universe or earthly life and remains with him or her well beyond the moment, perhaps permanently, thus it fits the Keltner and Haidt (2003) definition of a state that recognizes vastness and incites cognitive accommodation. The stories told suggest that moments of deep awe feed attachment to one's own life and faith in life's goodness and they support resilience in the face of difficulties. These experiences fill reservoirs of hopefulness, joy, and love and they support the person during trying times. Moments of awe are often engagements with nature, especially if we include human bodily processes such as birth and death as natural encounters. Two young women told of experiences of the Grand Canyon:

> Subject #1: Sometimes taking a moment to stop and appreciate something like the Grand Canyon or a clear, starry night can make you feel like a tiny part of a vast universe swirling around. That was exactly how I felt on my trip to the Grand Canyon. I was more amazed than I had ever been. I felt so small compared to everything around me. Yet at the same time I felt larger than life. After all, awe is defined partly by the fear one feels in the face of something larger than themselves. I felt so connected with the world at that moment. The birds had never seemed more beautiful. The sky had never seemed more wider. I had never been happier. A trip like that can make you appreciate everything about life.

> Subject #2: I have never been to the Grand Canyon but I have seen it in countless shows. It is so spectacular it can inspire awe through a TV screen. The best documentary I saw showed a lot of the views you would expect but it also showed a small waterfall dropping into a pool of azure water that looked more like Hawaii than the desert.
>
> The Grand Canyon alone is almost overwhelming, finding out that there is also a tropical-like lagoon within it was mind-boggling. I'm a devout atheist but things like that can almost make me believe in a higher power.

Characteristic of awe is the feeling of being small relative to another. Diminutive status can begin to feel threatening, as communicated by the second subject's feeling that the Grand Canyon is "almost overwhelming." The excitement and mild fear merge and evoke the sensations a child might feel being lifted into the air by a powerful adult. If the threat is limited and juxtaposed with an awareness of basic safety, the person relaxes the sense of self-delineation and may feel joined with the awesome universe and thus has a feeling of expansion. The paradoxical sense of being enlarged and diminished is characteristic of awe. Even when feeling dwarfed by what is awesome, people typically do not feel the shame we might associate with a diminished status. Attention is not on self-evaluation as is requisite for shame

The imbibing emotion: awe **121**

but on the great entity encountered. People who do feel shame in the presence of anything greater than they likely are not disposed to awe. Their attention moves to the small stature of the self so cannot sustain responsiveness to the grandeur beyond oneself.

Survival in the face of overwhelming forces was another stimulus for enlivening, sustaining awe, as were signs of new life under the shadow of death. An 18-year-old woman tells the next story:

> About 2 months ago, the Houston area flooded pretty badly. A few people lost everything they had. A few people even lost there lives. The whole situation was heartbreaking. The bayou close to my house also flooded and overflowed. I remember walking to the store one day and something caught my attention that had me in awe. It was a duck. Following behind the duck were her ducklings. It was amazing to me because this is something that I'd only seen in pictures books in elementary school. At first I thought I was seeing things, so I rubbed my eyes and blinked repeatedly for clarity and there it was. It was the most beautiful thing I'd ever seen. With everything that was going on in my city at the time, seeing those ducks brought me inner happiness. They were treading along the water in a line and the ducklings looked so happy. It was really amazing. All I could do was stare in awe and just think. I wondered how did they survive the storm. It was amazing to think of how so much can happen in a small amount of time but you have to continue on because life goes on.

In the narration, we encounter the theme of unlikely endurance. We also see the visual amazement that is common with awe. The woman thinks she is "seeing things." She rubs her eyes and blinks repeatedly. Finally, she stares in awe, taking it all in. Though the stimulus for her awe is materially small, its significance is great.

Another young woman's story at first surprised me as an example of awe. With its focus on something diminutive, it seemed uncharacteristic. But seeing elsewhere the theme of survival against odds offered some perspective on the anecdote. Hers is political awe and – like the little ducklings – the presidential candidate who awes her is "paddling along" despite obstacles. In this story and others, the power we associate with awe enters the story as a force that *opposes* something small but determined. Because the ordinary human or creature survives against that great force, it gains the stature of the power it surmounts:

> When the political campaigns started heating up in America, the first candidate whose candidature was often dismissed was Donald Trump and then suddenly he was the Republican nominee. I tried figuring out how such a candidate beat someone like Ted Cruz who somehow had a likeable character. Others like Jeb Bush would have made the cut based on their previous political connections but again, Republicans voted for Trump.

122 The imbibing emotion: awe

When launching his candidature, even standup comedians would find it funny that Trump was vying in the first place. They considered him to be the least likely candidate but when the primaries began, it was clear who was likely to win. Now it is up to the American people to choose between Hilary Clinton and Trump.

Donald Trump is the duck and ducklings still afloat in the floodwaters. No one thought he would make it but he has endured and flourished and as such is inspiring. Awe at survival against odds appears again in the narrative to follow, as does awe for natural forces that are both generative and deadly:

While living in Colorado, I had the good fortune to go whitewater rafting along the Colorado River. With round white sun overhead, we, a united group of strangers, floated along, each gripping a weathered yellow paddle, our one weapon against Mother Nature's force. Class 4 rapids embraced us, churned us, and propelled us while ice water slapped our faces with stinging pelts. A fierce vortex of angry whitecaps jumped and jabbed, overtaking our flimsy rubber sides, and after working together to steer clear from the jagged boulders that had threatened annihilation, fear-laced laughter erupted as defiant fists punched the air.

Weathered paddle in hand, she is very small, yet she gives herself over to the power of the river where she is lost in sensation. Merged with and dwarfed by the might of the river, against the odds she – the little individual, once again defined and separate – survives. She does not become ever-after a part of the torrent or a stain on the jagged rock. She re-emerges as herself after the exhilaration and fear of losing that self to the barrage of sensation. And she is changed abidingly – strengthened, tested, and forged. Had the waters overtaken the paddlers, their emotion surely would have shifted to comingled terror and horror.

Humans seek to preserve security and we do so by creating and protecting structure. But when we feel grounded and safe, we also seek to shed structure and familiarity, even the all-important architecture of self, which steadies us but also binds us to self-consciousness (Frosh, 2013). We soften our self-organization through sleep, drugs, and immersive experiences including movies, fantasy, nature, and infatuation. A 25-year-old research participant offered a vivid depiction of a life-altering experience of falling in love. She characterized her encounter as awe.

A time I felt I was in awe was the very first time I fell in love with my husband, before he became my husband. I didn't think he would ever enter my heart this way and once he did I felt I was in complete awe. My heart felt warm, my eyes could only see beautiful things around me, my ears would play back his voice over and over again like a broken record, I was completely falling for him. I just woke up one day and felt this. It was planned, it wasn't expected, but it felt so right.

The imbibing emotion: awe **123**

> What made me feel awe when I realized I was falling in love was the fact that I was falling in love! It was something I didn't expect at all. It came to me naturally and my heart took control over what my head usually controls. I had no idea what how but I didn't care because it felt so right and so amazing. I've never been in love before so of course I was in awe and I kept seeing fireworks and sparks flying. He was just so warm and inviting with his eyes and smile, his intelligence got to me, and how simple yet strong he was. All those things eventually marinated in my mind and probably got all the way down to my heart and that's how I felt in complete awe.

The young woman is fully engaged in absorbing everything about her new love. He is the lens through which she sees, the atmosphere in which she feels. She replays the sound of his voice. His beauty pervades her vision of the world. The boundary between the two of them softens. His loveliness enters her mind and "marinates" (another fusion), then enters her heart. She emphasizes the unexpectedness of her experience and her complete inability to anticipate its remarkable character. She had no map for these feelings, no frame of reference. They are category-bursting and overcome her and because they overtake her delightfully, not frightfully, she feels awe and not horror. She has never known anyone like her fiancée. He is the most marvelous person she has ever encountered. Awe expands for her the category of humanness and is an example of engaging the best in class.

Though it is wonderful to fall in love, people sometimes feel some relief (as well as loss) when emerging from that experience. Because the self can seem lost in love and also lust, the world outside the dyad can fall away, the person can neglect daily life and feel ungrounded and disoriented. These feelings come close to the oceanic in their quality of merger, but the fusion is with another person, one feels, not with the previously preconscious or unconscious, as described by Saarinen (2012). Of course, this distinction between types of merger encounters difficulty since falling in love can involve transference and regression and, from that perspective, may not be so far from immersion in one's own infantile object-world.

The story below is a good example of awe filling one's reservoir of appreciation of life. It also exemplifies awe as a response to confrontation with what is alien to one's experience, and it shows us the impact of softened self-boundary:

> I recently took a group trip to a tropical rainforest. I think that day was actually the best day of my life. When I entered the rainforest all I could do was state everything around me in awe. I'd never seen anything so amazing. As I walked deeper into the rainforest, I noticed how warm and moist the air felt—kind of like your bathroom after you take a shower. I felt like I was on another planet. It's not everyday that you get to experience nature like that. The trees were like towers. You could hear the sounds of the animals as if they were right in front of you. I got to see different birds, snakes, and

124 The imbibing emotion: awe

> I even saw a monkey up close. Never before had I seen one. I was able to take a tour of the entire rain forest and I had never felt more alive in my life.

The alien encounter is welcome and wonderful. She is visiting the rainforest, a world of abundant life, and the exposure to so much life leaves her feeling uniquely invigorated. She has become what she perceives.

Those severely traumatized and subjected to horror often lose the capacity for awe and must manage without its sustaining power. Fundamental assumptions about goodness and beauty have been shattered, therefore the universe cannot rise to the state of grandeur necessary for awe. Jean Améry (1980) said that "Any one who was tortured remains tortured." Whatever life offers up as awesome is met with doubt and discarded. As in the lives of Jean Améry and Primo Levi, suicide may follow after years of effort to regain a sense of hopefulness. Suicide is one powerful, self-defining act left to the individual, who at least can refuse the life that devastated his capacity for awe.

Powers of God and man

Human beings are creatures of fantasy and fashion with the imagination beings of inestimable power. To these, we relate ourselves in a state of awe, often a fearful awe. We feel awe as well for the vastness and natural powers of the created world. The grandness of what exists materially and energetically reflects itself in our awed view of whomever could have shaped it. The Creator must be magnificent to have made that to which our senses attest. He is thus entitled to our reverence. We, the worshippers, benefit because authority and grandeur order our lives. We derive some characteristics of the imagined Creator from our human relationships, assigning him, for example, the right to swagger, bully, and punish, to lavish and withhold love and sustenance, but also the disposition to *love and provide*.

If Gods create our reality, cult leaders and religious leaders interpret the established reality and the Creator. They are themselves subjects of awe. Baker (2007) studied cults and described their leadership thus:

> Cults are organized around a leader, typically a charismatic individual who maintains ultimate power and authority over the group. Within the cult, the leader is considered worthy of devotion and awe because of a superior capacity to comprehend the true nature of reality. Due to this purportedly unique and valuable knowledge, it is agreed in cults that the leader understands members better than they understand themselves . . . members are expected to reserve their unquestioning love and devotion exclusively for the leader who thus earns an elevated place at the center of their emotional lives.

> (p. 44)

The worship by some of gods others consider to be false elicits rage because it distorts an important world order, a hierarchy in which the deity's grandness is unchallenged. Such confrontation, like the unmasking of a powerful parent by a young child, is feared, because it would elicit God's terrible and deserved wrath and possibly dethrone him. To preserve God's greatness, we even allow our God to be greedy for worship and insistent upon human awe. Rage at those who promote gods we feel are false may, as Freud (1913) suggests, flow from ambivalence toward godly power. We dare not express our aggression toward them and do not tolerate the reflection of that antagonism in another's bold action. Our readiness to rage at the iconoclasts may betray as well our insecurity about how glorious our God really is.

In a radical critique of Islamic orthodoxy, a Muslim woman, writing under the pseudonym Sabbah (1984), relates her thinking about the relationship between worship and passivity. To adopt a state of worshipful awe is to assume a docile position:

> For a human being, will means the possibility of questioning the design or plan of someone else. The worship that God demands of man requires him to excise from himself his capacity to formulate conceptions, create alternatives, produce changes, and question relationships and the system underlying them. Worship, which is an affective capacity, the impulse of love toward another, inevitably implies the paralysis of another capacity – that of will, of the exercise of liberty. . . . Any manifestation of the will of the lover, the worshipper, can only be a weakening of the loved one, God.
>
> (p. 89)

Sabbah sees the relationship between man, who is the passive worshipper, and God, the revered, as mirrored in the relationship between woman and man, with the woman assigned the obedient and worshipful position. I have seen clinically several women from orthodox backgrounds – Jewish, Indian Catholic, and Muslim – who adopted an attitude of awe toward certain men and male capacities while retaining for themselves a childlike, diminished status associated with identity confusion and difficulty pursuing personal goals. Sabbah's analysis reminds us that awe is not so simple as apprehending in amazement what is. Some natural scenes elicit awe in almost everyone, but often the stamp of the individual (and culture) is on his or her determination of what is awesome. Not every man would see (and *feel*) Heaven's gate opening in the light streaming out from behind clouds over a grave.

Creation and creativity

A number of research participants spoke of the creation that human birth entails. Others spoke of grand artistic and architectural conceptions, for example, the

126 The imbibing emotion: awe

Egyptian pyramids. Creation may utilize a familiar, oft-repeated mode – as with the predictably-orchestrated gestation of a fetus. Creativity, however, is not a new instance of an old form, but is a novel construction. Great writing or art can be received as a wondrous form of creativity that inspires worship, not to a deity, but to the powers of the human creator. Some acts blur the distinction between creation and creativity by portraying a person assisting in the emergence of a form that is a blend of the familiar and the idiosyncratic.

I have a memory of taking an art class at the age of eight and experiencing great joy sculpting things from clay. At the end of each class period, we would cover our work-in-progress in layers of wet paper towel, then plastic, in order to keep it pliable for the next class, one week later. I was modeling two horses as a gift for my father and I loved this sculpture, my own handiwork, which was modeled on animals I admired and intended for a parent I treasured. I recall unwrapping the wet towel layers, ready to re-encounter my horses. Those moments of expect-ation and encounter were a state of awe. I could imagine no deeper pleasure. The sculpture for me had vast potential, which gave it power. To have capacity for creation was splendid. Pride was not at the center – though I felt some of that. More important was joy in the magical emergence from this clay of beautiful horses, images of another, natural creation, and my hope of carrying home this thing of my own making, to gift some of my delight.

A nature-loving client told a story about an event that for him was a creation assisted by human action. He had been taken birding by a man whose attunement to nature was so great that his ability to detect and discern birds and animals from fleeting sounds and subtle habitat changes left my client in awe of what this man could do. The guide brought forth for him a world that had been present all along, but was veiled and invisible to my client. I was not surprised that at the end of this recounting, the atheist narrator smiled and said, "It was a religious experience." He referred both to his awe at the powers of his guide, who he experienced as birthing a world for him, and awe at what had revealed itself under the guidance of this man. When the creation or creativity is our own – a child born or a poem written – we may feel jubilant and grand, a bit godlike, in our power and product.

Where novelty of form occurs, we walk the vibrant edge of *monstrous* creation, which risks disgust and horror. People fight over novel forms artists produce, as some revere the artist's creativity and others see the work as disgusting or blasphemous. Under some circumstances – especially with nature's most important creations – we have precise expectations about what aspects of a form can be original and what must be familiar if we are to feel awe and not horror or disgust. A newborn child can delight with an unexpected color or quantity of hair or a surprisingly long frame, but few deviations from the norm are tolerated before we veer into horror. Too many digits or even an unusual point to the ear, may deeply unsettle us. The child is such a new and unexplored package and so vital to our future that we fear some small deviation may signify a great deal about what is inside and what is to come.

The imbibing emotion: awe **127**

To create a new form, we or nature often destroy what exists. Creative art or music breaks the historical mold. Building an awesome railroad leaves scars on a dynamited mountainside. Performing a life-saving surgery produces a body riddled with cut, stapled tracks. Birthing a first child destroys the old family of two. Blechner (2005) talks of good sex as a creative but also destabilizing and risky act:

> The best sex destabilizes our world. Tristan becomes Isolde; Isolde, Tristan. Good sex disorients our neatly arranged world of categories. We may think that delight and disgust are diametrically opposed, but they are just around the corner from each other. Things we consider opposite become experiential neighbors through the magic of subjective alteration of experience.
>
> (pp. 43–44)

Developmental

When trying to understand his friend's description of oceanic feeling, Freud (1930) discussed his conception of the infant's relationship to his or her world. The child does not differentiate self from the external world: all is one. The boundary-loosening character of the state of awe, which prompts a person to soak up something vast from the outside, and to seek and hold contact with it, raises the question of whether awe might be associated with earliest human experience at the breast or in the arms of a parent, where touch, voice, heartbeat, and smells are central to the infantile world. During these earliest moments, might we experience emotional building blocks for later awe, which is a more complex state that requires a sense of relative size and of recognition that something new and life-altering has entered one's world? Curiously, the adult experiencing awe often opens the mouth as well as the eyes and takes in experience in a way that is suggestive of earliest nursing experience.

Benjamin (1995) states that separation–individuation theory is "infantocentric" (p. 32) and that it neglects to address the special pleasure of individuating *in relation to* a specific other who is herself or himself an independent center of feeling, action, and responsiveness. True awe is not an immature state but focuses on what is beyond the self and requires an alive and remarkable other, which may be human, otherwise animate, or wholly inanimate (but created by animate force). Stern (1985) tells us that symbiosis requires a sense of boundary that is formed, then surrendered. First comes the boundary, then the sense of union. Stern takes issue with earlier psychoanalytic assertions about infantile states of "symbiotic" undifferentiation between self and other, because no symbiosis can exist without first experiencing self-definition.[2] Stern's concept of symbiosis seems structurally related to the emotional state of awe in that separateness – which has been achieved – is abandoned, however transiently. Symbiosis of course implies boundary loosening on the part of *two* beings, which awe does not.

An alternative view of the ontogeny of awe conceives of it as maturing out of the emotional state Sylvan Tomkins (1962, 1963) called *interest-excitement* and not

128 The imbibing emotion: awe

beholden to any requisite infantile experience. Spezzano (1993) modified Tomkins's term by eliminating the hyphen (so we have *interest excitement*) in order to emphasize that interest is a *type* of excitement, one that is distinct from sexual excitement. He states that "I have adapted the term 'interest-excitement' from Sylvan Tomkins (1962, 1963), who also referred to this feeling state as a neglected affect, an element vital to creativity." Tomkins and Spezzano can be seen as following the trail established by Descartes whose attention to wonder posited no opposite or paired emotion. Fisher (2002) summarizes Descartes' understanding of wonder:

> [I]t amounts to the energy by which we are interested in something new and attentive to it. Not to feel this pleasurable interest is not to be aware of something new or surprising, rather than to notice it in some other way, since wonder is the means by which we single out, so to speak, the figure from the ground.
>
> (p. 28)

Interest excitement is the engaged orientation toward the world, of which awe and fascination are special cases.

Spezzano (1993) describes how interest excitement establishes personal agency. He is considering the developmental task of emerging from embeddedness within the mother–child dyad:

> the fundamental task of each person: to establish oneself as a subject rather than simply as the object of another's subjectivity. Establishing oneself as a subject involves authorizing oneself to bring new meanings into the world and then carrying those meanings into the subjectivities of the mother and all the other potential authorities that follow her in one's life.
>
> (p. 104)

As a type of interest excitement, awe figures in the child's establishment of herself as a center of subjectivity from which to evaluate scale. Awe is part of the human being's emotional equipment for coming to terms with a world in which we are relatively small and fairly powerless compared with much we encounter.

The child may direct awe toward a parent and in doing so is not fully embedded within the dyad but instead is positioned outside it while looking at and admiring a parent. A relatedness akin to worshipper and deity exists. Alternatively, a child may train awe away from the parent–child dyad and thus challenge the centrality of that pairing and of the parent herself. In doing so, she risks guilt over elevating something or someone non-parental to a higher level than the parent (Spezzano, 1993, p. 104).

Psychologists Keltner and Haidt (2003) posit that awe first appeared to humans as an emotional acknowledgment of greatness of high-status people. Multiple levels of influence may contribute to adult experiences of awe. These may include early nursing sensations that imprint rich pleasure associated with a drinking-in

The imbibing emotion: awe **129**

experience, evolutionary preparedness to respond with fearful admiration to high-status individuals, and a general readiness to engage in the world with interest-excitement (Tomkins, 1962, 1963).

Mid-childhood through adolescence appears to be a period of burgeoning experience of awe as the child's view of her world expands and she encounters things that are new and remarkable to behold including, at times, surprising personal capabilities and endowments such as the ability to feel romantic love or to manipulate mathematical concepts. The richness of the encountered world – including the inner world – takes expression through increasing characterization of experience as awesome.

I can do that – I'm awesome is a common feeling as the teen recognizes qualities of self with excitement, delight, and remodeling of the self-concept. These awed self-impressions help support the adolescent through moments of deep self-doubt, but likely do not have the sustaining power of later life awe as the teen swings between highs and lows in his or her relationship to self. Input from outside – from a parent or peer – often is needed to rescue the child from collapse of self-esteem. The *I can do that* awe of one day is washed away the next as the teen only gradually establishes a more enduring beachhead of self-esteem.

Adolescent views of others often swing between the attribution of awesomeness and the collapse of that admiration. One girl told me of all the people whose friendship she had sought, thinking each one "an awesome person," only to discover, in each case, "when I get to know you, guess what, you're not so awesome." Deep disappointment and anger attended the peers' falls from grace. She was left with no one awesome, indeed, no one even worth the effort of friendship. The breakdown of feelings that the peers were awesome seemed to follow from acute disappointments, partially denied, that made her want to withdraw from relationships. The developmental road forward would likely lead her to more moderation in her views, both of awesomeness and of worthlessness.

Developmental milestones such as falling in love and childbirth are category-bursting and greeted with awe. One woman offered this description of the impact of her sister's childbirth:

> When my sister first gave birth to my nephew, it was the most joyous day of my life. She was the first sibling to have a child and I was beyond excited. When she called me and told me she was going in to labor, I had to be there! I made my way to the hospital with the quickness. He was coming and everything around me was moving so fast. Most people don't like to see babies born but I think It was a beautiful thing. I stood at my sister in awe as she pushed and pushed. Childbirth is a natural part of life and the beauty of it all brought me to tears. Seeing the baby come out and then to hear his first cry was terrific. It was amazing and scary all in one. The moment had me in awe because once I reflected on everything around me, I just brought me to the realization if how wonderful life is and how blessed we all are.

130 The imbibing emotion: awe

The woman's milestone experience clearly lives beyond the moment. It leads her to reevaluate life itself and to see it in a more positive light. Fear is part of the moment but does not overwhelm the joy. The experience could easily trigger horror or disgust, given its liminal nature and elements including blood and bodily tearing. It demonstrates the thematic common ground often shared between emotions with opposing vectors.

Adults who have had earlier life experiences of awe, as most have, sometimes measure the quality of their lives by tracking their continued ability to feel awe. Upticks in awe experience are a reassuring sign that life is going well. Deadening of awe is a sign of trouble. Such insensibility is also a source of grief because awe experiences are highly valued and stand out brightly from the overall tapestry of life. Diminution of awe can occur either through the fading of once-bright memories or the inability to make new ones. Our accumulation of moments of awe over the course of life is an important part of a personal narrative.

Because he saw wonder as the response to what is new and surprising, Descartes believed wonder to be the province of the young (Fisher, 1998). Awe experiences, too, seem to become less common as adulthood progresses, as novel and genuinely surprising moments are fewer. Shifts in the experience of awe may also relate to the biochemistry of the aging mind in ways that have not, to my knowledge, been explored.

Awe in the fabric of lives

I treated Gary psychotherapeutically. He showed a remarkable conceptual split between what he regarded as awesome performance and all else that failed to meet the cut. Nothing short of awe-inspiring superiority held any value whatsoever. To fail at excellence was to be garbage, refuse, crap. No middle ground existed. He was the prisoner of fixed ideas of what was worthy. The valuable thing had already been established and set and could not be rethought. Gary's rigidity was consistent with Spezzano's (1993) descriptions of narcissistic personality. Though he retained the belief in his own potential awesomeness, he regularly failed to reach the standards he set and consequently suffered depression and crushing shame. He imagined he would feel excited awe over his own greatness, not simple pride, if he reached his goals. He distorted the normal nature of awe by substituting anticipation and preparation for surprise.

Gary did not lack interest-excitement, as discussed by Spezzano (1993), but showed an atypical development of it. He had no use for moderate interest-excitement and was contemptuous of such engagement as a lowering of high standards. Ordinary interest-excitement in life was itself devalued as a shadow of the desired state, that of great awe for himself, which would follow from superior performance. The extraordinary performance was more theoretical than real; most moments in his life fell short or were mere flashes in the pan. As much as he needed to succeed, he needed to fail. He did not rationalize his shortcomings, or deny them, but identified, even exaggerated them in order to return himself again and again to a

The imbibing emotion: awe **131**

depleted state that seemed associated with experiences of inability to delight his mother.

Some adults are too quickly in awe of other people and their activities. If the attitude of awe occurs easily, with little basis in extraordinary behavior from the recipient, it may tell us that a person has assumed a childlike posture. The awe says, I am small and insignificant and you are so very important and grand. Such an attitude can be paralyzing. Imagine an employee who is in awe of his boss. He may feel unable to function comfortably out of certainty that what he produces cannot meet expectations. In milder forms, such awe can lead to dedication to an idealized person or cause and to persistent action to support whoever evokes awe. In more extreme forms it will support passivity, collapse of ambition, and abandonment of critical thinking.

Awe plays a number of roles in the maintenance of unhealthy relationships. A woman might inflate the talents of her abusive husband, hold him in awe as gifted, successful, or charismatic, then use those awesome qualities to rationalize his abuse of her. She believes that she is stupid and slow compared with him. In her view, she frustrates him and necessitates the abuse. Because he is awe-inspiring in his capabilities, he merits her loyalty. Because he is vastly more able than she, she cannot manage without him. Perhaps she is quietly clinging to something she needs or desires while she stands in awe. One client believed that only as a small, traditionally feminine child would she be treasured and protected. In a state of awe, she remained that girl child. The posture ultimately complicated her life by keeping her dependent on idealized others and causing her to inhibit her capabilities. In contrast, the earlier quote from the man in awe of the beauty of the prairie shows us a young person receptive to an awe that enlivens and ultimately stirs in him a new capacity for creativity. He chooses to separate himself from his travel group and to lie down in the grass, ready for sensation and thought. He opens to the moment of awe that widens his path through life.

People who fear their own assertiveness – because it signifies aggression – may feel in awe of those who are free to strive. A person who holds himself back from ambition and striving out of fear – of aggression or perhaps wildness – may indeed be unaccomplished and unimpressive compared with others, since inhibition has real life consequences. Under those circumstances, awe of others' achievements may seem like a simple product of relative circumstances in life, but likely it is more than that. It is a necessary stance that maintains the safe anchorage of insignificance. The inhibited person sees another embark on a foreign trip, give a speech in public, or produce innovative artwork and he experiences the distance between self and other as awe.

Interpersonal awe can motivate or inhibit. In the research story below, we see inspirational awe in a young man.

> A time I felt awe was seeing my mother remarry. My mother was a hard working single mother of three and deserved to be happy. Upon her going back to church and becoming outgoing again after a bad divorce, she met

132 The imbibing emotion: awe

> someone that made her laugh and smile and glow again. After not seeing that side of her for years, seeing her with this new guy put awe in my heart that I would someday have what they still have to this day.

He does not envy the "new guy" who so delights his mom, but feels awed by what the couple have found in each other and awed by his mother's survival of a bad divorce and her new flowering. He looks at her as one might at a beautifully blooming shrub that has sprung to life in the spring sunshine, after a tough winter. His awe is of survival in the face of threat, of new life after death. His delighted awe over his mother's blossoming gives him hope for himself. He, too, can find love and can flourish. Perhaps he, like his mother, suffered greatly from the bad divorce. He, too, needs hope and inspiration. Might there be a defensive element to his wonderment at the situation, given the potential the marriage has to displace him in his mother's world? There might, but I would not rush to disregard the veracity of his awe.

Like all our emotions, awe can lack judgment. It may seem a matter of simple delight but troubled or hostile people – or ordinary people exploring extraordinary experience – can find themselves in awe of carnage or upheaval. Consider the remarkable ferocity terrorist groups have unleashed against civilians and their pride in merciless slaughter. Something akin to awe seems at work in these destructive alliances. They idealize unflinching, obdurate, iron ferocity – regarded as Godly might – that sustains awe for violence. For that to exist, natural human empathy must first be subdued by rendering alien some who are human. Our greatness as a species lies in rich connection with others. Our serious liability is in muting compassion under pressure of fear, insecurity, or envy. Such dehumanization operated rampantly in the Rwandan genocide as did intoxication with, and admiration of, violence. One perpetrator (Hatzfeld, 2006) recalled:

> Pio: We no longer saw a human being when we turned up a Tutsi in the swamps. I mean a person like us, sharing similar thoughts and feelings. The hunt was savage, the hunters were savage, the prey was savage – savagery took over the mind.
>
> Not only had we become criminals, we had become a ferocious species in a barbarous world. This truth is not believable to someone who has not lived it in his muscles. Our daily life was unnatural and bloody, and that suited us.
>
> For my part, I offer you an explanation: it is as if I had let another individual take on my own living appearance, and the habits of my heart, without a single pang in my soul. This killer was indeed me, as to the offence he committed and the blood he shed, but he is a stranger to me in his ferocity.
> (pp. 42–43)

Pio talks of how murdering "suited us" and tells of the ferocity and savagery that, during the murdering spree, could be admired.

The imbibing emotion: awe **133**

Other testimony suggests awe for the destructive power donned and for the new facility in reaping great rewards. Benefits took the form of plunder, abundant food, and flowing drink:

> Leopard: Through killing well, eating well, looting well, we felt so puffed up and important, we didn't even care about the presence of God. Those who say otherwise are half-witted liars. Some claim today that they sent up prayers during the killings. They're lying: no one ever heard an *Ave Maria* or the like, they're only trying to jump in front of their colleagues on line for repentance.
>
> In truth, we thought that from then on we could manage for ourselves without God. The proof – we killed even on Sunday without ever noticing it.
>
> (pp. 138–139)

Though previously devout, the killers had lost all awe of God and creation. They had become lords of ruthlessness who are able to meet all their own needs for self-regard, possessions, and food. Leopard shows us awe of oneself and one's own powers. As he states, they had become their own Gods.

Poet and naturalist Helen Macdonald (2015) wrote a compelling memoir of her immersion in falconry, which followed the death of her beloved father. In addition to pondering her own relationship to an adopted goshawk, she considered writer T.H. White, also an avid falconer. Discussing White's childhood travail, and his assumption of dictatorial power in breaking the will of a wild falcon, Gos, whom he both adored and subjugated, Macdonald explored the human capacity for awe of terrible power, especially for individuals, like White, who have been childhood victims of tyranny and need to become what they have feared. She said,

> For Gos was the dark and immoral child of ancient German forests. He was a murderer. He had all the glamour of the dictator. His laws were those of Hitler and Mussolini; he was the violence and irrationality of fascism made flesh.
>
> (p. 192)

White's heart is torn to shreds when he drives his falcon from him, through abuse. The tempestuous falcon is both the maltreated child and the child's persecutor. White is equally in awe of the free-flying bird – the child escaped – and the tyrant of dark and malign power.

John, introduced earlier, was subjected to emotional and physical abuse in childhood and took great delight in offending and unsettling others with violent, often threatening commentary. He, too, was awed by violence. He felt buoyant in moments of power and experienced a delighted self-awe over his ability to unsettle others. He was enraged by the idea of surrendering any of his weapons, whether material or psychological. As mentioned earlier, he had a habit of tormenting a

134 The imbibing emotion: awe

friend with fantasies about making stew out of human brains and serving it to him. He also liked to intellectually humiliate anyone who had slighted him and he delighted in adeptness in this practice. He would tell of his behavior and laugh gleefully at the images of tossing others about as if they were leaves in the path of a ruthless wind.

In the 2016 US election season, we saw the attraction – indeed, awe – with which a segment of the population responded to Donald Trump's imagery of unbridled aggression and force, both verbal and physical. He seemed to represent for many the permission to unleash one's most primitive aggression against fellow humans, who have been thoroughly dehumanized. The license to aggress was given from above, from a place of paternal power. We saw the great hunger some feel for permission to throw aside humanity and conscience and wreak mayhem and vengeance. Presumably, the appeal of guilt-free and shameless tyranny would be strongest for those struggling with humiliation, envy, or feelings of insignificance.

Awe over destructive power has been normalized in US culture in our appreciation of military might. George W. Bush proudly named our post-9/11 incursion into the Middle East, the campaign of "shock and awe," likely aiming to counterbalance or deny the shock – mixed with awe? – we felt at the massive destructiveness of the 9/11 attacks that laid low towering buildings and killed thousands. We take pride in dropping the MOAB – mother of all bombs – in Afghanistan while our domestic politics are in shambles. Often people talk of being "awestruck" or "overawed." These extensions of the word, awe, suggest the emotion's association with power that can overwhelm, which we may decry or admire.

The person without awe is missing a dimension of humanity. This absence may follow from atypical mental endowment, from early deprivation that keeps spirit and mind from kindling, or from later trauma and horror, which lead the heart to close in self-defense. Love ignites moments of awe. Depression and grief will abort them. Those with damaging personal insecurity, who need to be at all times "the greatest," may resist awe (except for self) since awe's posture is that of humility in the face of what is grand in the human, natural, or spiritual world. Though his own mind and his accomplishments were far more impressive than most, Albert Einstein (1931) spoke of his wonder and awe of the world:

> The most beautiful thing we can experience is the mysterious. It is the source of all true art and all science. He to whom this emotion is a stranger, who can no longer pause to wonder and stand rapt in awe, is as good as dead: his eyes are closed.

5

THE FIXED EYE OF FASCINATION

> There seemed to be no use in waiting by the little door, so she went back to the table, half hoping she might find another key on it, or at any rate a book of rules for shutting people up like telescopes: this time she found a little bottle on it . . . and round the neck of the bottle was a paper label, with the words "DRINK ME" beautifully printed on it in large letters. It was all very well to say "Drink me," but the wise little Alice was not going to do that in a hurry. "No, I'll look first," she said, "and see whether it's marked 'poison' or not". . . .
>
> (Carroll, 1929, p. 30)

Fascination is the wish to take in through the comprehending mind, often aided by the senses. To see, to study, to learn, to master is to respond to the world that says, like Alice's transformative bottle of potion, DRINK ME. The power of the object – the other – commands my entire interest. I want to know its every secret so that I and it are united, as gambler and cards, tattoo artist and ink.

Awe, too, involves drinking in but targets the grandeur of an object and the need to accommodate the fact that such a mighty thing exists. Fascination does not require greatness in relation to myself or a change in my conceptual frame; it requires a highly interesting encounter that captivates my attention. Awe and fascination co-occur if what impresses me as grand and life-changing also stirs my desire to learn. Like awe, fascination is a subtype of interest-excitement (Tomkins, 1962, 1963), the fundamental attitude of engagement with the world.

Regarding wishes for contact, disgust and fascination are opposites. Disgust asserts, go, get away from me, I want nothing of you, I judge you to be bad and want to turn my eyes away. Fascination implores, come, stay with me, I want every bit of you, I want to keep and comprehend you. Fascination extends and deepens closeness and engagement. It sparks inquiry and learning. Fascination is abundantly gifted to those who become learned. What is beyond current understanding will fascinate a lively mind.

136 The fixed eye of fascination

In some instances of fascination, the captivator is replete with energy; in other instances, life inheres in the gaze of the fascinated. Witchcraft speaks to the power of the witch, whose psychic and bodily energy compels the subject's attention and renders the subject helpless to the witch's desires and directives, like hypnosis or brainwashing might. When the witch is active, the subject has no independent will; he is in her thrall. Cult leaders often depend on a combination of fascination and awe to control vulnerable individuals. The awe speaks to the leader's elevation, grandeur, and power. The fascination regards the longing to understand the leader's unique qualities.

The word, "fascinate," has magic in its roots. *Webster's Third New International* dictionary makes the connection to the Greek, *baskainein*, to bewitch, to speak evil of. The online etymology dictionary offers this view of the word's history:

> fascinate (v) 1590s, "bewitch, enchant," from Middle French fasciner (14c.), from Latin fascinatus, past participle of fascinare "bewitch, enchant, fascinate". . . . Earliest used of witches and of serpents, who were said to be able to cast a spell by a look that rendered one unable to move or resist. Sense of "delight, attract and hold the attention of" is first recorded 1815.

Some aim to fascinate others. We see this dynamic portrayed in a passage from Oscar Wilde's (2015/1890) *The Picture of Dorian Gray*. Lord Henry intends to fascinate Dorian:

> He felt that the eyes of Dorian Gray were fixed on him, and the consciousness that amongst his audience there was one whose temperament he wished to fascinate seemed to give his wit keenness and to lend colour to his imagination. He was brilliant, fantastic, irresponsible. He charmed his listeners out of themselves, and they followed his pipe, laughing. Dorian Gray never took his gaze off him, but sat like one under a spell, smiles chasing each other over his lips and wonder growing grave in his darkening eyes.
>
> (pp. 714–715)

Both the fascinator and the fascinated gain gratification from the interaction. The fascinator feels his own power and magnificence and is paired, rather than alone. The fascinated, too, is joined with another. Additionally, he experiences enrichment of his world by the wonderful and complex.

The Sirens of Greek mythology are the most renown of fascinators. Odysseus learns of them from Circe, daughter of Helios, and goddess of magic, who tells this story:

> But Circe, taking me by the hand, drew me away
> from all my shipmates there and sat me down
> and lying beside me probed me for details.

The fixed eye of fascination **137**

I told her the whole story, start to finish,
then the queenly goddess laid my course:
"Your descent to the dead is over, true,
but listen closely to what I tell you now
and god himself will bring it back to mind.
First you will raise the island of the Sirens,
those creatures who spellbind any man alive,
whoever comes their way. Whoever draws too close,
off guard, and catches the Sirens' voices in the air—
no sailing home for him, no wife rising to meet him,
no happy children beaming up at their father's face.
The high, thrilling song of the Sirens will transfix him,
lolling there in their meadow, round them heaps of corpses
rotting away, rags of skin shriveling on their bones . . .
Race straight past that coast! Soften some beeswax
and stop your shipmates' ears so none can hear,
none of the crew, but if you are bent on hearing,
have them tie you hand and foot in the swift ship,
erect at the mast-block, lashed by ropes to the mast
so you can hear the Sirens' song to your heart's content.
But if you plead, commanding your men to set you free,
then they must lash you faster, rope on rope."
(Homer, 1996, pp. 272–273)

In this ancient story we learn that fascination can divide us internally into one who is willing to remain rapt and one who would pull away in apprehension of danger. We discover the great peril of fascination, which can leave us among the corpses, our skin shriveling. Alice's encounter with the DRINK ME potion is similarly replete with warnings about the dangers of imbibing.

Everyday fascination was described in the research narrative to follow, written by a 65-year-old woman. She makes a clear distinction between awe and fascination. The object of her interest is not awesome; she holds it in mild contempt, wishing it were something more worthy, a great novel perhaps; and yet she cannot resist it:

It is sad to admit this, as a very well-educated person, that my attention these days is drawn to high quality serial dramas on TV/screens. According to the 19th century psychologist, William James, such focused, un-distracted attention – or what I would call, "fascination," is almost inadvertent: you can't help yourself. I wish I could say the same degree of fascination is true for books, such as novels. While they do draw me in and keep me there, it is easier to be distracted by thoughts, sounds, and sights in the surrounding environment (including my own head). With video programs, as watched on a big or small (tablet) screen – with headphones! – for me, there is much

138 The fixed eye of fascination

> less likelihood of experiencing distraction: immersion is more common.
> I believe this is one reason why people "binge" on these programs.
>
> A time when I felt such fascination was in watching "The Americans"
> or "Orange is the New Black" (as examples). Everything about these shows
> is fascinating to me, from the characters, to the plots, to the settings. Even
> when I remove myself a bit and observe the acting, the direction, etc., they
> are still fascinating.

The writer emphasizes her powerlessness. The nature of the shows is to captivate
and she cannot resist. She recognizes some danger in the fascination. She wishes
she could be riveted elsewhere but she cannot choose. The best she can do is take
comfort in the shows' "high quality." She also emphasizes her full immersion and
the pleasure of the state of diminished self-awareness. Such absorption and relaxing
of self-consciousness is also seen in horror and awe.

The self is differently constituted moment to moment. During times of fascination, the self is strongly identified with the senses, especially the eyes. The self
is also equated with the attentive and inquiring mind. Fascinated, I become "all
eyes" or a piercing intellect. Attention narrows and distractions fall away. The mind
lingers and wants to sustain contact, unlike in disgust, which hastens to turn us
away. The fascinated one has stopped watching the clock. If the clock beckons,
she can respond only by tearing herself away from beguilement.

Obsession and fascination can overlap or diverge. Obsession connotes preoccupation, which signifies fascination only if intellectual energy is engaged. I can
be obsessed with chocolate cream pie but it will not fascinate me. Retaliating against
someone who hurt me may obsess me, but the endeavor need not fascinate. If I
am obsessed with Medieval poetry, likely I am fascinated as well because my curiosity
is excited by something with complexity. If fascination is directed inward, the self
is bifurcated into observer and observed. I look at my own mathematical gift and
find its presence and contours fascinating, just as I might consider another's talent.

Fascination and the extraordinary human

Monsters and heroes deviate from the ordinary and hold great powers of fascination.
They expand the category, *humanity*, the salience of which we have seen in horror,
disgust, and awe. In looking at disgust and horror, we have considered monsters
and the intercategorical or marginal space they occupy. The power of the margin
is twofold. What is outside the edge of normalcy disturbs us, but also tends to
engage our sharp curiosity. Indeed, our welfare is served by attending closely to
anything that strays too far from the normative. In such divagations lie physical
and social dangers, as well as unique opportunities.

Interest in monsters has bred the field of "teratology," from the Greek, teratos,
meaning monster or marvel, a root that conveys the convergence of disgust and
fascination. The elephantiasis narrative presented in Chapter 1 illustrates well the
co-occurrence of the two emotions. Remember that the young storyteller says:

> I can't recall what he said, but as he talked the film would focus in on the afflicted limbs of the individuals. At first this sight repulsed me so much I didn't want to look, but I didn't look away or close my eyes – it was sickening, but somehow it fascinated me, never having seen such things before.

She is both repulsed and fascinated. She attributes her fascination to novelty. These limbs are not those she is accustomed to seeing and taking for granted. They are new, altered, and deformed and she must look at them and try to comprehend them; she must acknowledge their weird power, that of disease and damage, of expectations defied.

Abnormality seen in another person may result from projection of one's own disavowed impulses. Perceived deviations thus composed often fascinate as well as repel. The structure of these fascinations is that of projective identification, which allows me to retain engagement with my disowned impulse. Externalized characteristics – for example, ugliness – may also fascinate. In extreme cases, we see those people onto whom we project or externalize as true monsters, who belong within the class of aliens.

Like monsters, heroes operate outside the bounds of normalcy. They neither disgust nor horrify; they only fascinate and awe us. They are our ideal selves, ideal parents, or both. They speak to us of what we can become, or cannot possibly become. They talk to us of what can *be* in the world, and thus they awe us, and if they bind our attention in deep curiosity they fascinate as well. Heroes emerged as subjects of fascination in several research narratives.

Fascination and identity

Fascination with the heroic or the merely intriguing may derive from hunger to define a personal identity. To view with fascination temporarily collapses the distance between me and another as I drink in what you are. Here is a young woman fascinated by a popular performer:

> It had always been a dream of mines to meet Beyonce. I knew she was headed on tour so when she came to my city to perform, I had to be there. Even tho the ticket prices were high, it was worth it. The show was sold out. It was my first time being at a concert and the atmosphere was amazing. She did several numbers that I was very familiar with. I was fascinated by her every move. She kept so much energy during the performance, I couldnt help but wonder how she did it. She is really an amazing performer. She has the voice of an angel. It fascinates me how long she can hold a note. It is very different seeing an artist perform live than over the TV or radio. It was a wonderful experience. I left the show feeling overwhelmed and speakless.

140 The fixed eye of fascination

The narrator does not tell us she wants to be *like* Beyonce, but her emphasis on Beyonce the person and her capabilities – not on the music – suggests that the writer finds in her a heroine, someone with whom to identify. The other's impressive qualities enhance the listener; they don't diminish her, which might lead to envy (or result from envy). This woman's fascination overlaps with awe: she both studies what occurs in the moment and feels its life-changing grandeur.

Another example of fascination that aimed to define a women's place in the world came from a young, intellectually-challenged African-American woman I tutored. This young woman had urgent questions about race. She feared asking her questions, believing that simply to notice aspects of race made her "racist," but the questions would not release her from their grip. One day, having watched African-Americans being pushed and dragged out of Trump rallies by people with furious faces, she let me know she had an urgent question, though it was "racist." She wanted to know why white people hate black people and want to hurt them.

She herself occupied a unique place racially. Due to a skin condition, her "black" skin was white to the eye. Understanding skin color and race was central to her efforts to make sense of herself. In her approach to me as well, fascination stirred. She knew me to be Jewish and had many questions about Jews. She puzzled over whether a person could be both white and Jewish or were these categories as mutually exclusive as white and black. How could I be white and not hate her, white but also Jewish? How could she be black when her skin was white? She told me these questions burned in her. She hungered to learn about this subject so she could understand how the world works and try to secure her place in it.

One research participant described how a moment's fascination with a crime scene investigation led him down a career path. Given the opportunity, we would want to ask why that particular exposure fascinated him so, when it might not have affected others similarly:

> A time I felt fascination was a couple of years ago when I saw police working at a crime scene near my house and when the Crime Scene Investigators came out I thought their suits and the gadgets they carried were so cool. I started watching all of the police and crime shows, especially CSI (all versions) and Law and Order (all versions), and Dexter. I will be studying law and forensics in school and hopefully pursue a career as a CSI.

What path was the young man traveling when his fascination erupted? Was he in search of an identity? Or perhaps something in his world felt secretly criminal and in need of investigation. Had he, as a young child, encountered something that smacked of forbiddenness but also elicited proscribed curiosity? Might a career of criminal investigation speak to his urgency to know and to find a justification for zealous looking?

The fixed eye of fascination **141**

When he saw the police investigators and their equipment and attire, his fascination was immediate. We don't know whether he was in search of an identity, but often fascinations do appear to answer latent questions such as, who am I? What might I become? Which of the world's symbols, decorations, and emblems might I attach to myself to gain meaning?

The veiled and the forbidden

I recall from childhood an old couple who lived on my street, who seldom were seen but were reported to hate children. They had a particularly tempting swing in their yard that made us long to trespass. We also wanted to lay eyes on this monstrous couple, then run like the wind. They fascinated and horrified, though nothing in their physical appearance set them apart from the kindly old couple at the other end of the street. Still, they deviated from our behavioral norms and had qualities of high import to us – a reputed dangerous antipathy toward children and a wondrous piece of play equipment – and so we wanted both to avoid them in fear and to see and study them and show our capacity to outrun their malevolence if need be. The swing alone did not draw us; the swing's illicitness and the forbidding character of its owners did. We see in this story fascination with the dangerous and the pleasurable, but also with the interdicted.

The forbidden and the veiled are related. Both involve something out of reach. Either we cannot know about it, or we cannot access it and its pleasures. The concepts merge because the veil forbids the eyes. The shrouded might be a lovely woman, an equation with unknown solution, or a swing half-seen in deep shade. It has often been remarked that uncloaking makes things ordinary. The covering of Muslim women prohibits the gaze but also invites searching attention and powerful curiosity and fantasy. To allow free access diminishes fascination. Stay-at-home parents often complain that it is the absent parent, less known to the child and in some sense veiled, who is most desired.

One client told a story of fascination with what occurred in therapy groups led by her individual therapist, to which she was not privy. She had fantasies of planting a "spy" in these groups who would report back to her and reveal what was secret and off-limits, both cloaked and forbidden. The excitement about such reportage contained some of the thrill children can feel about stolen access to the world of adults or older children. It was rich in fantasy about what could not be seen.

Marginal status

I have spoken about monsters and heroes but human deviation is not the only marginal status that fascinates us. Captivation with the liminal (Leach, 1964) points us toward the bearded woman, the living dead, anything at the edge of one category or suspended between two. Fascination with the intercategorical illustrates the allure of what confuses or unsettles our thinking. We feel compelled to attend because

142 The fixed eye of fascination

we must make sense of what is initially unfathomable; we want to bring it into relation with familiar experience. Sears (2015) describes the concurrence, in the nineteenth-century US, of anti-cross-dressing laws co-occurring with fascination with cross-dressing. The person who challenged typical gender categories needed to be regulated, but also held great allure. Interrogating our categories also serves to reinforce their importance.

To the anthropologists' focus on the naturally intercategorical, we must add man's psychic need to *generate* such intercategorical and marginal foci of fascination. We don't just happen across oddities; we create them as well, often building them from dissociated aspects of self. We must remember Sartre's (1948) statement, "if the Jew did not exist, the anti-Semite would invent him" (p. 10). Great is the human need to find what lies beyond the border of familiarity in order to abhor and adore it.

The next story explores boundaries between life and death, physical definition and dissolution, the rotten and the nutritive. Another might read of the woman's experience and feel revulsion. For her, fascination prevailed:

> We were living in transition, had just sold our house, and rented a small place for 8 weeks, just until my daughter graduated and we could move to Michigan. A baby bird lived in a nest, just outside our window. His cries for food were endless, until one silent morning, I stumbled upon his pink, feathery body lying at the base of the tree. The ants had made the same discovery, and working in teams around the clock, they dismantled the little body. As hours passed, Mother Nature's armies dissected while winged scavengers took their fill and left fresh eggs as payment. As each did their part, the small patch of earth surrounding the baby bird seemed to create a cradle, a grave, a swallowing of sorts, which in the end finally closed the space this little guy occupied in life.

The baby bird is an exquisite blend of life and death, matter and energy, and thus it fascinates. The woman is herself in transition and is concerned for a daughter in in flux, thus the transformation of the very young, very vulnerable bird may have been of special interest.

The narrative below shows a person fascinated by the apparent rout of ordinary rules that pertain to the physical universe:

> As a child I always loved magic. I remember my first ever magic show. I was fascinated! The performer had a certain charisma and charm and I couldn't take my eyes off him. He did tricks that I had never been seen or heard of. He sawed a woman in half. I couldn't believe my eyes! The magician had my full attention and I became obsessed. He had the whole crowd under his spell. It was unbelievable. The show got better and better with every minute that passed. I was fascinated by his wonderful talent. He put on a great show that I will remember for years to come.

The fixed eye of fascination **143**

She is enthralled by the man himself – his charisma and charm – but also by the magic, the ability to do what cannot be done (slice a woman in half without harming her!), which pushes past the edge of normal experience. So the gestalt – the magic and the man – cast their lasting spell over her. As always, we must ask, what did the individual bring to the viewing? A curiosity about male power in relation to women? Would it be delightful (charismatic and charming)? Or might it be deadly (women cut to pieces)? Did she experience the kind of excitement we call "counterphobic," which comes when something you fear, such as mortal wounding of the body, is faced and escaped?

In the narrative of his life in the Nazi concentration camps, Elie Wiesel describes a torturous forty-plus mile winter march of starving prisoners evacuated from a camp due to the approach of Russian troops. On this interminable march, which killed most, 15-year-old Wiesel describes the fascination he began to feel with the idea of dying:

> Death wrapped itself around me till I was stifled. It stuck to me. I felt that I could touch it. The idea of dying, of no longer being, began to fascinate me. Not to exist any longer. Not to feel the horrible pain in my foot. Not to feel anything, neither weariness, nor cold, nor anything. To break the ranks, to let oneself slide to the edge of the road. . . .
>
> (p. 92)

Death is always of consequence to us but for this young man its allure was enormous. He had fought death mightily yet began to see its other dimension: its vast power to relieve him of his suffering. As such, it was a form of magic that lay within his exhausted grasp, the sole power left to the suffering, to the slave of earthly masters. Yet he recognizes death as an ugliness as well. It stifles, it sticks, it speaks to him unbidden. It is the great edge of known experience, over which he might choose to pass, changing everything.

Moving from the horrific to the quotidian, in the realm of marginal experience, I think of a neighbor child who visited me regularly and felt a compulsion each time to search inside the seat of an exercise bike, underneath its black cover, to find, squeeze, and squeal in fascinated disgust over a mysterious, mobile, jelly-like material within, even to reveal to another visiting child this alien substance with its unique textural allure. Or I think of a woman who felt fascinated delight in the extravagant molds that could be found growing in food dishes of those with ill-kept refrigerators. These unusual forms, which represented the transition of material from one state to another, captivated her. No untended refrigerator was safe from her explorations.

Sexual fascination

In consideration of awe, I discussed Sabbah's (1984) treatise, *Woman in the Muslim Unconscious*. She analyzes certain widely-consumed erotic literature that portrays

144 The fixed eye of fascination

women as sexually voracious; she calls this woman "the omnisexual woman" or "the slit" because she is no more than a greedy, muscular vagina and engorged vulva craving orgasm. The sexually voracious woman is obsessed with erotic satisfaction, especially with the search for the enormous phallus, even if the quest takes her to the barnyard, which it does regularly in this erotic literature and mythology. The woman's sexual parts are personified and become a dramatic and fascinating character.

Rather than acknowledge fascination with this imaginary character, patriarchal societies treat the rapacious female as a reality that justifies strict control of women, who cannot be trusted to manage themselves sexually and thus are a threat to men's pride and their lineage. The omnisexual nature of the woman requires that she be covered, homebound, silenced, and married only to a male-selected partner. The woman's purported sexual wantonness is used to justify brutality toward women – ranging from domestic violence to honor killings.

A number of important elements contribute to this portrayal of women as insatiable (Sabbah, 1984), but among them is fascination with female sexuality and anxiety about what satisfies women. Can an ordinary man satisfy her? Will she be a source of humiliation to the man through infidelity or through demonstration that he cannot fulfill her? Will she be a source of unending delight to the man by directing her desire exclusively to him? Denying the intensity of his own sexual interests, curiosity, and insecurity, the man casts himself as a relatively helpless victim of the Siren female, either of her sexual voracity or her sexual infidelity. He is prey to the witch's spell. Thus he is fascinated in the passive sense of the word. Rather than owning that his captivation rests in *his* nature, he blames it on the woman's inclination to fascinate. He is tied up, passive, victimized, and spellbound. He feels, *I am bound by you,* and he legislates, *you will be constrained by me.*

In the Jim Crow South and into the present, the sexual danger that white men presented for black women was denied, while emphasis was placed instead on the black man's sexual aggressiveness toward white women, and on black women's alleged hypersexuality (Thompson-Miller, Feagin, and Pica, 2015). Black men learned to avoid even eye contact with white women, coming to call such activity "reckless eyeballing" to reflect its danger. Despite such caution, men were regularly accused of rape, then castrated or lynched (Thompson-Miller, p. 22). Minor sexual offenses – often fabricated – were used to justify beating, mutilation, and murder. As with Muslim violence against women, Jim Crow aggression toward purportedly hypersexual black males, and the brutal rape of black women, had complex roots, among them the sexual insecurity of the white male who might use rape to assert such sexual power and combat insecurity. The white man fascinated with the black man's alleged hypersexuality and sexual menace likely is projecting his own illicit impulses or betraying envy. The black man often was assigned the white man's sin and punished ruthlessly for it. Fascination was denied, but indulged under the guise of attention to social order and preoccupation with castigating supposed sexual reprobates.

The fixed eye of fascination **145**

Sartre (1948) understood that one driver of French anti-Semitism was the need to use the Jew to embody all those forbidden improprieties the anti-Semite finds so interesting, including sexual licentiousness:

> But he [the anti-Semite], manning the outposts of Society, turns his back on the pure virtues he is defending: his business is with Evil, his duty, to unmask and denounce it, to appraise its extent. His sole concern, therefore, is to amass anecdotes which reveal the lubricity of the Jew, his greed for money, his guile and treachery. He immerses himself in filth. Read Drumont's La France Juive: this book, labelled "An expression of the highest French morality", is a collection of vile and obscene stories.
>
> (p. 37)

Sartre goes on to say:

> But Evil, on the other hand, is something he can contemplate untiringly, something for which he has not only the intuition but, one would say, the taste as well. With an energy touching on obsession, he returns again and again to anecdotes of obscene or criminal actions, which excite him and satisfy his perverse leanings: but since, at the same time, he attributes them to the same infamous Jews on whom he pours his scorn, he gluts his passion without compromising himself.
>
> (pp. 37–38)

The psychological dynamics Sartre sees in the anti-Semite apply as well to those who degrade Blacks, Muslims, women, or others. They also have applicability to whoever focuses his distaste – but also his fascination – on a particular individual who he has concluded – unburdened by evidence – is guilty of horrible behaviors or in possession of grotesque character traits. The fascinated one has no idea that he is enticed by what the hated person represents. He sees himself as the nucleus of moral umbrage, thus he is free of shame, guilt, and self-disgust. We saw earlier the role disgust plays in condemning projected impulses. Fascination is the partner in the dance of projective identification. What is projected is indicted as disgusting, but retains an allure that betrays its origins.

Developmental

Fascination is an easy emotion to ignore. It tends to be quiet, approved by elders, and seldom evocative of concern. It doesn't assert a clear relationship to human development, as disgust might when we consider its reaction-formation function. So where do we place fascination developmentally?

Like awe, fascination is a form of what Tomkins (1962, 1963) called interest-excitement and Spezzano (1993) modified to interest excitement. Fascination can

146 The fixed eye of fascination

be thought of as quietly excited interest. Infants who study the world with full and focused attention may be displaying an early form of fascination. By toddlerhood, unusual life forms such as dogs often elicit an excitement that seems to convey fascination with what this creature *is* and *does*. Toddlers sometimes pick out idiosyncratic subjects of great interest. I knew one young boy who was fascinated by vacuum cleaners. Any house he visited he entered with the urgent question "va?" which was his way of asking whether a vacuum cleaner might reside in that house. Years later, he switched his fascination to *The Music Man*. Every element in the production was of greatest interest to him, whether the costumes, the instruments, or the music. By that point, important identifications could be expressed through his connection with this show, which centered on an intriguing male figure.

If childhood fascination becomes obsessive and must find and fixate an object, it can interfere with learning, which requires mobile attention. But the capacity for fascination, if it remains flexible, is pure gold for the educator. Young minds fascinate easily. Much is new to them and nature seems to have equipped them for rapid, energized absorption. Fear and the need to master it drives them as well. Bright, well-functioning children often mix idiosyncratic areas of fascination, which may take the form of hobbies, and an openness to shifting fascinations that respond to what life and its teachers present.

The idiosyncratic beguilements of childhood are diverse. Some reflect prominent developmental or familial issues; others may reflect a native bent of the child's mind. Even if rooted in conflict or fear, early fascinations may lead to rewarding mastery experiences as learning and problem-solving advances and fears are mastered. Such early fascinations, vigorously pursued, may lay the groundwork for adult abilities to master complex material. The subjects studied by children may abruptly lose their glow (in part, due to changing intrapsychic needs), but not infrequently such fascinations will form a solid base for life-long interests.

Puberty brings a rising interest in sexuality, but not all interest is fascination. Fascination requires more than the wish to gratify desire: one must intend to learn all about a subject. Sexual fascination is fueled by the normative veiling of sexual information in many cultures. What remains concealed never becomes ordinary. Sexual excitement combines with sexual shrouding to feed fascination. Inhibition, if pronounced, will counter sexual fascination or cause it to follow a diverted course.

We remarked earlier that some forms of awe may diminish as the years advance. Fascination, though, is a low-drama, high reward emotion that often persists and contributes to a life rich in intellectual engagement and delight. Specific fascinations such as those with monsters and heroes may, however, lessen with maturity as a young adult's identity issues become settled and those individuals the young tend to idolize or fear are revealed to be human beings with feet of clay.

Fascination in the fabric of lives

To fasten one's attention on something and absorb its offerings is a great human ability, a tool of learning, and a generator of attachment. But inclinations that are

The fixed eye of fascination **147**

powerful inevitably will, at times, deliver us into danger. When we cannot tear our attention from something, we are at risk of getting lost in ways that interfere with balance in life. Our judgment may falter, as may our self-control. Fascination may rocket us to the land of obsession or addiction where we are unable to turn away from the video game, Internet sex sites, or the gambling table. Some activities are naturally alluring and difficult to resist. Toy makers and video game designers understand this as do purveyors of sex. They study how to hold human attention. And some people are more ready than others to fall prey to fascination – or to a particular enticement – due to their lasting or momentary psychological needs.

Helen Macdonald (2015) describes her falconry addiction in her memoir, *H is for Hawk*. She explores the fascination with her goshawk, Mabel, that takes root while she is reeling from the death of her beloved father:

> It is a rush. You lose yourself in it. And so you run towards those little shots of fate, where the world turns. That is the lure: that is why we lose ourselves, when powerless from hurt and grief, in drugs or gambling or drink; in addictions that collar the broken soul and shake it like a dog. I had found my addiction on that day out with Mabel. It was as ruinous, in a way, as if I'd taken a needle and shot myself with heroin. I had taken flight to a place from which I didn't want to ever return.
>
> (p. 176)

"Losing oneself" is key to addiction. Macdonald shows us how she disappears into the world she makes with Mabel. There she shelters and wants to remain, veiled and safe.

At least in the early stages of a fascination, the experience tends to seem like benign and controlled activity. With destructive fascinations, awareness may later dawn of their out-of-control elements. Shopping exemplifies an addiction that creates security and delight. A person hungers to engage joyfully in life, but seeks a safe investment that poses no emotional risks. So she shies away from seeking a new friend, lover, or hobby; instead, she shops for beautiful things she can possess permanently. No risks to self-regard, no chance of loss occur. The objects are personally chosen, purchased, and possessed. The situation is low risk, however the pleasure achieved may be fleeting. So another purchase follows, and another, until perils of over-spending or preoccupation materialize.

Acquiring objects can also enhance identity. A teenager imagines herself in possession of a lovely matching bedroom set like the one featured on the web site her friends visit. She will have that bedroom and know she is desirable to her friends; she will belong. Once acquired, the bedroom set holds less magic than she imagined and she finds herself fixated on a new phone, then a new make of jeans, a new backpack, and so on. Her fascinations are driven by the urgency of wanting to be somebody special, someone who will fit in and be admired. These examples of acquisition are at the border between obsession and fascination and will shift one way or the other depending on the nature of the engagement with the object.

148 The fixed eye of fascination

Does she want to know all about it? Where was it made? Who designed it? How did it come to market? If the object itself holds great allure, in all its particulars, it is a fascination. If the object is just a means to the end of belonging or feeling pretty, it is an obsession or preoccupation.

Fascination is both a capability and a vulnerability. If we can feel its force, yet maintain balance in life, if we can watch that it does not disregard laws, flout financial responsibility, or short-change relationship needs, then fascination can greatly enrich our experience. But if equilibrium is lost, others in one's life will resent the fascination, exhaustion may occur, and specific calamities such as bankruptcy or damaged health may ensue.

Fearing and resisting fascination can play a part in psychological difficulty. Timothy, discussed in Chapter 3, came to represent to me the perils of fighting the natural human fascination with sex. Raised Catholic, he was so fearful of the fascinating power of sexuality that he drove himself to the brink of psychosis trying to control his sexual thoughts, and he bolstered his need to do so with an irrational idea that sexual indulgence of any kind would lead to social incompetence. His inner calculus was that he could be socially successful only by quashing sexuality, therefore, he was highly motivated to resist the hugely motivating force of sexual attraction. But the fascination of sexuality refused to subdue and thus his conflict was perpetual, as were his symptoms. Strange mental blanknesses would overtake and frighten him and seemed to be an emergency response to the temptation to allow his mind to flood with sexual fantasy.

We explored the religious education that had oversold the impropriety and power of sex. Accepting this belief contributed to his configuring any sexual interest as a muscular constrictor that would embrace and bind him. His belief that he would suffer dire consequences for sexual interest carried the deep mark of guilt over indulgence of impulses. We talked time and again about the inner judge or disciplinarian that insisted he pay painfully for his sexual pleasures. My work with Timothy also centered on building tolerance for sexual fascination and its various expressions. He feared that allowing any attention to sex would mean he would never get free of mental bondage. His fascination would send his life swirling down the drain. He would forget his schoolwork, his family, his friends. Interestingly, his primary sexual fantasies were about being physically bound, while his fear of fascination was that it would psychically bind him. I talked to him of normal satiation, of allowing the fascination to live, with confidence that he would get his fill.

We also noted that Timothy's role as youngest in the family made the idea of submission familiar, acceptable, and easily sexualized, whereas assertiveness put him in competition with his siblings. Active production of pleasure through masturbation or an initiator's role in sex brought punishing ideas about loss of social competence, as well as actual social paralysis and compulsive thought patterns. These responses served to return him to the submissive position, which kept him connected to his family with minimal interpersonal friction. As Timothy began to experiment with more active social and sexual roles, his fascination and excitement

The fixed eye of fascination **149**

over sadomasochistic Internet imagery diminished, which brought him some relief from the idea he would be hopelessly and helplessly captivated by his sexual desires.

A counterpoint to Timothy was John, bathed in adolescence by his mother, whose capacity for non-sexual fascinations helped him survive an abusive childhood. Nature enthralled him and he embraced his excitement. He rode his aptitude for fascination in order to find physical and psychic spaces that his rageful and erratic parents could not invade with their insults, blows, or battles. His fascination served as the door to a magic land, an image that suggests the narrative of many beloved children's books about lonely children. So while Timothy was terrified that he might be fascinated with something that would, in his eyes and in the imagined view of others, turn him into a monster or animal, someone beneath human dignity, John embraced safe fascinations and became a lifelong scholar whose interests were a defining characteristic of his personality. When under stress, his adaptive engagement veered into an obsession with leaving the country to go to the jungle, where he – Robison Crusoe-like – could leave behind the fickleness of human society and immerse himself in nature. At these times, his fascination worked in opposition to human relatedness and represented a mental security vault in which he tried to lock himself.

Oscar Wilde's (2015/1890) character, Dorian Gray, demonstrates a deep retreat into fascination. His childhood had been painful and had frayed his trust in others:

> For these treasures, and everything that he collected in his lovely house, were to be to him means of forgetfulness, modes by which he could escape, for a season, from the fear that seemed to him at times to be almost too great to be borne. Upon the walls of the lonely locked room where he had spent so much of his boyhood, he had hung with his own hands the terrible portrait whose changing features showed him the real degradation of his life. . . .
>
> (p. 815)

Dorian is entranced by his collected treasures, which help him escape the world. He is captivated by his beautiful self-portrait as well and hangs it among his cherished items, but the painting signifies the impossibility of rescuing himself through fascination, since it soon will reflect his dissolute life.

Some may hunger to fascinate others. Quests for love or fame may rest on a coveted portrayal of the self as captivating. We want to be persons of great allure to others and may feel that if we do not fascinate others, we are of no worth. We constantly look for the mirror that smiles back, but never are satisfied. Discussed in Chapter 4, Gary needed to be in awe of his own performance but aimed as well to fascinate others. If he could not bind another's attention and evoke awe, he was worthless. Self-awe followed from fantasied, measurable achievement, but also from seeing fascination reflected in another's eyes. The legacy of his inability to engage his mother's delight and interest was evident.

150 The fixed eye of fascination

To fascinate can become a burden. I think of an attractive young Muslim woman, living in a largely Christian country, who wrapped her hair as part of her religious observance and drew from others a response of fascination with her "exoticism." Her foreignness was read as a highly intriguing forms of alienness. She was seen as holding fascinating secrets within, from the hidden hair to the unknown doctrine and way of life. This young woman felt she barely knew herself. She believed she lacked clear identity and that Islam – which she had chosen, not inherited – might be a route to such distinctiveness. To be an object of fascination was more stressful than pleasing. The idea that others expected to find treasures beneath her "veil" sharpened her self-consciousness and self-doubt. She feared she was an imposter, now under a magnifying glass, and would be found out and humiliated. She was aware of no urge to fascinate others, though clearly the potential for such a desire needed consideration.

The person who cannot be fascinated deserves a few words. He sees nothing and no one in life to excite his interest. He will find life drab and may seek stimulation compulsively or pursue new love objects because the old ones bore him. Much of the richness in life is in feelings evoked when we observe the world we inhabit. The person who does not stir in response to a poem, a tree, a child, the night air – whether with awe, fascination, interest, even disgust – is lacking typical sensitivity and his life is flat. Such unresponsiveness can follow from an atypical neurological status. It also can derive from early trauma or neglect, which can lead either to the failure of some personality aspects to develop or to the use of inhibition to dull sensitivity to a disturbing world. Narcissism can interfere with the ability to find the world engaging (Spezzano, 1993). A person may care about nothing unrelated to self-aggrandizement (why would I care about the stars in the firmament or some Hollywood star. I want to shine myself – that is all that matters). The person may even dislike the notion that anything other than he could fascinate. If I can be captivated by a falcon's flight or another man's talents, what does it say about my own gifts? I have failed in my quest for uniqueness. But the person who cannot be fascinated is bored and restless and missing much in life.

6

CONCLUDING COMMENTS

The four emotions at the center of our discussion are the instruments and signs of our engagement with the world. They characterize vivid encounters and say to us, this I want, this I spurn; this is me, this is not me; this destroys, this sustains. They evaluate whether and how these transactions will enrich or threaten our identity, security, or satisfaction. I have approached these four emotions via the key concepts of self and its boundary, humanity, and category-breaching.

The self-boundary speaks to what happens to my experience of being me when I am in the grip of an emotion. Disgust implores me to stiffen and spit out, wipe off, or protect some vital core from soiling and invasion. Or I may lasso something bad that has ventured inside and eject it, thus using disgust as a rescue emotion. Horror signifies that I am helpless because I am already overtaken and in the process of being altered in some awful way that I must try to absorb. The disturbance may be a physical incursion, an alteration of consciousness, or an event that deforms the outside world so profoundly that the self is agitated and the delicacy of the line between self and other becomes apparent. Awe says, come, enter me, expand me. I invite you. It is a lover in the sphere of emotion. I open my eyes and spirit when in its embrace. It both shrinks and enlarges me. In the words of one research participant, "I felt so small compared to everything around me. Yet at the same time I felt larger than life." Fascination speaks of wanting and needing to know everything about a topic. I focus my mind and my eye to that purpose. For the moment, I am nothing but the agent of that attention.

The emotions can be glossed as well by how they comment on humanness, our own and others'. Disgust speaks to what is humanly undesirable – the soiled, the aged, the alien, the bleeding and torn. We do not want to integrate these things into our experience of mind or body. If we aim to assert superiority over a person, or license ourselves to aggress toward him, we may need to render him inhuman and disgusting. Inter-group violence flows from this dynamic. Horror responds to

152 Concluding comments

humans become inhuman, whose presence profoundly alters our world. When people are inhuman, we stand on unsteady ground. If the distance from normalcy is great, horror is a common response. Awe focuses on the heroic – the best of what is human – or on what is superhuman and stirs our astonishment. Awe may stretch or clarify our concept of humanity, as we absorb what is humanly grand. Fascination, too, focuses on what interests us about both extremes of humanity – the monstrous or abhorrent at one end of the spectrum, and the astounding at the other. It hungers to grasp the essence of what we encounter.

Self and humanity are two essential categories but are not the only fundamental classifications: guilty and innocent, clean and dirty, young and old are among those that matter greatly. Category theorists say it is the in-between spaces that bother us most: the half-guilty or somewhat dirty more than the thoroughly condemned or sullied. We want our classifications to be distinct so they can do their job of organizing our experience. Thus we focus with disgust on the in-between, unsettled states that refuse to declare themselves. They disquiet us because our organizing impulses have been thwarted.

Category breaches *energize* experience and bring it to life. Such vitality can trigger disgust over what is charged with life due to its unstable position. Fascination, too, is engaged by what occupies an indefinite or liminal space. The odd is always interesting. We must figure out what to make of it and how to relate to it, therefore it compels our attention. The intercategorical status is less crucial to horror and awe than to disgust and fascination. Awe trains its light on *best in class*, on the extreme positive or ideal. Horror reaches for the abject, sometimes for the alien, the explicitly not-me, which may also be inhuman. What I have called category-bursting is one breach that does figure in awe and horror. Powerful forces break through ordinary boundaries and radically reconfigure categories so that the young abruptly ages or the pure is contaminated. In magically recasting reality, such powers engender awe, horrify, or both at once. Dorian Gray's portrait was a category-bursting thing that turned young to old, beautiful to hideous without regard for the normal laws of time and nature.

Behavioral overreach brings contact between an emotion and one of its opposites. Too much fascination may leave us unable to extricate ourselves. We become imprisoned, helpless, or bound. We may become disgusting, to ourselves and others, as we sink into addiction. A surfeit of awe means we have aggrandized one thing above all else and lost perspective. We are worshipful and perhaps blind to the limitations of what we revere. If we self-worship, we are absorbed in narcissism. If we venerate another – human or not – we may be naive and bound in a helpless simplicity of mind. Once again, disgust may be the voice that attempts, in its rough manner, to limit our indulgence. If too much damage has been done so that our overreach has made us, or our creative endeavor, a monstrosity, then horror will arise. William Day (1985) stated, in his study of Gothic literature, "The possibilities of the underworld, particularly of voyeurism . . . turn quickly into horrors, and the protagonist is paralyzed, caught between desire and fear, seemingly opposite emotions that have fused" (p. 25).

Concluding comments **153**

We can work backward from the alarmed emotions – disgust and horror – and find their pleasurable partners. We start with something disgusting but cannot deny that it engages our great interest, our sharp attention, our fascination. Or we begin with what horrifies or disgusts but find in the monstrous a transformative power, a destructive and creative capacity that arouses an element of awe.

In our individual lives, and in society, the four emotions appear as powerful expressions of our core human needs, interests, and liabilities. Disgust tells of our urgent desire for some control over what touches us physically or stirs our imagination. Fascination evinces our readiness to risk deep immersion, even feelings of fusion, as we commit ourselves to engagement. Awe, too, says we are prepared to absorb what the world offers and will chance losing ourselves in appreciation for what is grander than we are and vaster than we had imagined. Finally, horror says we have had too much of the world and are threatened to the core. We barely tolerate the life surrounding us or within us, which threatens our sanity and our survival. Together, these emotions speak of human fragility, and convey as well our hunger for richly engaged and informed lives despite our vulnerability.

NOTES

Chapter 1

1. A number of writers within psychology and neuroscience have offered schemata that characterize the broad range of emotional phenomena I have described. Neuroscientist Jaak Panksepp (1998) believes that emotion is subcortically produced, and this assertion links human emotion with the cognitively-unelaborated emotion assumed to exist for other mammals. Panksepp states, "Even though cortical processes such as thoughts and perceptions (i.e., appraisals) can obviously instigate various emotions, to the best of our knowledge, the affective essence of emotionality is subcortically and precognitively organized" (p. 26). Panksepp's neuroscientifically-derived model is consistent with my inclination to separate emotion and cognition, but also with the idea that emotion very quickly gains cognitive representation so that the named emotions, with their intrinsic cognitive structure, become possible. Psychoanalyst Charles J. Spezzano (1993) argues for the primacy of affect over thought from a developmental perspective. He states that "Psychological life begins for all of us with affect. Before idea or object, there is affect, a confusing swirl of fluctuating positive and negative feeling states" (p. 77).

2. Developing the "constructionist perspective," psychologist Russell (2015) talks of "core affect," which refers to "a neurophysiological state that is consciously accessible as a simple, non-reflective feeling that is an integral blend of hedonic (pleasure–displeasure) and arousal (sleepy–activated) values" (p. 196). Though core affect is accessible to consciousness, "people do not always attend to it" (p. 197). The idea of a process that exists at a nonconscious level but can, at times, be consciously accessed and *then* become emotion, is a plausible conjecture that remains for the neuroscientists to explore. The "simple, non-reflective feelings" to which Russell refers bear a relationship to what I have called "cognitively-unelaborated feeling." However, I do not see such feeling as being qualitatively restricted to pleasure and displeasure. Russell postulates that core affect is an ongoing process that can be brought into consciousness or not. It operates like a stream that flows below ground at times and above ground at other times. Only when above ground would I apply the words feeling and emotion.

3. Freud (1913) rooted his understanding of taboo in the idea of ambivalence. He believed that taboo objects are the subject of highly ambivalent emotions. Regarding the contact prohibitions that link taboo with obsessive-compulsive disorder, he tells us:

> Behind all these prohibitions there seems to be something in the nature of a theory that they are necessary because certain persons and things are charged with a

156 Notes

> dangerous power, which can be transferred through contact with them, almost like an infection. The *quantity* of this dangerous attribute also plays a part. Some people or things have more of it than others and the danger is actually proportional to the difference of potential of the charges. The strangest fact seems to be that anyone who has transgressed one of these prohibitions himself acquires the characteristic of being prohibited—as though the whole of the dangerous charge had been transferred over to him. This power is attached to all *special* individuals, such as kings, priests or newborn babies, to all *exceptional* states, such as the physical states of menstruation, puberty or birth, and to all uncanny things, such as sickness and death and what is associated with them through their power of infection or contagion. (pp. 21–22)

Focused as it is on nuclear family dynamics and conflict between love and hate, desire and prohibition, Freud's theory of ambivalence disregards the evocation of complex feelings by whatever disrupts our fundamental categories of experience.

Freud spoke of the "taboo conscience" (p. 67) and said that the breach of taboo brought "a taboo sense of guilt" (p. 67) – thus introducing an emotional component that helped him make sense of the parallels between taboo and obsessive-compulsive disorder. I would suggest that some breaches of taboo in fact bring guilt (e.g., incest taboo) or other emotions, including shame and disgust, but many bring only concern about danger.

Chapter 4

1. Pascal's (Fisher, 1998) view of wonder stands apart in terminating in a fearful place, since wonder, he feels, positions man as horribly small in relation to the heavens and discomfortingly massive in relation to the minuscule. Pascal's recognition of the ways that horror and wonder interweave moves us closer to the terrain I and other contemporary thinkers (Keltner and Haidt, 2003) would stake out for awe.

   Earlier concepts of *the sublime* show that concept used as awe is employed currently. Fisher (2002) says of the sublime that, "Within aesthetics, the romantic notion of the sublime spiritualized fear by removing from it personal interest and danger and then imagining conditions within experience that blend fear and wonder" (p. 146). Fisher explains Kant's view of the sublime:

   > Kant's theory of the sublime merges experiences of wonder – especially in the case of the mathematical sublime – with the more traditional, Lucretian experience of the forces of nature that so outweigh the tiny human force that the imagination feels its own annihilation in standing in their presence. (p. 147)

2. Some descriptive confusion may figure in this apparent controversy. The fusion state Freud (1930) describes and the "symbiotic" state described by Mahler, Pine, and Bergman (1975) do not seem to require an "I am with Mother" conception, just a rich experience of sensations that is absent any idea of boundary between internal and external. Thus these states would seem plausibly to precede the development of much sense of boundary between what I am, feel, and do and what surrounds me and is apart from me. They are boundaryless without representing merger between mother and baby.

REFERENCES

Améry, J. (1980). *At the Mind's Limits, contemplations by a survivor on Auschwitz and its realities.* Bloomington, IN: University of Indiana Press.

Anzieu, D. (1989). *The Skin Ego* (Chris Turner, trans.). New Haven, CT: Yale University Press.

Atlas, G. and Benjamin, J. (2015). The "too muchness" of excitement: sexuality in light of excess, attachment and affect regulation. *International Journal of Psychoanalysis*, 96 (1), 39–63. doi: 10.1111/1745-8315.12285. Epub 2015 Feb 20.

Baker, A. (2007). *Adult Children of Parental Alienation Syndrome: breaking the ties that bind.* New York: W.W. Norton & Co.

Barrett, L. (2015). Ten common misconceptions about psychological construction theories of emotion. In L.F. Barrett and J.A. Russell (Eds), *The Psychological Construction of Emotion.* New York: Guilford Press.

Benjamin, J. (1995). *Like Subjects, Love Objects: essays on recognition and sexual difference.* New Haven, CT: Yale University Press.

Blechner, M. (2005). Disgust, desire, and fascination – psychoanalytic, cultural, historical, and neurobiological perspectives commentary on Muriel Dimen's paper. *Studies in Gender and Sexuality*, 6 (1), 33–45. doi: 10.1080/15240650609349264.

Butler, J. (1993). *Bodies That Matter.* New York: Routledge.

Butler, J. (2002). Melancholy gender-refused identification. In M. Dimen and V. Goldner (Eds), *Gender in Psychoanalytic Space* (pp. 2–20). New York: Other Press.

Carroll, L. (1929). *Alice's Adventures in Wonderland, Through the Looking Glass, The Hunting of the Snark,* New York: Random House, The Modern Library.

Casey, L.S. (2016). The politics of disgust: public opinion toward LGBTQ people and policies (unpublished doctoral dissertation). University of Michigan, Ann Arbor.

Cecil, R. (Ed.) (1996). *The Anthropology of Pregnancy Loss.* Washington, DC: Berg.

Cohen, D. (2017, March). Before straight and gay. *The Atlantic.*

Corbett, K. (2009). *Boyhoods: rethinking masculinities.* New Haven, CT: Yale University Press.

Corbett, K. (2016). *A Murder Over a Girl.* New York: Henry Holt and Company.

Corngold, S. (1972/2013). Introduction to Franz Kafka's *The Metamorphosis*. In F. Kafka, *The Metamorphosis* (pp. xi–xliii). New York: Modern Library.

Creed, B. (1993). *The Monstrous-Feminine: film, feminism, psychoanalysis.* New York: Routledge.

158 References

Darwin, C. (1872). *The Expression of the Emotions in Man and Animals*. London: Fontana Press.

Davies, J. (2017, April). Relational theory and clinical approaches. Paper presented at the meeting of the Michigan Council for Psychoanalysis and Psychotherapy, Ann Arbor, Michigan.

Day, W. P. (1985). *In the Circles of Fear and Desire*. Chicago, MI: University of Chicago Press.

de Kretser, M. (2003). *The Hamilton Case*. New York: Little, Brown and Company.

de Maupassant, G. (2015). *Le Horla. The Necklace and Other Stories* (S. Smith, trans.) (pp. 288–316). New York: Liveright Publishing Corp.

Dimen, M. (2002). Deconstructing difference: gender, splitting, and transitional space. In M. Dimen and V. Goldner (Eds), *Gender in Psychoanalytic Space* (pp. 41–62). New York: Other Press.

Dimen, M. (2003). *Sexuality, Intimacy, Power*. Hillsdale, NJ: The Analytic Press.

Douglas, M. (1966). *Purity and Danger*. New York: Routledge.

Douglass, F. (1999). The claims of the Negro ethnologically considered, address delivered at Western Reserve College, July 12, 1854. In P.S. Foner and Y. Taylor (Eds), *Frederick Douglass: selected speeches and writings* (pp. 282–298). Chicago, IL: Chicago Review Press.

Douglass, F. (2010). *Narrative of the Life of Frederick Douglass, an American Slave, and Other Writings*. New York: Fall River Press.

Du Bois, W.E.B. (1986) *The Souls of Black Folks*. New York: The Library of America (Penguin Books).

Du Maurier, D. (1938). *Rebecca*. Philadelphia, PA: The Blakiston Company.

Einstein, A. (1931). In H.G. Leach (Ed.), *Living Philosophies, a series of intimate credos*. New York: Simon & Schuster.

Ekman P. (1992). An argument for basic emotions. *Cognition & Emotion*, 6, 169–200.

Ekman, P. (1999). Basic emotions. In T. Dalgleish and M. Power (Eds), *Handbook of Cognition and Emotion* (pp. 45–60). Chichester, UK: Wiley.

Ekman, P. (2003). *Unmasking the Face: a guide to recognizing emotions from facial expressions*. Los Altos, CA: Malor Books.

Fast, I. (1984). *Identity: a differentiation model*. Hillsdale, NJ: The Analytic Press.

Fisher, P. (1998). *Wonder, the Rainbow, and the Aesthetics of Rare Experience*. Cambridge, MA: Harvard University Press.

Fisher, P. (2002). *The Vehement Passions*. Princeton, NJ: Princeton University Press.

Freud, S. (1905). Three essays on the theory of sexuality. *Standard Edition*, 7: 125–245. London: Hogarth Press, 1953.

Freud, S. (1913). Taboo and emotional ambivalence. *Standard Edition*, 13(1913–1914): 18–74. London: Hogarth Press, 1953.

Freud, S. (1919). The 'uncanny'. *Standard Edition*, 17: 217–256. London: Hogarth Press, 1955.

Freud, S. (1930[1929]). Civilization and its discontents. *Standard Edition*, 21: 59–145. London: Hogarth Press, 1961.

Frosh, S. (2013). *Hauntings: Psychoanalysis and Ghostly Transmissions*. New York: Palgrave Macmillan.

Gass, N. (2015, June 2). *Politico*.

Geiko (2016). Televised advertisement.

Geurts, K.L. (2002) *Culture and the Senses: bodily ways of knowing in an African community*. Berkeley, CA: University of California Press.

Goldner, V. (2002). Toward a critical relational theory of gender. In M. Dimen and V. Goldner (Eds), *Gender in Psychoanalytic Space* (pp. 63–90). New York: Other Press.

Green, A. (1999). *The Fabric of Affect in the Psychoanalytic Discourse* (A. Sheridan, trans.). New York: Routledge.

Haidt, J. (2013). *The Righteous Mind*. New York: Vintage/Knopf Doubleday.

References **159**

Hartmann, H. (1958). *Ego Psychology and the Problem of Adaptation*. New York: International Universities Press.

Hatzfeld, J. (2006). *Life Laid Bare* (L. Coverdale, trans.). New York: Other Press.

Hatzfeld, J. (2008). *A Time for Machetes* (L. Coverdale, trans.). London: Serpent's Tail.

Himmler, H. (1946) *In Nazi Conspiracy and Aggression*. 1943 speech.

Homer (1996). *The Odyssey* (R. Fagles, trans.). New York: Penguin Books.

Izard, C. (1971) *The Face of Emotion*. New York: Appleton-Century-Crofts.

Izard, C. (1992). Basic emotions, relations among emotions, and emotion–cognition relations. *Psychological Review*, 99, 561–565.

Jacobson, E. (1964). *The Self and the Object World*. London: Hogarth Press.

James, W. (1950/1890). *The Principles of Psychology*. Gloucester, MA: Peter Smith.

Jeffery, P. and R. Jeffery (1996). Delayed periods and falling babies: the ethnophysiology and politics of pregnancy loss in rural North India. In R. Cecil (Ed.), *The Anthropology of Pregnancy Loss* (pp. 17–38). Washington, DC: Berg.

Jianzhong, Q. (2003). On the social constructivist theory of emotion, 11(05), 541–544. http://journal.psych.ac.cn/xlkxjz/EN/.

Josephs, L. (2016). The treatment of Oedipal disgust: when one person's sexual delight is another's disgust. *Psychoanalytic Dialogues, International Journal of Relational Perspectives*, 26 (4), 410–426.

Kafka, F. (1998/1935). *The Trial*. (B. Mitchell, trans.). New York: Schocken Books.

Kafka, F. (2013) *The Metamorphosis*. (S. Corngold, trans. and Ed.). New York: Modern Library.

Keltner, D. and Haidt, J. (2003). Approaching awe, a moral, spiritual, and aesthetic emotion. *Cognition and Emotion*, 17 (2), 297–314.

Klein, M. (1986). The psycho-analytic play technique: its history and significance (1955). In J. Mitchell (Ed.), *The Selected Melanie Klein* (pp. 33–54). New York: The Free Press.

Kristeva, J. (1982). *The Powers of Horror, an essay on abjection*. New York: Columbia University Press.

Layton, L. (2002). Gendered subjects, gendered agents: toward an integration of postmodern theory and relational analytic practice. In M. Dimen and V. Goldner (Eds), *Gender in Psychoanalytic Space* (pp. 289–312). New York: Other Press.

Leach, E. (1964). Anthropological aspects of language: animal categories and verbal abuse. In E. Lenneberg (Ed.), *New Directions in the Study of Language* (pp. 23–63). Cambridge, MA: The M.I.T. Press.

LeDoux, J.E. (2015). *Anxious*. New York: Viking.

Lemma, A. (2010). *Under the Skin, a psychoanalytic study of body modification*. New York: Routledge.

Lessing, D. (1999). *Mara and Dann*. New York: Harper Perennial.

Levi, P. (1989). *The Drowned and the Saved* (R. Rosenthal, trans.). New York: Vintage International.

Levinson, J. (1997). Emotion in response to art: a survey of the terrain. In M. Hjort and S. Laver (Eds), *Emotion and the Arts* (pp. 20–36). New York: Oxford University Press.

Lidz, T. (1973). *The Origin and Treatment of Schizophrenic Disorders*. New York: Basic Books.

Macdonald, H. (2015). *H Is for Hawk*. New York: Grove Press.

Mahler, M., Pine, F., and Bergman, A. (1975). *The Psychological Birth of the Human Infant: symbiosis and individuation*. New York: Basic Books.

Martin, W. (1984). *The Mind of Frederick Douglass*. Chapel Hill, NC: University of North Carolina Press.

McCarthy, C. (2006). *The Road*. New York: Vintage Books.

Miller, S. B. (1985). *The Shame Experience*. Hillsdale, NJ: The Analytic Press.

160 References

Miller, S. B. (1986). Disgust: conceptualization, development, and dynamics. *International Review of Psychoanalysis*, 13, 295–307.

Miller, S.B. (1996). *Shame in Context*. Hillsdale, NJ: Analytic Press.

Miller, S. B. (2004). *Disgust: the gatekeeper emotion*. Hillsdale, NJ: Analytic Press.

Miller, W. I. (1997). *The Anatomy of Disgust*. Cambridge, MA: Harvard University Press.

Oliver, M. (1994). *White Pine*. Beside the waterfall, p. 6; Porcupine, p. 11; The sea mouse, p. 41. New York: Harcourt.

Panksepp, J. (1998). *Affective Neuroscience*. New York: Oxford University Press.

Plutchik, R. 1980. *Theories of Emotion*. New York: Academic Press.

Rozin, P. and Fallon, A.E. (1987). A perspective on disgust. *Psychological Review*, 94, 23–41.

Rozin, P., Haidt, J., and McCauley, C.R. (1999). Disgust: the body and soul emotion. In T. Dalgleish and M. Power (Eds), *Handbook of Cognition and Emotion* (pp. 429–445). Chichester, UK: Wiley.

Rozin, P., Haidt, J., and McCauley, C.R. (2000). Disgust. In M. Lewis and J.M. Haviland-Jones (Eds), *Handbook of Emotions* (pp. 637–653). New York: Guilford Press.

Russell, J. A. (2003). Core affect and the psychological construction of emotion. *Psychological Review*, 110, 145–172.

Russell, J.A. (2015). My psychological constructionist perspective, with a focus on conscious affective experience. In L.F. Barrett and J.A. Russell (Eds), *The Psychological Construction of Emotion* (pp. 183–208). New York: Guilford Press.

Saarinen, J. (2012). The oceanic state: a conceptual elucidation in terms of modal contact. *International Journal of Psychoanalysis*, 93, 939–961.

Sabbah, F. (1984). *Woman in the Muslim Unconscious* (M.J. Lakeland, trans.). New York: Pergamon Press.

Sartre, J. (1948). *Portrait of the Anti-Semite* (E. de Mauny, trans.). London: Secker & Warburg, Lindsay Drummond.

Sartre, J. (1966). *Being and Nothingness* (H.E. Barnes, trans.). New York: Washington Square Press.

Scarantino, A. (2015) Basic emotions, psychological construction, and the problem of variability. In L. Barrett and J. Russell (Eds), *The Psychological Construction of Emotion* (pp. 334–376). New York: Guilford Press.

Schaller, M. and Murray, D. (2010). Infectious diseases and the evolution of cross-cultural differences. In M. Schaller, A. Norenzayan, S.J. Heine, T. Yamagishi, and T. Kameda (Eds), *Evolution, Culture, and the Human Mind* (pp. 243–256). New York: Psychology Press.

Schieffelin, E. (1985) Anger, grief, and shame: toward a Kaluli ethnopsychology. In J. Kirkpatrick and G.M. White (Eds), *Person, Self, and Experience* (pp. 168–182). Berkeley, CA: University of California Press.

Schneider, S.J. (2004). *Horror Film and Psychoanalysis*. Cambridge: Cambridge University Press.

Sears, C. (2015). *Arresting Dress*. Durham, NC: Duke University Press.

Seligman, M. (1971). Phobias and preparedness. *Behavior Therapy*, 2, 307–320.

Sereny, G. (1975). *In quelle tenebre*. Milan: Adelphi.

Shevrin, H. (2000). The experimental investigation of unconscious conflict, unconscious affect, and unconscious signal anxiety. In Max Velmans (Ed), *Investigating Phenomenal Consciousness: new methodologies and maps. Advances in consciousness research*, Vol. 13 (pp. 33–65). Amsterdam: John Benjamins.

Sobo, E. (1996). Cultural explanations for pregnancy loss in rural Jamaica. In R. Cecil (Ed), *The Anthropology of Pregnancy Loss* (pp. 39–58). Washington, DC: Berg.

Spezzano, C. (1993). *Affect in Psychoanalysis: a clinical synthesis*. Hillsdale, NJ: Analytic Press.

Stern, D. (1985). *The Interpersonal World of the Infant*. New York: Basic Books.

Stoker, B. (2013). *Dracula*. First published, 1897. London: Vintage.

Styron, W. (1990). *Darkness Visible: a memoir of madness*. New York: Random House.

Thompson-Miller, R., Feagin, J.R., and Picca, L.H. (2015). *Jim Crow's Legacy, the Lasting Impact of Segregation*. Lanham, MD: Rowman and Littlefield.

Tomkins, S. (1962). *Affect Imagery Consciousness* (Vol. 1). New York: Springer Publishing Co.

Tomkins, S. (1963). *Affect Imagery Consciousness* (Vol. 2). New York: Springer Publishing Co.

Tomkins, S. (1992). *Affect Imagery Consciousness* (Vol. 4). New York: Springer Publishing Co.

Tyrrell, M. (2015). PTSD: Horror in the Mind: the psychology of post-traumatic stress disorder, and the ethical way to lift it. Uncommon Knowledge, www.uncommon-knowledge.co.uk/bio/mark_tyrrell.html.

Walton, K. (1997). Spelunking, simulation, and slime, on being moved by fiction. In M. Hjort and S. Laver (Eds). *Emotion and the Arts* (pp. 37–49). New York: Oxford University Press.

Wiesel, E. (1960). *The Night Trilogy*. New York: Hill and Wang.

Wilbur, R. (1988). October Maples, Portland. In *Richard Wilbur, New and Collected Poems*. New York: Harcourt Brace Jovanovich.

Wilde, O. (2015). The picture of Dorian Gray. In *The Penny Dreadfuls, Tales of Horror: Dracula, Frankenstein, and the Picture of Dorian Gray*. First published, 1890. New York: Skyhorse Publishing.

Williams, W. (1986). *The Spirit and the Flesh: sexual diversity in American Indian culture*. Boston, MA: Beacon Books.

INDEX

abortion 5–6, 20
addiction 103–104, 147
admiration 110
adolescence: awe 129; disgust 52–54, 56–57, 60–61, 68–69; fascination 146; horror 83–84, 99
affect (definition) 3
aging process: awe 130; disgust 54–56; horror 78, 82–83, 99–100
Alice's Adventures in Wonderland see Carroll, L.
alienness 6: awe 114–115, 123–124; disgust 38–39, 47–50, 67; fascination 150; horror 80, 94–96, 114; *see also* humanity
aliens (extra-terrestrials) 119
Améry, J. 118, 124
anal stage of development 51–52
animal cruelty 30–31, 76, 79
anti-black racism: defensive reaction to 18; disgust 34–35, 48–49; fascination 140, 144; horror 87–88
anti-Semitism: disgust 34, 47–48, 49, 65–67; fascination 145
anxiety 18, 84
arachnophobia 82, 104
artistic creativity 92, 126
Atlas, G. 61–62
awe 109–110: absence of 134; category-breaching 114–115, 118, 123–124, 129–130, 152; compared with other emotions 110–113; and

creation/creativity 125–127; developmental stages 127–130; excessive 131, 152; and fascination 135; and horror 114–115, 116–119; and humanity 115–116, 152; life-affirming 110, 120–124, 131–132; as a reaction to power 113, 118, 131; and religion 115, 124–125; and the self-boundary 7, 113–114, 127, 151; and violence 118, 132–134

Baker, A. 124
"basic emotions" 21–24
Benjamin, J. 61–62
Beside the Waterfall see Oliver, M.
Beyoncé, fascination with 139–140
biological primacy theories 31
birth 115, 126, 129–130
blank face 76–78, 85, 98, 102
Blechner, M. 127
Brod, M. 92

carnage: awe 132–133; horror 87, 100–102
Carroll, L. 135
Casey, L. 39–40
category breaches 5–7: awe 114–115, 118, 123–124, 129–130, 152; disgust 36–42, 67, 152; enlivening 43, 152; fascination 41, 138, 141–143, 152; horror 75, 87, 90–96, 152
category-bursting 6, 7: awe 115, 129–130, 152; horror 82, 152

164 Index

causation 16–17
change 86
child abuse: disgust 32–33, 60–61; horror 78, 98
child development: awe 127–129; disgust 30, 50–52; fascination 145–146; horror 97–99
climate change 84
clowns 75–76
cognitively-unelaborated feelings 15–16, 83
consciousness 3; *see also* unconscious feelings
"constructionist" theory 21–22, 155n2
contagion 32–35, 51, 68
Corbett, K. 40
core affect 155n2
counterphobia 104, 143
Creed, B. 97–98
crime scene investigation 140–141
cross-dressing 40–41, 142
cult leaders 124, 136

Davies, J. 63
Day, W. 85, 103, 119, 152
death: awe 115; fascination 142, 143; horror 79, 85–86
defensive emotion 18
definitions of emotion 3–4
dehumanization 39, 100–102, 132–133
de Kretser, M. 54, 78
de Maupassant, G. 118–119
dementia 78, 82–83
depression 16, 83
development 24–25: of awe 127–130; of disgust 30, 50–56; of fascination 145–146; of horror 96–100
dirt/dirtiness 32–33, 38, 42, 46, 51
disavowed identification 67–72
disease: disgust 10–11, 11–12, 59–60; fascination 138–139; horror 78, 81
disgust 27–28: and the alien 38–39, 47–50, 67; and atypical gender/sexuality 39–42, 64–65; a basic emotion 24; and contagion 32–35, 51, 68; as a destructive force 30, 40, 47–50, 65–67; developmental stages 30, 50–56; and dirt 32–33, 38, 42, 46, 51; and disease 10–11, 11–12, 59–60; and fascination 59, 138–139; and horror 43, 75, 78–80, 87, 102–103; and humanness 39, 48–49, 52, 62, 151; and the intercategorical 36–38, 39–42, 152; and life uncontained 42–45, 60–63; moral 29–32, 44, 45–50; proneness to 57–58, 69–70; protective

functions of 28, 56, 58–72; and the self-boundary 7–9, 27, 28, 35, 52, 151; self-disgust 54–55
dissociation 100–102
diver–ocean relationship 111
dogs: disgust at eating 36–37, 44; wild nature of 116–117
Douglas, M. 6, 33, 46, 90
Douglass, F. 44–45, 48–49
dreams (nightmares) 2–3, 104–106
drunkenness 44–45
Du Bois, W.E.B. 18
du Maurier, D. 88–90

Einstein, A. 134
elephantiasis (case story): disgust 10–11, 11–12, 59–60; fascination 59, 138–139
emotion (definition) 3–4
emotional operating systems 23
enthrallment 119
environmental disasters 84
esprit de corps 67
evil spirits 80–82
evolutionarily-conserved emotions 14–15, 31
excess 44–45, 60–63
extra-terrestrials *see* aliens

facial expressions 22: blank face 76–78, 85, 98, 102; false smiles 22, 75
fascination 2, 135: absence 150; and alienness 150; and awe 135; developmental stages 145–146; and disgust 59, 138–139; etymology 136; fascinators 136–137, 149; with the forbidden or hidden 141, 150; with heroes and monsters 138–139, 152; with the intercategorical 41, 138, 141–143, 152; negative aspects 147–150, 152; and obsession 138, 146; and personal identity 139–141, 147–148; resisting 148; with sex 143–145, 146, 148; with TV shows 137–138
fear: and awe 112; and horror 73, 74, 82; real or imagined 5
feces: anal stage of development 51–52; disgust 38
feeling (definition) 3–4
fiction: used for illustrative purposes 25; writers' vocation 92
Fisher, P. 4, 13, 112, 128, 156n1
Frankenstein 119
Freud, S.: on disgust 28; on oceanic feelings 111; on taboo 3, 37, 113,

Index **165**

155–156n3; on the uncanny 74–75; on the unconscious 17–18
Frosh, S. 91

gender issues: awe in religiously orthodox women 125; categorization 5, 11; *Rebecca* as horror story 88–90; sexuality of women 143–144; transgender people 39–42, 64–65, 142
genocide: Holocaust 49, 65–66, 85, 118, 143; Rwanda 80, 92–93, 100–102, 132–133
Geurts, K.L. 46
ghosts 81–82, 91–92
global warming 84
God (and false gods) 115, 124–125
Grand Canyon 120
grandeur 112
Green, A. 3
grief 85–86
group identity 67

Haidt, J. 45–46, 112–113
Heaven 115
Hell 103
heroes 139
Himmler, H. 49
H is for Hawk see Macdonald, H.
Holocaust 49, 65–66, 85, 118, 143
Homer (*Odyssey*) 136–137
horror 1–3, 73–74: and the alien 80, 94–96, 114; of the altered self 82–84, 94–96; and awe 114–115, 116–119; and carnage 87, 100–102; case studies 106–107; of change 86; and contrasting powers 92–94; defenses against 100–106; defensive value of 100; developmental stages 96–100; of deviance from family/sexual norms 83–84, 85, 88–90, 94–96; and disgust 43, 75, 78–80, 87, 102–103; of inhuman humans 75–80, 152; lacks intentionality 84; of malign spirits 80–82; of margins 90–92; of moral disorder 87–88; nightmares 2–3, 104–106; and the self-boundary 7, 12, 73, 151; the uncanny 74–75; of an unsustaining environment 84–86
Huckabee, M. 64
humanity 9, 12, 151–152: awe 115–116; disgust 39, 48–49, 52, 62, 151; fascination 138–139; horror at the inhuman being 75–80, 152; *see also* alienness

impurity 33, 46
incest 85
infancy, and development of: awe 127–129; disgust 30, 50–52; fascination 145–146; horror 97–99
intentionality 43, 84
intercategorical status 5–6, 152: awe 118; disgust 36–38, 39–42, 152; fascination 41, 138, 141–143; horror 75, 87, 90–96
interest-excitement 127–128, 130–131, 145–146
Islam 125, 144, 149–150

Jews: anti-Semitism 34, 47–48, 49, 65–67, 145; Holocaust 49, 65–66, 85, 118, 143
Jim Crow laws 34–35; *see also* anti-black racism
Josephs, L. 54

Kafka, F.: *The Metamorphosis* 94–96; *The Trial* 77–78
Kant, I. 156n1
Keltner, D. 112–113
Klein, M. 97
Kristeva, J. 36, 97

labeling (naming) of emotions 4–5, 11, 15–16, 19–20, 24
Leach, E. 19, 36, 91
LeDoux, J.E. 22–23
Lemma, A. 97
Levinson, J. 3–4
Levi, P. 20–21, 65–66
life trajectories 25
love, falling in 122–123

Macdonald, H. 133, 147
magic 91–92, 142–143
malign spirits 80–82
marginality 6: fascination 138, 141–142; horror 90–92
Martin, W. 48, 49
menopause 54
mental illness 83
mental simulation 5
Metamorphosis, The see Kafka, F.
Meyer, J. 110
Miller, S.B. 9–10, 25, 43–44, 62–63, 70–71
Miller, W.I. 42, 45
miscarriage 5–6
miserliness 70
modes of emotion 13–14, 57
monsters 9: fascination 138–139; horror 78, 95–96, 119

166 Index

monstrous-feminine 97–98
moods 15
moral disgust 29–32, 44, 45–50
moral horror 87–88

naming of emotions 4–5, 11, 15–16, 19–20, 24
narcissism 150
natural world: awe 109, 110, 113, 116–118, 120–121, 122, 123–124; horror 84, 89
neuroscientific research 19, 22–23
nightmares 2–3, 104–106
novelty 113, 126

obsession 138, 146
oceanic feelings 111–112
Odyssey see Homer
old age: awe 130; disgust 54–56; horror 78, 82–83, 99–100
Oliver, M.: *Beside the Waterfall* 116–117; *Porcupine* 117–118; *The Sea Mouse* 93–94
opposite emotions 13
oral stage of development 30, 50–51

Panksepp, J. 23, 155n1
phobias 57–58, 82, 104
Picture of Dorian Gray, The see Wilde, O.
piggishness 50–51
politics: awe 134; disgust 29–30, 31
poltergeist activity 81–82
Porcupine see Oliver, M.
post-traumatic stress disorder (PTSD) 87
precursor states 4
projective identification: disgust 30, 40, 47–50, 66–67; fascination 139, 145
puberty: disgust 52–54; fascination 146; horror 83–84, 99; *see also* adolescence

racism: defensive reaction to 18; disgust 34–35, 47–50, 65–67; fascination 140, 144–145; horror 87–88
rape 34, 144
reaction-formation 51, 64
Rebecca see du Maurier, D.
religion: awe 115, 124–125; horror 103; and sexuality 83–84, 148
restraint 50–51
robots 75
Russell, J.A. 22, 155n2
Rwandan genocide 80, 92–93, 100–102, 132–133

Saarinen, J. 111
Sabbah, F. 125, 143–144

sacredness 46
Sartre, J.-P.: on anti-Semitism 34, 47–48, 66–67, 145; on slime 44
Sea Mouse, The see Oliver, M.
Sears, C. 40–41
self-boundary: awe 7, 113–114, 127, 151; disgust 7–9, 27, 28, 35, 52, 151; horror 7, 12, 73, 151
self-disgust 54–55
self-protection 18, 28; *see also* projective identification
sexual abuse/harassment: disgust 33–34, 60–61; horror 78, 98
sexual behavior/deviance: destabilizing 127; disgust 39–42, 64–65; fascination 143–145, 146, 148; horror 83–84, 88–90; as viewed at puberty 52–54, 99, 146
shame 54, 55, 120–121
shopping addiction 147–148
Sirens 136–137
slime 44
smiles, false 22, 75
social breakdown 85
Spezzano, C. 14–15, 128, 155n1
spider phobia *see* arachnophobia
splitting 21
Stryon, W. 16
sublime, the 156n1
suicide 124
supernatural events: awe 119; horror 81–82, 91–92
survival in adversity 121–122
symbiotic state 127

taboo 3, 20, 21, 36, 113, 155–156n3
tactile experiences 30, 51
teenagers *see* adolescence
termination of pregnancy *see* abortion
terror 82, 84
terrorism 132
thought and feeling 15–16
thrill-seeking 91
Tomkins, S. 127–128
transgender people 39–42, 64–65
transvestism 40–41, 142
trauma: horror 80, 100; PTSD 87; unable to feel awe 124
Trial, The see Kafka, F.
Trump, D.: awe 121–122, 134; disgust 29, 31, 41

uncanny, the 74–75
uncertainty 86
unconscious feelings 4–5, 17–19, 22–23

unethical behavior (moral disgust at) 29–32, 44, 45–50

vastness 112
violence: awe 118, 132–134; disgust as trigger for 40, 47–50, 65–67
vomit 37

Weisel, E. 85, 143
White, T.H. 133

whitewater rafting 122
Wilbur, R. 109
Wilde, O. (*The Picture of Dorian Gray*) 55–56, 83, 119, 136, 149
witches 91, 136
wonder 112, 128
worthlessness 46–47, 62, 68

zombies 76

# Taylor & Francis eBooks

Helping you to choose the right eBooks for your Library

Add Routledge titles to your library's digital collection today. Taylor and Francis ebooks contains over 50,000 titles in the Humanities, Social Sciences, Behavioural Sciences, Built Environment and Law.

Choose from a range of subject packages or create your own!

Benefits for you
- Free MARC records
- COUNTER-compliant usage statistics
- Flexible purchase and pricing options
- All titles DRM-free.

Benefits for your user
- Off-site, anytime access via Athens or referring URL
- Print or copy pages or chapters
- Full content search
- Bookmark, highlight and annotate text
- Access to thousands of pages of quality research at the click of a button.

 Free Trials Available
We offer free trials to qualifying academic, corporate and government customers.

eCollections – Choose from over 30 subject eCollections, including:

Archaeology	Language Learning
Architecture	Law
Asian Studies	Literature
Business & Management	Media & Communication
Classical Studies	Middle East Studies
Construction	Music
Creative & Media Arts	Philosophy
Criminology & Criminal Justice	Planning
Economics	Politics
Education	Psychology & Mental Health
Energy	Religion
Engineering	Security
English Language & Linguistics	Social Work
Environment & Sustainability	Sociology
Geography	Sport
Health Studies	Theatre & Performance
History	Tourism, Hospitality & Events

For more information, pricing enquiries or to order a free trial, please contact your local sales team:
www.tandfebooks.com/page/sales

 | The home of Routledge books | www.tandfebooks.com